POLO WISDOM

YOU CAN TALK, BUT CAN YOU PLAY?

BY

R. D. LUBASH

with Photographs by
David Lominska
and
Biomechanical Drawings by
Alejandro Gambarini Lóizaga
with
additional Digital Images by
the author
and
Cover Painting by
Paul Hickman
from the collection of the author

Polo Wisdom

FIRST EDITION
2003

Copyright © 2003 by Robert D. Lubash

TITLE
Polo Wisdom, an all encompassing title depicting
rules, styles and training skills endorsed and used
by the Polo Training Foundation.

ISBN: 0-9645332-2-2

Library of Congress
Cataloging-in-Publication Data-pending

Carl W. Miller, American Yearbook Sales Inc.
321-779-8061
Jostens Printing and Publishing
Published and Printed in the U.S.A.

In Memory of

James A Bachman	Alfred G. Pennell
(1947 - 1991)	(1923 - 2000)
Thomas B. Glynn	**Robert S. Skene**
(1905 - 2001)	(1914 - 1997)

Without Tommy Glynn, Herbie Pennell, Bob Skene and Jimmy Bachman this book could never have been written… nor would I ever have been on a polo field. All four, recently deceased… were monumental in honing my game.

Tommy had an unequaled vantage point, having been on the polo scene for over seventy years. A fine horseman and judge of horseflesh, he was an invaluable and never-ending source of information. His encouragement made me continue in spite of my early frustrations. He played with most of the greats of the "Golden Age of Polo" and went on to manage Boulder Brook, Ox Ridge, Saratoga and Greenwich polo clubs. He was instrumental in Peter Brant becoming the highest rated amateur polo player in the world and his White Birch team winning more tournaments than any other team during the nineteen seventies and eighties.

It was Herbie who invited me to stick 'n' ball in the old Squadron 'A' Armory all those years ago. Needless to say, I bought my first polo pony from Herbie. Naturally shy, he wasn't a man given to idle chatter and it took some prying and a lot of patience before he would take you into his confidence. He doled out his wisdom in dribs and drabs, as though they were pieces of gold. Several of us "kids" used to hang out around his tackroom on the mere chance of picking up some gold dust. He was unbelievably gifted with a mallet and able to exert his control of any game in which he participated. Herbie made me play my first chukkers without a mallet so that I would learn what to do and where to be on the field.

The great gentleman Bob Skene was most influential, not for his 10-goal skills or the fact that he held that rating for seventeen years, but for his ability to communicate that knowledge in such a way as to make it easy to follow his instructions. He was able to dissect every nuance of a maneuver and impart that knowledge in easily understandable bites. He was the first to use technical theory to analyze a swing. "Hurricane Bob" was so intuitive on the field that he once played one horse for four chukkers in a row. He seldom went faster than a slow canter nor hardly went past mid-field and, when finished, the horse hadn't broken a sweat yet Bob was able to be on every ball/line first!

Jimmy Bachman was the hardest working polo player that I have ever encountered. Sometimes he played three games in a day and then worked green horses until it was too dark to see. And, when he wasn't playing he was at the barn. He walked the aisles constantly doing up a leg here, mucking there, administering medication or just making sure that his string was comfortable and happy. A master at keeping horses in playing condition, he was highly regarded for his ability to work on a pony's legs. His ability to control a game was extraordinary given the fact that often he played horses that other players couldn't or wouldn't ride.

DEDICATION

For C. F. F.

ACKNOWLEDGMENTS

It would have been impossible to write this book without the help, knowingly or otherwise, of the entire polo community, but I would be remiss without giving special mention to those who gave their time and energy and were instrumental in bringing this book to fruition.

Initially, it was Dennis Banks who lead me out of the tall grass by helping sort my disparate notes into readable words and Thomas Thornton, who edited those words into some semblance of flowing prose and critical mass.

Tony Coppola and Audrey Melvin, Gil Johnston, Horace Layffaye and Steve Krause all gave the manuscript a read to make sure that I didn't speak out of turn and added their specialized expertise.

All of the above would have gone for naught had it not been for Carl Miller, whose prior book, _The Classic Experience_, about the Hampton Classic Horse Show paved the way. Printing and publishing presented a steep learning curve and the finished book would never have looked as it does without my Mac and the imaginative help of Jim Gooch and his team at Josten's, especially Toby Walk who gave meaning to the word pagination and did it all with a big smile.

Mr. Loizaga's wonderful _biomechanical_ drawings originally appeared in the book _Polo de alto handicap de argentino_. I am grateful to Markus Tödtli of Bank Hoffman, the books publisher and to Alberto Pedro Heguy and Daniel Martinez Páez, the book's authors, for their kind permission to reproduce some of Sr. Loizaga's artwork here.

Not only did PTF Boardmember 'Old Eagle Eye' Lynn Thompson cross every "t" and dot every "i", without her "fresh eyes," the collective lot of us would have all looked like we dropped out of school in the third grade. And then there is the indefatigable Danny Scheraga. The minute he first learned of _Polo Wisdom_ he threw his support and considerable knowledge behind the project and infused the Polo Training Foundation Board with such enthusiasm that my nascent scribbling, much to my surprise, actually became a book.

R. D. Lubash
Stamford, CT
August, 2003

TABLE OF CONTENTS

PART THREE: THE GAME

PART SIX: POLO QUOTES

Preface:

My father played polo until the early 1950s. Although I rode occasionally, I was more interested in high school sports, so I never paid close attention to polo. A dozen years later a friend, whose father had played with my father, and I decided to treat our dates to something different from the usual movie. Under mild protests from the distaff side, we went to the venerable Squadron 'A' Armory in New York City for an evening of arena polo.

The featured match was an All-star collegiate team taking on a Squadron "A" 0-goal team. It seemed that none of the players could connect with the ball and, needless to say, the match was a bore. The girls complained that the arena was cold and smelly. The only excitement came from the numerous spills and wrecks. Surely, my friend and I thought, we could be overnight sensations if we decided to take up the game. So, after the match, we went back to the stable area. Some of the veteran players, remembering our fathers, were very solicitous and invited us to "stick 'n' ball" the following week.

My friend, having much more sense than I, declined the offer while I accepted and proceeded to make a fool of myself. For the better part of a month I religiously came to "stick 'n' ball." Indeed, it was great fun to ride around the arena trying to hit the ball...and very frustrating, too.

Although other riders effortlessly galloped around the arena hitting the ball and negotiating traffic, I couldn't hit the ball ten yards. And, if I ever did manage to connect, the ball would careen off the mallet at some odd angle, causing me to ride into someone's path.

Embarrassed and possessing a greater respect for the sport, I was about to throw in the towel when a grizzled old gentleman rode up to me. Saying that he had known my dad, he wondered if I would mind if he gave me a few pointers. I gratefully accepted his kind offer only to become more embarrassed when he pointed out that the ball is meant to be hit with the flat side of the mallet rather than the little round end!

Naturally, this little tidbit helped enormously. But what stuck in my mind was the fact that I had been riding around the arena for a month while many players, including several high-goalers, watched and said nothing.

Over the ensuing years it became evident that polo players were content to keep their know-how to themselves under some misguided guise of one-upmanship. The professionals, players and grooms alike, had come by their knowledge the hard way and seemed especially insular. *Patróns* feel that they have paid for it dearly. Even the sparsely available books on the subject were written before the advent of modern polo and are more concerned with the rudiments and recaps of important matches from a bygone era. It is no secret why there are so many successful polo playing families: they can pass the information from generation to generation.

Not being blessed with great natural ability, and like most poloists, having taken up the sport fairly late in life, caused me to become an inveterate student of the game. In the forty years that I have been trying to play polo I have managed to amass considerable information that, hopefully, will enable the reader to improve and, more importantly, safely enjoy the sport of kings.

Today there are many good books on polo (see Bibliography), and there are several polo schools around the world and clinics offered by the Polo Training Foundation. Most of these options are geared for the first-timers and are considered a success if they turn you onto the sport to the point that you will become a customer or, better yet, a *patrón*. There are also some books, mainly of interest to the advanced poloist, on the breeding and '*making*' of the polo pony. This book, however, was written to fill the gap in between. Somewhere in this gap it is assumed that the reader knows how to ride (if not, learn real fast!), has been exposed to polo, and knows the difference between the off-side and near-side. This book contains no revelations, but rather is a compendium of advice from many sources. If you can remember it all and put it to use under the pressure of game conditions, you will be a much sought-out player.

Polo Wisdom is about outdoor polo. Not that arena, bicycle, cowboy polo and polocrosse aren't great sports, but there is nothing like grace under pressure and the thrill of a chase down a long, wide open field of outdoor polo. To facilitate writing this book I have taken some liberties. Gender has been thrown out the window, not meaning any slight toward female polo players who, for the most part, are better horsemen (there, I did it again) than their male counterparts due to the fact that they don't have the compensatory brute strength to cover up their lack of riding skills. If it is any compensation, I have referred to all horses in the masculine. Also, subjects appear in more than one chapter [e.g., becoming one with the horse is covered in chapters not only about riding, but stable management, conformation, etc.] Current polo vernacular is generally rendered in quotation marks.

Although there are many qualified oracles in the polo community, it is difficult for novices to obtain useful information because they don't know what questions to ask. If nothing else, I hope that this book will help answer most questions and impart enough understanding of the game to know what to ask of your local professional so that you can have more fun and be a better polo player.

Note: A numeral followed by the letter h and a period (10h.) indicates a player's handicap (ten goals). The letters following (UK) indicate the player's affiliation (England). In all instances, the player's highest rating attained is used.

R. D. Lubash
Giant Maple Farm
Stamford, CT
Fall 2003

Part One:

The Equine Athlete

"Look back at our struggle for freedom,
Trace our present day's strength to its source;
And you'll find that man's pathway to glory
Is strewn with the bones of the horse."

Anonymous

The horse was first domesticated, odd as it may seem, not as a conveyance but as a warrior. Look at the references to the horse dating from man's first cave drawings through mythology and the Bible. The references are not to tilling the soil or hauling heavy loads, but to carrying mounted fighters. Somehow it became apparent early on that the big, powerful and fierce horse was capable of utmost bravery under fire and possessed the willingness to totally submit to a physically weaker human master. (It has been suggested that horses perceive humans with ears permanently pinned back.)

In the days when wheeled vehicles were pulled by oxen and asses, the horse was an unprecedented weapon of war. The prophet Mohammed realized the importance of horses in battle and instructed his followers to take extraordinary care of their horses. The first recorded horse race was in 624 B.C. at the Greek Olympiad. Surprisingly, it took almost a thousand years before the horse was used for work or pleasure. Yet, from the very beginning, horsemen devised games to show off the horses' athleticism. Polo, in its primordial form, was among the first of these games and the oldest game, mounted or on foot, played with a stick and ball.

There are many animals that depend on people for food, shelter and medical care. None but horses will carry a person through danger with such a brave disregard for their own safety and remain able to unflinchingly respond to a rider's commands. If this statement needs further testament consider that in the 1854 Charge of the Light Brigade, regarded by many as one of the most horrific cavalry battles of all time, only 260 horses out of 700 survived the Russian artillery. In the course of the Peninsular War (1808–14), Napoleon's armies took the best of the Andalusian horse stock and nearly decimated the entire breed. And, a little more recently, half of the three million horses used in World War I perished!

Probably the only thing that otherwise individualistic polo players agree about is that the horse is the single most important factor of the game. Some say "pony power" counts for as much as seventy-five percent of success in the sport. Surely this is a gross understatement for the high goal professional player. He values horsepower more than anyone because he, more often than not, is pitted against an opposing player of equal ability. In those instances the horse may be the only difference and, therefore, account for one hundred percent of the game. Obviously, if you can't get to the ball, it doesn't matter how good you are with a mallet.

The term "polo pony" dates back to just prior to the First World War, when Hurlingham (UK) rules limited the size of horses to 14.2 hands (large pony). However, after the War, during which polo suffered a hiatus, there was a dearth of horseflesh, so the governing bodies saw fit to make the size unlimited (1916 in the USA; 1919 in the UK) and it has remained that way to this day.

Horse breeds are divided into three different categories: coldbloods, warmbloods and hotbloods. No single breed has established itself as *the* polo pony, but it is no coincidence that in today's high goal matches most of the ponies are *Thoroughbreds* (hotbloods) or, at least, *near Thoroughbred* (warmbloods). The term thoroughbred came into use around 1750 to indicate an English racehorse whose pedigree could be unequivocally traced to the so-called "foundation sires," Byerly Turk, Darly Arabian and Godolphin Arabian.

Many polo ponies are fully registered thoroughbreds (tattooed on the inside upper lip)..."off the track." But the majority of polo ponies are non-papered and often crossed with other breeds, most notably the Argentine Criollo, known as one of the toughest and soundest breeds in the world, and the American Quarter Horse. It is not unusual, for example, to see a Quarter Horse head suspended on an Arabian neck with Thoroughbred body conformation. Still others are crosses with Moorland, Morgan,

and the English Barb. Argentina is the number one polo pony exporting country and has been since the 1920s. It is safe to say that the most prized type of polo pony is nearly as full Thoroughbred as possible.

In the 1960s, Woody D. was one of the most renowned ponies of all time. Although a Thoroughbred, he began life as a parson's horse, then a range stallion, a cowpony, as well as a top high goal polo pony that played in his last U.S. Open championship game at age twenty for Bob Skene (10h. USA). His illustrious career was immortalized in the Walt Disney movie *Stormy*, in which he starred, adding yet another talent to his varied list of skills before his final career move to top polo pony sire for the Oxley Stables in Oklahoma. In 2000 Woody D. was inducted into the Museum of Polo and Hall of Fame.

Cold-blooded horses, descended from the "Forest Horse," are generally not well suited for polo. They are bred for superior strength and durability rather than speed and athleticism. Accordingly, in high-goal polo, where world-class speed, stamina, athletic ability, and "heart" are mandatory, most ponies are "Thoroughbreds." It is not unusual to find a "clean-bred" or "papered" Thoroughbred on the polo field. Below the top, high-goal level warm-blooded horses are somewhat more common, because usually they are not as high-spirited. Like Thoroughbred mares, stock and Quarter Horse ponies may adapt to polo more readily due to their calmer disposition, but unlike Thoroughbreds, they rarely have the speed for high goal competition. Indeed, good ponies love the game as much as the players. While it may be an overstatement that some ponies actually

CRIOLLO

The Spanish conquerors brought horses descended from Barb and Andalusian stock to The New World. Beginning on the island of Hispaniola (Haiti/Dominican Republic) these small horses were left to roam wild and soon populated all of Latin America. Called by different names–Crioulo in Brazil, Corralero in Chile, Costeño in Peru and Criollo in Argentina–they all demonstrate an independent character, ability to adapt to their environment and unparalleled longevity. Criollos have been known to live to be forty years old!

Criollo, pronounced in *cri-o-jo* in Argentina, horses have temperaments that are similar to other breeds, (Camargues, Mustangs, etc.) that have remained wild for generations. They are independent, brave, tenacious, resourceful, and are noted for their endurance and resistance to illness.

The criollo's conformation–muscular, compact and well proportioned–and the fact that they are also hardy make the criollo the perfect horse for ranch work. With their malleable personalities and great balance it is no wonder that they have become the preferred horse for sport and war. In fact, it was the criollo that was chosen by the English remount for the Australian Light Cavalry that served so notably with valor and tenacity in WW I.

It is no wonder that the *petiseros*, as horse trainers are called in Argentina, sought out criollos. Because of their propensity for domination and relatively ease of training, criollos were the preferred stock for Gauchos, Indians and European settlers alike.

In a process similar to the evolution of the American Quarter Horse, the English settlers brought thoroughbred racing stock to the New World and soon began cross-breeding with native criollo horses resulting in today's world renowned Argentine polo pony.

Most modern criollo polo ponies have been crossed with thoroughbred blood for so many generations that today they are closer to thoroughbred than criollo. In fact, most of the polo ponies played today are mixed blood...meaning that in addition to criollo and thoroughbred some Arabian and Quarter Horse blood is probably present. However, purebred criollo stock is still preferred for pato, paleteada and jineteada (native games).

follow the ball, the really great ones have at least embraced the concept that they may have to follow the play.

Although the horse has the largest eyes of any land mammal, his eyesight is not particularly well suited for the game of polo. Even though his visual acuity is better than a dog's or cat's at distance, the wide-set placement of the eyes, his long nose and inability to parallel-adjust closer then forty feet, give the horse poor depth perception. This shortcoming, coupled with poor color differentiation and directional hearing (ears that are able to rotate toward the direction of the sound), could make the polo field a scary place. To further exacerbate the problem, the horse, who smells like what he eats (grass), is an easily recognized prey animal. He is a coward whose natural reaction to danger is to "turn tail" and run as fast as he can. Man, who smells like what he eats (meat), is a predator and, therefore, a primordial enemy. With a prey animal's mindset, the horse has a raised level of awareness and often recognizes danger before his rider does.

Conformation, Sex, Age, Size

"In judging the polo mount, consideration is given to
conformation, but the emphasis is on performance."
Cyril R. Harrison (8h. USA) (1909-1965)

A polo pony is not a pony at all, but a full-grown horse of any size, breed or color. "Pretty is as pretty does" certainly applies to polo ponies, but most who exhibit good athletic ability do so because they are "built so they can," as Harrison liked to point out. The basic qualities to look for in any performance horse are a good place to start when appraising a polo pony's abilities. Remember that perfection, as always, is illusive.

Conformation

The shape and proportions of a horse's body are called conformation. Good conformation enables a horse to perform efficiently at maximum athleticism, whether it is on the track, over a fence, or on the polo field. It is easier for a properly proportioned horse to collect and extend himself at all gaits. But each horse discipline is favored by a particular type conformation. Musculature also affects performance. Chunky muscles won't make it in this sport. Flat, angular muscles seen on Thoroughbreds and Arabians are preferred because they are slow-twitch (oxygen-burning) muscles that operate with a constant flow of oxygen, which enables them to travel faster and farther. Lean muscling enhances a horse's cooling ability. This type of musculature is inherited and points to another reason why a preponderance of Thoroughbred blood is prized.

The polo pony should appear evenly balanced over all four legs, front to rear and side to side. He should have a lithe neck that tapers into fairly narrow, but prominently high withers (withers should be about the same height as the croup or rump) and a short back; a broad and deep chest connected by a long sloping shoulder with a slight curve up to the withers and a flat loin; broad croup should slope into muscled hindquarters; and straight, not too widely spaced legs. By comparison, a jumper needs particularly developed hind quarters, and a race horse a longer back and longer legs. The polo pony's legs should *appear* too short for the body due to a broad girth of well-sprung and rounded ribs. The pony's top and bottom lines should be parallel.

Ideally, the forearms should be long and straight when viewed from the side. The cannon bone should be thick, short and flat and display good definition between the bone and tendon. Pasterns, the

Ill. #1: Parts of the Horse

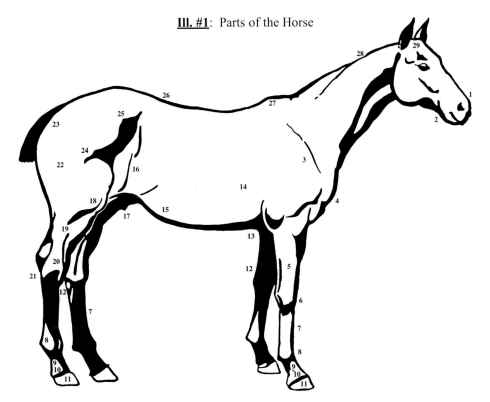

1. NOSE	7. CANNON BONE	13. ELBOW	19. GASKIN OR SECOND THIGH	25. POINT OF HIP
2. CHIN GROOVE	8. FETLOCK	14. RIBS	20. HOCK	26. LOINS
3. SHOULDER	9. PASTERN	15. BELLY	21. SEAT OF CURB	27. WITHERS
4. POINT OF SHOULDER	10. CORONET	16. FLANK	22. QUARTER	28. CREST
5. FOREARM	11. HOOF	17. SHEATH	23. DOCK	29. POLL
6. KNEE	12. CHESTNUT	18. STIFLE	24. HIP JOINT	

horse's shock absorbers, should be sufficiently long and slope at about a fifty-degree angle for the front feet and sixty-degree angle for the hind. The hind legs should be on the vertical plane of the cannon bone, through the hock to the point of the buttock. Too great an angle to the hind legs is called, "sickle hocked," and should be avoided. Knees should be broad and flat.

The stomach (belly) should be reasonably flat and long (longer than the back) and not angle up sharply to meet the flanks. The stifle (hips) should be long and wider than the rump. Medium length pasterns are best. Short increases concussion and too long creates more stress on tendons and joints. Dark colored or striped hoofs are considered a sign of good breeding. Light-colored hoofs can be soft and not hold up well under the stress of polo. A foot that is round, wider at the bottom and in proportion to the horse will afford the best support. Likewise, a smaller-hoofed pony is likely to be more agile.

The head should be small and the face line straight with large wide-spaced eyes topped by small alert ears, like a pony's. A medium-length neck aids the horse to balance and affords the rider the most control. The neck should be longer on the top than the bottom. Avoid at all costs a "ewe" shaped neck because it aids neither the horse nor the rider. Many believe that large nostrils help a horse take in more oxygen, "breathe the wind." While not fully substantiated, it has been proven that a well-defined jugular and large windpipe help a pony enormously. You should be able to put a full fist sideways between the jawbone cavity.

Would that it were possible if you found such an animal, you could also afford it.

Sex

*"I just seem to have better luck with mares,
and if I could, I'd buy all mares."*
Billy Wayman, father of 10 goaler Tommy (USA)

Polo is one equine sport where males and females compete without prejudice. If there is prejudice it is in favor of the mare. In fact, mares are more prominent because most polo trainers find their temperament better suited to the adjustment necessary for polo. Mares are usually less temperamental. Geldings, on the other hand, are considered by many to be easier to handle. Still others argue that because geldings are not considered "whole horses," they care less, making them stubborn learners. A somewhat less obvious reason for some players preferring mares is that mares physically mature quicker than their brethren, so training can begin earlier. However, trainers do agree that horses that are calmer and less emotional are faster learners. An indication that there is no hard-and-fast rule was a recent meeting of two internationally ranked high goal (22) teams, where each team brought twenty-four horses. One string consisted of twenty-two mares, and the other seventeen geldings and only seven mares.

Another reason that there are many more mares on the polo field is conformation. Mares tend to have wider stifles and less body weight than geldings. The wide hip placement facilitates stopping and turning. Furthermore, as with all athletes, less body weight increases speed and agility. Mares usually have less massive necks than geldings and certainly stallions. A narrow throatlatch attachment of the head makes the neck more flexible, which further aids maneuverability. Mares are especially coveted in cold climates as their lower body temperature enables them to better withstand the cold.

Ill. #2: Luna, mare out of Top Secret and Guach Acha, bred by Héctor & Susan Barrantes and played by Gonzalo Pieres took first prize AACP in 1987 and 1990. Good conformation was only one of her attributes.

A somewhat more practical reason why mares are so popular is that a good mare can still be of value, well past her playing time, for breeding purposes. Many players hold on to mares longer than they would to a comparable gelding because they hope they can eventually breed the mare to a suitable stud. However, good stallions are hard to find, and breeding has become so expensive and time-consuming that the practice is not as common as one would think. Another factor may be that stallions and geldings require higher import tariffs from some countries. "I've had more male champion horses than anyone," states Memo Gracida (10h. USA), but currently counts only three geldings among his top ten ponies.

Also, there are fewer geldings. According to the Jockey Club of the 72, 825 thoroughbred starters in North America in 2002, 18,786–or 25.8 percent–were geldings. Most horses develop a heavier front end, usually about 65 percent or more of their weight is carried over the front legs. One current popular theory is that castrated horses distribute their weight more evenly, which may be why many horsemen believe that gelding stay sounder longer.

One of polo's oldest and most heated debates centers around the question, "Does the horse follow the ball?" We won't even attempt to settle the issue here, but if some do indeed follow the ball, trainers say that they would more likely be mares. Proponents of this theory point to the fact that in a wild herd mares are followers while stallions lead. Whether this tendency to follow a moving object translates to a polo ball may be debatable, but many Western cutting horse trainers say it is easier to teach a mare to "cow" than a gelding.

Mares, of course, are subject to hormonal changes when they are in season ("in heat"), which may render some mares unplayable on certain days (see Some Common Ailments, Part Five). This may give some credence to the theory that geldings give a more consistent performance. Currently the prevailing view is that while geldings are more reliable, they regularly give only eighty percent of themselves while mares are more apt to give one hundred and ten percent.

Aggressiveness and gutsiness are two qualities that are more readily attributed to mares. Some say that this is because geldings are usually at the top of the pecking order and they are used to other horses making way for them. Therefore, they are less likely to go into a crowded play or meet an on-coming horse.

Bedouin horse breeders, noted for their highly evolved breeding programs, selected mares for stamina and courage. Stallions were chosen for their beauty and intelligence. Last, but not least, there are those that believe that women players get more out of a gelding while male players have better luck with mares.

Age

"Polo ponies usually go bad in the legs
before they do from old age."
Harold L. "Chico" Barry (9h. USA)

Far too much attention is placed on age. In his last Argentine Open, the youngest horse on Juan Carlos Harriot's (10h. ARG) string was fourteen! Yes, the youngest! The rigors of polo require a sound, durable horse. One that is sound at ten will probably stay that way for the remainder of his playing career.

Horses do not reach their full physical maturity until they are about four or five years old. Since it takes a season or two to "make" a polo pony—to finish training so the horse, once he has reached the necessary height, is ready to play—the youngest "made" prospect you will probably see is six or seven. While it is possible to determine a horse's exact age up to about ten years, it is almost impossible to be precise after age ten, and all horses over ten are designated "aged." Aged horses have probably forgotten more polo than most novices will learn, and therefore make excellent horses for beginners.

Lt. Commander Robert de Pass's famous horse Tarquin played by 7 goal Englishman Paul Withers in the 1966 Argentine Open won best playing pony honors. Tarquin repeated this feat in 1971 at Deauville and finally retired from polo at age twenty-eight! Obviously, an aged or elderly horse will need some special feeding supplements, because he cannot store and synthesize certain nutrients as well as a younger horse. Older horses' organs may not function as efficiently and often have difficulty maintaining weight, therefore requiring a special diet. Older horses can also be more prone to lameness and not withstand intense work. However, prominent horse dealer Dave Rizzo (5h. USA) admonishes, "If the pony has had six or more years in polo and is still sound, it probably has a better chance of staying sound well into old age than a fresh five–year-old." Generally, a polo pony is considered old at fifteen years of age—five years after being designated "aged."

AGE OF MAN	20	40	50	60	70
AGE OF HORSE	5	10	15	20	25

As a horse ages, the angle of the teeth increases and the teeth become discolored. Determining the true age of any given horse is an art for anyone but the experts, except when it comes to Thoroughbreds. Although formed in 1894 (four years after the USPA), it wasn't until 1971 The Jockey Club began registering all thoroughbreds that expected to race by tattooing their inside upper lip with a letter followed by four or five numbers. Starting with the letter A they reached the letter Z in 1996 and in 1997 started the alphabet using the letter A.

Tattoos are notoriously hard to read. Viewing them in the dark or with a black light can help...but not always. By regulation, every Thoroughbred is said to be one year old on the January 1st following its birth regardless of when in the previous year the horse was foaled.

The following is a list of the recent and coming breeding years and their corresponding letters:

1985 – O	1990 – T	1995 – Y	2000 – D
1986 – P	1991 – U	1996 – Z	2001 – E
1987 – Q	1992 – V	1997 – A	2002 – F
1988 – R	1993 – W	1998 – B	2003 – G
1999 – S	1994 – X	1999 – C	2004 - H

Size

*"The perfect polo pony is a 16 hand horse that
plays like one that's 15 hands."*

Tommy Wayman (10h. USA)

An old axiom in the polo community is that "a good big one is better than a good small one." Certainly a horse with longer legs will cover a distance faster than one with shorter limbs. While this may be generally true, there are more than enough exceptions to the rule to make size a matter of personal preference. Obviously, stride for stride, a larger horse will get to the ball first on the flat greensward. Another factor to consider is that large animals, because energy demands of each cell in the body are correspondingly less, lose heat more slowly. And, while being big may produce a speedadvantage, there is an equally big mechanical disadvantage. The advantage of longer legs may be totally canceled out by an increased clumsiness. Usually a horse of greater quality can afford to be smaller in size. As in racing, light horses, because the don't have to bend their knees as much as heavier types, are preferred because they are usually faster.

In any case, the horse should be of sufficient size to easily carry the rider. Remember that the horse was never intended to carry a rider and, in fact, is poorly designed to do so. A small boned ("typey"), barely fifteen-hand thoroughbred may not stay sound very long under a two-hundred-pound rider. Also, in a ride-off/bump, a small pony and rider combination will have to travel faster to offset a bigger pairing.

Ricardo Santamarina, breeder/trainer at Argentina's famed La Fortuna *estancia* (who produced many outstanding horses for Harold Barry and Tommy Wayman) cautions, "Not too big...compact. But not so compact as to lack agility." Smaller and proportionately shorter-coupled horses are likely to be "handier" and turn within a smaller radius, which enables them to be quicker to take up the new line of the ball.

Believe it or not, size is often a matter of fashion as much as anything else. After height limitations were abolished, polo pony size continued to grow until a peak was reached in the mid-1930s when the cream of the crop of high-goal players demonstrated a decided preference for 16-hand-plus horses.

Today, most players are apt to fault a horse for being too big rather than too small. Personal preferences aside, 15.1 or 15.2 hands is the ideal size to enable a six-foot person to reach the ground with a 52-inch mallet with maximum extension.

Stamina, Speed, Agility

Stamina

> *"A polo pony has got to have the speed of a race horse, the tough, quick response of a cow pony and the agility of a show jumper. Then he's got to have more stamina than any of them."*
> Cecil Smith (10h. USA) (1904-2000)

Stamina refers to a horse's ability to sustain a high level of performance over an extended period of time. This implies the capacity to withstand fatigue without loss of proficiency.

Mr. John Watson, the pre-eminent poloist and sportsman of his day (1880s), was reported to have played his famous pony Fritz (Kinsman) for forty minutes without getting off his back! (Twenty to thirty-minute "chukkas" were not unusual during the Victorian era of polo!) More recently, Northrup R. Knox (8h. USA) played his famous pony Ragamuffin, bred by John Oxley (2h. USA), three periods in the 1957 U.S. Open.

While the pace of the game has quickened since then, a well-conditioned, sound pony should be able to play two hard chukkers of medium goal polo on a regular basis. During big tournaments, when it comes down to do or die, many high goal players play the same pony two or three times! Julian Hipwood (9h. UK) played Galen Weston's famous New Zealand–bred pony, Spice, in chukkers 2, 6 and 7 in the 1986 Gold Cup. And, as if that weren't enough, Spice played another double chukker match the following week in the International! But, warns Tommy Wayman (10h. USA), "It shortens a pony's playing life by half if you 'double up'" (play one pony multiple chukkers).

It is said that one period of polo is equivalent to a "season" for a conditioned racehorse. A "season" at a race meet might consist of eight race outings or only twenty minutes of actual work. Horses are usually exercised only at a slow gallop between races. Racetrack trainers worry about the threefold increase in stress on a horse's legs during their first step out of the starting gate. In athletic horse show disciplines, like jumping and cutting, riders also worry about stress injuries in spite of their mounts wearing special protective devices. All this and the maximum time the horses are worked is under two minutes. Most race horses are retired after only two years of racing. Polo players ask for, and receive, a full seven and a half minutes of constant starts, stops and turns every chukker. So be kind to your hard-working ponies. They are athletes, perhaps the greatest animal athletes of all, not machines. Learn to feel when they are tired. During a stoppage of play stand still or walk slowly and let your pony take a breather. After two or three months of continual conditioning and tournament play turn them out for rest and relaxation.

Speed

"In polo, it's not always the speed down the field
(sc. that counts), it's the loose ball and
who's going to get it."
Stewart B. Iglehart (10h. USA) (1914-1993)

All things being equal, the player on the faster horse will get to the ball first and control the play. One of the most exhilarating spectacles in a polo match is to see top thoroughbred ponies racing flat out down the field at speeds of thirty-five to forty miles per hour.

However, flat-out speed is not as important as acceleration. The ability to take the first quick step—often in a new direction—is frequently more important than flat-out speed. When tension on the reins is relaxed, a polo pony should be quick to take the first step into a gallop in one stride when cued. If top speed is a significant factor at all, it is mostly for the One and the Back: The Number One to outrun the back and the Back to catch the One.

Agility

"There is nothing in which a horse's power is
better revealed than in a neat, clean stop."
Michel Eyquem de Montaigne (1588)

An agile horse demonstrates a capacity to turn, change direction, and stop while maintaining perfect balance. Doing this while carrying a rider defines its handiness. Agility and handiness constitute a horse's athleticism.

A racehorse is considered under an immense burden when asked to carry a maximum of 126 pounds in one direction. A polo pony must be a miraculous animal when asked to carry a 180-plus -pound person while stopping and turning under top speeds. To do so with great agility defines the best ponies.

A horse uses its neck to aid in maneuverability and to balance from front to rear. The more athletic horse will carry his head low on a strong but flexible neck. Overall, athleticism can, to some extent, compensate for lack of speed.

"Green horses and green players don't mix."
Bart Evans (8h. USA)

Unless someone is already in the horse breeding business, breeding a pony is the least cost-effective, the most time-consuming, and the riskiest way to find a good polo mount. Green horses are another type of gamble and almost equally time-consuming. For the purposes of this writing, it is assumed that the buyer is looking for a "made" pony.

The majority of polo ponies are bought from two types of professionals, either breeder/trainers and dealers or from other players who are "trading up." Very often the person you purchase a horse from will wear many of these different hats simultaneously.

Sometimes trainers are also breeders working with bloodlines that they have had particular success with in the past. Many times they have their best playing mares bred to a successful stallion. Trainers take great pride in their ability to "make" polo ponies. By buying from a trainer, players can get a fresh made pony without the vices often found on ponies that have had many owners. If the trainer is also one who makes his living on the playing field, he is likely to keep the best ponies for himself and sell the ones that don't quite measure up. If you know the specific type pony you want, a trainer may be the best place to look.

Dealers offer the added advantage of being able to take a horse in trade. Often they are also trainers and will buy "green broke" prospects to finish for polo. Sometimes trade-ins need to be retrained and freshened up. Usually dealers have a large and varied inventory and a greater turnover.

Of course, there is the famous story of Jack-in-the-Box. Supposedly, an Irish horse dealer noticed the horse pulling a butcher's cart, bought him for $250, and sold him to George and Col. E. D. Miller, author of the authoritative book *Modern Polo.* Miller trained and played the horse for several seasons before reselling the horse to another noted player, Col. Henry Thomas Fenwick, for the then (1911) unheard-of price of $2,500.

While there are many such tales, they are the exception rather than the rule, and it is recommended that you seek out a reputable dealer in your local area who is willing and able to stand behind his product. Visiting professionals may be willing to guarantee your satisfaction, but great traveling distances can render any guarantee moot.

Remember the old adage, "A buyer needs a hundred eyes, the seller not one."

Evaluating the Prospect

"Pay for how they play, not how they look."
James "Jimmy" Bachman (7h. USA) (1947-1991)

After you have played the horse, preferably two chukkers or more, and are content with the prospect's conformation, it is time to have the horse "vetted" (prepurchase exam). It is best to use a veterinarian familiar with polo ponies. It is equally important that you and the vet have developed a communicative relationship previously and he knows how you will use and *maintain* the prospect. If that is not practical, try to find a veterinarian that is not beholden to the seller.

Initially, the veterinarian should view the horse in his stall. Check the wood for signs of cribbing. Look at any dropping and for excessive wetness. Is there partially eaten feed in the manger? Check for any unusual pattern in the displacement of the bedding that might show signs of such vices as weaving or pacing. The eyes should be examined when the pupil is dilated in the darkness of the stall.

The veterinarian should perform a general exam of ears, lungs, heart and abdomen. Special attention paid to the mouth and teeth can reveal more than just the horse's age. Pull the tongue out and to one side and feel the bars of the mouth to see if they are slightly concave and smooth and have not been rounded or otherwise damaged. Are there sores or ulcers under the tongue? A cut tongue, gums or lips could be a sign of a "puller" or horse with an insensitive mouth. It can also reveal a pony usually played in a severe bit, but not fitted with one at the time of the test.

Next observe the pony under saddle along with your veterinarian. Ask the rider to trot. Check for lameness with the horse trotting toward and away from you and then turning left or right. A horse will raise his head perceptively when stepping on a sore leg attempting to minimize stress to the injured area. If the horse "paddles" or throws his feet out to the side instead of straight forward and back, it could indicate a prior injury and/or conformation deformity.

While still at a trot, notice the prospects "action." It is desirable that the horse be a "small mover," with little knee action as opposed to a "high stepper" and a medium to small stride. The closer to the ground the horse carries his hoofs, the more stable platform from which to strike the ball. Then view the same traits at a canter and finally at the gallop. Watch for smoothness and ease with which the pony turns and stops. The prospect should bend around turns following a turned-in nose and not hold his head too high. The pony's proficiency should not decrease with increased speed. Some veterinarians suggest performing these tests on two different surfaces; one soft greensward and the other hard-packed ground, to see if the prospect will maintain soundness on both.

The prospect should change leads appropriately and not "drag a lead" (take more than a stride to complete the change) or "cross canter" (change front legs and not the hind or vice versa). Ask the rider to execute an abrupt stop from full speed and then a turn. The pony should stop and turn with his hocks well underneath his body. Is the horse capable of doing a "roll back" or stopping and turning over his hind legs, thereby reversing direction and retracing his hoof prints?

Assuming that the prospect has acceptably passed the above evaluation, try the pony yourself. Check how the pony is bitted. If it is severely bitted, this may indicate a desensitized mouth. From a gallop bring the pony to a sudden stop, back up and then start up again at a gallop. The pony should jump forward into a gallop in one stride. In addition to being able to test the prospect's responsiveness, this maneuver will reveal the horse's ability to balance.

Now that the prospect has been worked for a while and is "heated up" (pulse and respiration are elevated) and you have been able to discern any differences in the horse's manner of going and personality when stressed, it is time for the second part of the veterinarian's check. After a season of play a well-conditioned pony will have a pulse rate of about 25 at rest. A "green" horse will have a slightly higher resting pulse rate (about 40). After a chukker of play the pulse rate will elevate to between 150 and 180. How quickly the pulse rate drops after exercise is an indication of good conditioning and can foretell cardiovascular problems. One minute after exercise the rate should drop to the mid-sixties.

It is too difficult to evaluate an unconditioned horse that has been turned out to pasture for an extended period of time to obtain any meaningful results. So don't look to purchase a horse not in training. A prospect that is sound in the pasture may not stay sound under work. Besides, if he is such a good pony, why is he turned out?

Soundness

Polo is a dangerous sport for player and horse. Even when using the best protection equipment available and despite high-quality caretaking, injuries do occur. We all, horses and players alike, play with a few minor ailments. The longer we play the more these "issues" begin to add up.

Soundness in a "made" polo pony that has a few seasons under his belt is a relative term. In addition to the stress that polo puts on a horse's legs many have incurred blows from mallets, balls, and other horses. Thus the term "polo sound" has come into use to signify a pony that has blemished, scarred, or otherwise imperfect legs but is still very much playable. For this reason, many poloists feel that a thorough veterinarian exam is unnecessary and a waste of money or, at best, only warranted for very expensive horses. Yet chances are that you will keep the horse for many years. If you amortize the cost of the prepurchase exam over the time you expect to keep the pony, it is in fact a very inexpensive way to insure happiness.

As in all performance horses, ninety percent of unsoundness in polo ponies is located from the knee down. Run your hands over the entire horse paying special attention to the legs to look for any bumps, lumps, mushiness or puffiness. The outside of the horse's bones are protected by a thin membrane called the periosteum. Injuries to this membrane result in irregular bone growth that can create bumps and other protrusions called exostosis, splints, spavins, ringbone, etc. Feel down the back of the cannon bone. The tendons should be straight and hard. If the tendon is not straight and perpendicular it could indicate a previously bowed tendon. The skin should be taut and you should be able to feel the indentation between the suspensory ligaments on the inside of the tendon. The space should be even and without any deposits or interruption. Look for any tiny holes or scars that might indicate that the pony has been "blistered" or "pin fired." Both of these remedies are used to restore damaged tendons by causing irritation. The healing of the irritation (calcification) promotes hardening of the tendon sheath, but usually leaves scarring.

Pinch the underside of the hoofs with a hoof tester to locate any tender spots and look for signs of thrush around the frog. The sole of the hoof should be white. Pink spots indicate bruising. Check for soreness around the coronet band and check the hoof for any cracks or uneven growth rings in the wall. Hoofs that appear spread out at the base with a series of differing spaced ridges may indicate founder and/or laminitis—or just a remnant of a past fever or change in feed. Lifting and stretching the front and rear legs (flexation test) can reveal tenderness or joint problems.

If the above hand and eye check has shown any imperfections or if the prospect is an older horse, the veterinarian should perform a laboratory check consisting of blood work-up, ultrasound and radiograph analysis. Certain conditions such as navicular disease can only be detected by radiography. It is always a good idea to save the radiographs. When the horse is eventually sold, the prospective owner can compare old radiographs to new ones. Blood analysis can reveal if a horse was medicated at the time of the exam.

A pre-purchase exam is not just a question of pass or fail. (It is much easier for the vet to fail the prospect than pass it and have his evaluation questioned later.) Determining the length of time a horse that is "polo sound" today will stay useful is the toughest question for the veterinarian to answer. That is why it is important for the vet to know your ability and willingness to manage health and soundness problems.

While an unsound, unplayable pony is worthless, there are many good playing ponies that will never pass a veterinarian's pre-purchase exam but, with proper care (see "Grooms"), will remain that way for many years.

Cost

"A good animal is cheap at almost any price."
Sir Walter Gilbey, 1900

The polo horse is a commodity affected by the current economic conditions and supply and demand. Obviously, a "made" pony between the ages of six and nine with good conformation, that plays well, has a good disposition, and is sound is a commodity able to demand top dollar. That is, if the owner will sell the horse at all, which is highly unlikely if he is a professional making his living (handicap) on the playing field.

Just because a pony is "made," sound and priced right or played in top-flight competition doesn't necessarily mean that the horse will suit you or respond favorably to your riding style or ability. The single biggest mistake made in purchasing a polo pony is buying "too much horse." Being "over mounted" takes all the fun out of polo and is a danger to the rider and other players alike. The rider must have a high level of confidence to lean far out from the horse, as is often required in polo. Being over-mounted causes apprehension and inhibits the rider's ability to concentrate on playing the game. However, an experienced rider may seek to purchase a horse that is slightly more accomplished than he is in an effort to improve his skills. It is figured that the rider will soon "play up to the horse," thereby raising his level of play. The theory is that better horses make better players. The aforesaid not withstanding, being over-mounted is the biggest and most dangerous error any player can make and unfortunately, one of the most common!

A beginner needs a different type pony than a high goal player. If you plan to play low-goal polo (4- to 8-goal) a horse that has successfully competed at the 22 goal or higher level may be a detriment. The position you are more likely to play also impacts on a prospect's suitability. The One and Two require quicker horses with more top speed. A Three might need a handier horse, while a Back might prefer a bigger, sturdier horse with high top speed.

Bear in mind that it costs a trainer/dealer about $3,000 to $4,000 a year just to keep a horse. Famous polo pony trainer for such stars as the Dorignac's, Pieres' and Ernesto Trotz, Cato Morzano (5h. ARG) advises, "It takes three months to teach a horse to play polo, but it take three years to get one able to play in the *Abierto*." A four- or five-year-old green horse will probably cost the professional about $2,500 to $5,000. If it takes two years to turn the green horse into a "made" pony, the professional will have at least $10,000 invested in the horse before it is salable. If it is a high-goal prospect that number could be closer to $50,000.

If the professional makes his living playing, he will be loath to sell the horse at all until he has used up some of the pony's potential. At that point the pony may come to the market place. While no longer suitable to the professional, he might be just perfect for you. In the United States today, top high-goal ponies fetch prices of between $20,000 and $40,000, while the vast majority of lower goal ponies sell for under $10,000. Of course, there are notable exceptions. In 1991 David Jamison (3h. UK)

Photograph by David Lominska

Chesney, who won races on the flat, was bought at Ascot for £2,000 in 1986 to be trained for polo by David Morley. Although his owner, David Jamison (3h. UK), only played the horse one chukker the 15.1 black gelding won five Best Playing Pony Awards ridden by Carlos Gracida (10h. USA) Note the large ring Balding gag with bit guards, drop noseband and draw reins.

refused £250,000 for his famous black gelding Chesney that he bought off the racetrack in 1986 for £2,000. Chesney, winner of five Best Playing Pony Awards in the British Open, played many seasons under Carlos Gracida (10h. USA) and is now 22 years of age retired in Gloucestershire, England much to the chargrin of the Australian newspaper magnate Kerry Packer, the whispered bidder.

Although there have been rumors of recent sales at the $200,000 level, the modern validated record is still the 1928 sale by Luis L. Lacey (10h. ARG) of his famous pony Jupiter to Stephen "'Laddie" Sandford for $22,000, which in today's terms would be $235,000! Another interesting benchmark was set in 1930 during the Great Depression, when forty-eight of John Hay (Jock) Whitney's famous Greentree ponies were sold at auction. The top price paid was $14,500, and the average was $3,479. If it serves as any consolation, in 1878 James Gordon Bennett, the father of American polo, sold his best horse for $85. At the other end of the spectrum, La Luna may be the most expensive horse ever. She was leased at $50,000 per year for only five years and then returned to her owners Gonzalo Pieres (10h. ARG) and Susan Barrantes to be bred.

Argentine horses, once a never-ending source of high-quality horseflesh at inexpensive to moderate prices, have become almost as costly as homebreds. Although Argentina still has an abundant supply of horses and maintenance costs are cheaper, the cost of transportation (to the United States about $4,000, including quarantine) must be factored into the equation. Argentina's recent financial crisis and currency devaluation may have made imports attractive once again. Still, Argentina produces the greatest number of polo ponies in the world in all price ranges and, not surprisingly, players too.

The most accurate price barometer can be determined at polo pony auctions that are held with increasing frequency at big tournaments. Here the open outcry auction market pitting buyers against each other establishes a fair market price. If you plan to use the auction market to find a pony, be sure to allow sufficient time to try out the prospect and have him vetted before the bidding begins.

Stabling

Although polo players who campaign in inter-circuit and international tournaments are often forced to accept makeshift, semi-permanent stabling, for the purpose of this writing we are only addressing the "home" or permanent stable. Like any athlete, a performance horse's conditioning and temperament are greatly affected by stable life, nutrition, and exercise. Whether you are renting, buying, or building a new stable from scratch, the same criteria apply. Your "string" will appreciate peaceful and serene surroundings while being protected from the elements, staying high and dry even on the wettest days, with ample room. In addition, abundant day and electric light and extensive ventilation are imperative. The surface area of a horse's lungs are roughly the same size as a tennis court, so they need a tremendous amount of fresh air that is free from draughts.

In addition to the number of horses to be stabled, local climate and building codes may dictate how a barn may be constructed. The two simplest and most cost-efficient styles in the U.S. are shed row and center aisle.

A shed row barn has all stalls side by side with all doors on the same side and a slanted roof that has extended eaves or overhang. Ideally, the row is laid out on a north/south axis with the doors placed on the east, or afternoon, shady side. In larger barns two sets of shed rows are placed facing each other.

A center aisle barn style consists of two facing shed rows connected by a gabled roof with an open space between the two rows wide and high enough to drive farm vehicles in and out through the back door. Aside from this obvious feature, center aisle barns offer the advantage of creating a loft for storage. They also save space while reducing the time wasted walking from end to end of a long row.

Photograph by David Lominska

A typical temperate climate shed row style barn. The ample overhang and tie rail provide a sheltered work area close to each horse. Full height sliding doors limit aisle passage problems. Just past the gray is a pass-through to shortcut walking around the ends of the barn to get to the opposite side stalls. The porous floor makes for easy cleanup.

However, if ground space is not at a premium, shed rows are less expensive to erect and an extra stall can be quickly added.

Various types of wood, fiberboard, cement, cinder block, stone, and metals or a combination thereof have been successfully utilized in stable construction. In areas that are hot year round, "summer" barns are popular. "Summer" stabling usually employs cinder block, cement and tin roofs with the walls and partitions constructed with slats or pipes to allow for maximum airflow. Horses like peace and quiet for rest. For this reason, corrugated metal roofing should be avoided because of the excessive noise it makes during rainstorms. Stall walls made of wood can break or splinter, presenting potential danger. On the other hand, cement or cinder block walls are unforgiving if kicked and can also be dangerous. Consequently, many horse owners cover their hard walls with wood, fiberboard, rubber, or other padding.

Stall doors should be wide enough to allow a handler to fit through the opening simultaneously with the horse (about four feet). While it may look attractive to see a row of stalls with horse heads protruding, doors that keep horse heads inside at all times are much less problematical. Likewise, ledges, bumps, niches or other protrusions should be avoided wherever possible (see note on cribbing in "Evaluating the Prospect," page 10). Water and feed bucket hangars and other stall devices should be carefully installed so as not to provide protrusions in an otherwise smooth box.

If the barn is erected on relatively high ground it will not be susceptible to flooding during rainy periods and, if above the local water table, will drain easily during the day when the horse is 'turned out'. Each stall, or box as it is called in England, should be large enough to allow the horse to lie down to rest or roll and get up easily without danger of becoming "cast" (see "Stabling," page 15). The most popular stall size in newly constructed barns is an inside measurement of ten feet by twelve feet. While sufficient for a polo pony or large horse, this "standard" 10 x 12 size should be considered a minimum and many players opt for 12 x 12, 12 x 14 or even 14 feet square. The ceiling should be high enough and unencumbered so that a horse can fully stretch his neck without banging his head.

Several different types of flooring are preferred depending on local availability and cost. Most of the popular materials fall into one of two categories: porous, allowing for drainage through the floor, and non-porous, which traps the urine for evaporation. Traditionally, porous stall flooring such as clay, dirt, sand, gravel, and crushed seashells has been the most popular. With the advent of affordable thick rubber matting to absorb shock, non-porous flooring such as cement, macadam and pressure-treated woods have gained favor. Both types have their adherents; preference depends largely on the type of bedding used (see "Stabling," page 15).

Interior stall fixtures should be placed in corners to make them less obtrusive. Placing the fixtures in different corners forces the horse to move around the stall. Automatic waterers or buckets should be about three feet and six inches off of the floor. Many players prefer buckets, because this facilitates monitoring the amount of water being consumed. Feed mangers should be slightly higher than water buckets and have an inner retaining ring or lip to minimize grain waste. A great controversy surrounds the feeding of hay. Some say that the hay should be placed on the floor. After all, the horse is a natural grazer and can't get hung up in a net or rack. Others say that a raised net or rack makes the horse eat more slowly and gives him something to do. The floor feeders argue that raised hay causes seeds and dust to fall into the horse's eyes and nostrils. Both methods work sufficiently well, so the final decision is up to the individual owner. The final mandatory stall fixture should be a sturdy tie ring away from the water and feed corners (see "Daily Routine," page 43).

When it comes to latches and fasteners, it is wise to buy the very best hardware you can find. Steel (iron) is the cheapest, but will rust. Stainless steel (iron and chromium) is more expensive but rustproof. Aluminum, also expensive and rustproof, is usually bulkier due to its lighter mass. Brass (copper and zinc) and bronze (copper and tin) are strong and virtually immune to weather and, except for their higher cost, are ideal.

In addition to the stalls, space should be provided for feed, hay, bedding, and tack, as well as for washing a horse and keeping horse clothes. Besides rodent-proof storage bins, the feed room should have space to prepare meals (mix grains, add supplements and medications, etc.). Hay and bedding take up the most space and have to be kept dry. To avoid mold, hay should be stored off the ground to allow air to circulate. The "wash rack" should have both hot and cold water taps and a trap drain floor. It should be large enough to allow for a horse to easily turn around. A large, heavy-duty washer is desirable for cleaning blankets, leg wraps and saddle pads.

Many more sophisticated or "professional" stables have manager's offices(s), veterinary rooms, living quarters for grooms, and clubhouses with trophy rooms, but one problem they share with even the smallest barn is manure and its disposal. Disposal may be less of a problem if you are fortunate to have a very large farm and can utilize a spreader to distribute the manure over the property as fertilizer. The manure pit is best constructed downwind from any living quarters. It should be far enough away from the barn so as to not draw flies and insects, yet close enough for the groom not to have to struggle with a wheelbarrow over a long arduous track. In many areas Environmental Agency approval (EPA) is required. In order to save loading time, many horse owners rent or buy empty containers that can be hauled away when filled. Whatever solution you choose, your groom(s) will greatly appreciate a pit that is easy to empty into without lifting the wheelbarrow.

Finally, introducing the horse to its new home involves a psychology of its own. Horses like the security of their own space but, unfortunately, polo demands that horses be often shifted from one location to another. Nevertheless, try to introduce a horse to a new location during daylight hours and give him some time to look around before putting him into his new stall. Make sure that he is put in his proper location initially so that he doesn't have to be shuffled again before he has had a chance to get used to his new surroundings. Hay and/or feed should have been placed in the stall before the horse is brought into his new home.

Pasture

Polo ponies should be turned out daily so they can rest their minds and to allow them to walk around rather than stand in a stall all day. Ponies are also turned out for longer periods of time, usually between seasons, to rest and rejuvenate their limbs and mouth. There are two types of "turn-out": pasture and "skin" paddocks. Many players prefer their horses not to eat too much grass on the theory that there are better methods of supplying protein while minimizing bulk. A dirt paddock affords the horse room for mild exercise and relief from the boredom of being in a stall all day without opportunity to stuff his belly. The paddock should be large enough for the horses to run freely and let off steam. If a horse is to be primarily turned out he will require a minimum of 3 acres of pasture. A paddock can never be too large unless, of course, you are trying to catch a horse. Either type should be level and not prone to wet, muddy areas during inclement weather.

Given the luxury of choice, most players prefer a grass paddock in spite of its higher maintenance, because a horse will relax more while enjoying his natural pastime of grazing. The type of grasses in the paddock should be carefully chosen to provide the proper balanced diet for the amount of time they are "turned out". Whether the famous Kentucky Blue, Bermuda, rye, or clover will depend mostly on local soil and climate. With some lush pasture grasses it will be necessary to limit the amount of time that a horse is turned out in the spring. On the other hand, in winter, hay and other supplements may be required. The paddock will have to be mowed regularly. Horses are partial to about a six-inch stalk and don't like long, stemmy grass that lie flat. In addition, manure droppings will have to be picked and removed to minimize parasites. An overused pasture may become mineral-deficient, and lime and fertilizer will have to be spread to rejuvenate the soil. To maintain top quality, weed-free pasture it is necessary to practice "rotation" by allowing the field to go fallow one season and replanting the next.

Nutrition

One of the factors anthropologists attribute to the successful evolution of the horse is that it could survive where ruminants (antelope, buffalo, camel, cattle, giraffe, goat, etc.) could not. Prehistoric wild horses, in competition for food with ruminants, invariably chose the very worst, lowest protein, and highest fiber roughage. A horse can survive on grasses that a cow would starve to death on. As the following tale implies, a horse can be conditioned to eat almost anything.

> A young cowboy rode up upon a run-down farm. It was obvious to the cowboy that it wasn't very much of a farm. The only crop to be seen was cabbage. The equipment was rusty and in various stages of disrepair. Even the dogs and chickens looked like they had seen better days. The cowboy rested his horse for a while watching the farmer plow the field behind an uncharacteristically finely turned-out team. The horses seemed well muscled. Their manes, tails, and coat shone as they happily put tremendous effort to the task at hand. The cowboy shouted out to the farmer as he completed a row nearest to him to inquire what he fed his team to make them perform and look so good. The farmer replied just one word, "Cabbage." "What", asked the cowboy in disbelief, "I didn't know that a horse would eat cabbage?" "Neither did I," shot back the farmer, "for the first thirty days."

This story not withstanding, given free choice, a horse will eat what smells, tastes, and feels the best—in short, what is most palatable. Unlike owners of non-performance horses, polo players have to be especially concerned to supply sufficient amounts of energy-producing feedstuffs (see Chart 1a in "Daily Ration," page 20). If a pony uses up more energy than it receives, its performance will decrease, as will its weight. Conversely, excess intake of energy-producing feedstuff can lead to colic, founder, and obesity.

An adult horse needs to eat about two percent of its body weight (about twenty pounds) every day. In order to insure that a horse eats a sufficient quantity of feed to be able to maximize energy intake, the ration must be palatable. The horse has three basic taste experiences: sweet, an appetite enhancer; bitter (sour), which detracts from intake; and salty, which can work both ways. The aroma of molasses, clover and alfalfa are the horse's favorite smells. When given a choice, it prefers the texture of grasses and seeds. All of these factors influence which of the feedstuffs will work best for a particular pony. Once a horse is healthy, happy, and in good condition he has a natural tendency to maintain that state. Nutritionists call this level of fitness *homeostasis* (see "Determining the Daily Ration," page 25).

Daily Ration

All horse feeds consist of proteins, carbohydrates, fats, vitamins, and minerals. Protein is the horse's body builder and accounts for about twenty-two percent of its body weight. Not only does it build muscle, skin, hair, and hide, but it is a vital component of the blood. Protein is used to repair body cells. The horse has the ability to store proteins but usually expels any excess. Because of protein's storage capabilities, polo ponies do not require a diet higher in protein than other horses. However, in periods of extreme stress, protein content can be increased from an average of ten percent to about fourteen percent. This is often accomplished with additives such as soybean or linseed meal, which have a super-high protein content (forty to forty-six percent) compared to that of oats (ten percent).

The horse's principal energy providers are carbohydrates (sugars). They are found in starch and glucose, which are easy for the horse to digest. (Cellulose is more difficult to break down into simple sugars.) There are two types of carbohydrates: simple, or water-soluble, and complex (fiber). Fats, or lipids, are important because they aid in the absorption of vitamins and minerals and, more essentially, are the source of the digestive acids that the body cannot produce on it own. Lipids like linseed, cod liver, and vegetable oils have high fat content that can easily be broken down into glucose and, together with the fatty acids, converted into energy. Minerals such as calcium, phosphorus, or potassium are essential for all horses, but are especially important for polo ponies because they also affect muscles, most notably the heart. Total nutritional value depends on varying the amounts of these substances so that a balance of all of the essential nutrients can be achieved without one particular ingredient leading to an imbalance. Concentrates such as pellets (nuts), grains, and sweet feeds are heavily weighted to provide large amounts of carbohydrates and proteins and are, therefore, fed in smaller amounts than roughage.

Grains

> *Mohammed wrote that, "a man would be*
> *forgiven one sin in heaven for every grain*
> *of barley fed to his horse".*

Grains such as oats, corn, barley, wheat, rye, or milo contain simple carbohydrates that are easy for the horse to digest. Grain is rated by numbers according to its quality. Better quality grains have higher weight per bushel, which indicates lower moisture content. Grains, like all feedstuff, should be free of mold, debris, dust, odor, and discoloration.

Oats are the tried and true high-energy horse feed. They are low in fat, about ten percent protein and palatable because they smell like grass. Best of all, they are safe to feed because thirty percent of their volume is made up of husks that add bulk. Because of this high fiber content, about eleven percent, it is almost like feeding roughage. Oats are practically void of vitamins and are low in calcium, phosphorus and carotene. Crimping oats (flattening them between heavy rollers) increases the nutrient value by about five percent, and is beneficial for older horses and those with poor teeth (see "Getting the Pony Fit to Play," page 27). Although oats can be fed whole, and many polo players feel that whole is more beneficial, horses tend to prefer them crimped, rolled, and/or steamed because the resulting flat kernel is easier to digest. Although the weight of oats can vary widely depending on their area of harvest and type of processing, a bushel averages about thirty-two pounds. A heavier bushel of oats will contain a greater proportion of kernels to hulls. Since most of the nutrient value is contained in the kernel, it is easy to see why the heavier bushel is preferred.

Because corn (maize) is the most widely grown crop in the United States its nutrient value varies as to the climate and soil content of the area in which it is grown. Corn is low in protein but high in carbohydrates and has less bulk because it lacks hulls. Because of its high energy content, corn is a common feed for draft horses and mules and is good for any kind of horse doing strenuous work like polo. Yellow corn is rich in vitamin A and moderate in the vitamins E, thiamin, niacin, and riboflavin, but, because of its low protein content, should be fed only with legume hay or a supplement. Corn meal, made by grinding corn ears, is usually mixed with molasses to add bulk and reduce the dustiness. Unlike oat hulls and wheat bran (feeds without bulk often called "heavy feeds"), shelled corn does not form hard-packed masses in a horse's stomach.

Many players feel that corn is "too hot" to feed most horses and can cause high-strung thoroughbreds, so popular in polo, to become less manageable. To a certain extent, this is true. Since corn is richer than, say, oats, feeding the same _size_ measure of corn will "fatten up" a horse and a fatter horse will produce more heat, especially in warmer summer months. A horse with a higher body temperature will also have a "hotter" temperament. If, however, the amount is figured by weight, corn is also a safe feed that can boost energy.

Although classified as a "heavy feed," barley has a hull and, like oats, is a good, safe feed with a slightly higher (11%) protein content. It is less toxic than oats and low in fat with a moderate carbohydrate level. However, barley is very hard and should be fed only in rolled form. A bushel of high-quality barley will weigh about forty-seven pounds. By itself, barley can form a pasty lump in the horse's stomach, reducing its digestibility. Most often barley is fed as a component in combination with oats (25%) and wheat bran (15%).

Milo, a variety of sorghum, is a popular and inexpensive feed in the Southwest and Plains area of the United States, where it grows abundantly. It is a hard round grain lacking bulk that must be rolled or steamed to make it palatable to horses. Nutritionally, it is more similar to corn than oats. Milo has a tendency to constipate horses that are not used to eating sorghum or conditioned to it gradually with small incremental increases over a period of time. Unprocessed milo is difficult for the horse to masticate and should not exceed twenty-five percent of the ration.

Wheat is a dense, small, expensive feed that, like barley, is technically classified as a "heavy" feed with an average bushel weighing in at sixty pounds. Only bran or middlings, byproducts of milling the coarse outer coating of the wheat kernel, are used for horse feed. Because wheat bran is a mild laxative, "bran mash" (made by pouring hot water over the wheat bran and letting it stand covered for about a half hour) is usually fed only once a week to "clean out" the digestive system. Wheat can be fed

Chart No. 1a/Total Digestible Nutrients

FEED TYPE	DIGESTIBLE PROTEIN	%TDN	CALCIUM %	PHOSPHORUS	FAT
OATS (Crimped)	9.4	71.5	.09	.33	.05
CORN (Cracked)	6.8	82	.02	.28	.22
WHEAT (Bran)	13.7	67.2	.14	1.29	
BARLEY	9.3	77.8	.06	.38	
SOYBEAN (Meal)	30.8	77.2	.39	.87	5.8
COTTONSEED (Meal)	34.2	72.6	.19	.96	
BEET PULP	5	65	.70	.10	.30
TIMOTHY HAY			.23	.20	
ALFALFA HAY			1.47	.24	
RED CLOVER HAY			1.21	.18	

cracked, rolled or steamed, but never ground. When mixed with other grains, it should not exceed ten or fifteen percent of the ration. On non-work days (see "Daily Routine," page 29]) this ratio can be as high as thirty percent. Because wheat bran is high in protein and phosphorus, it is frequently used to balance a high calcium diet. A bran mash is not a better feed than any other, but most horses enjoy the change in feed and mixing a bran mash with alfalfa cubes or beet pulp is a specially enjoyable and filling meal.

As mentioned above, molasses, a byproduct of cane sugar refining, is often a component in horse feeds to reduce dust and to aid palatability. It is also an inexpensive source of energy and horses seem to like the flavor. Like bran, however, it is a laxative and should not make up more than ten to twelve percent of the daily ration.

Because of their convenience, commercial feeds are rapidly becoming the most popular feedstuff in the polo universe. Somewhat like "sweet feed," commercial concentrates offer a complete nutritional mix of proteins, minerals, and vitamins. The various components are compressed into pellets with molasses or soybean oil often used as binding agents. In addition to their convenience, the nutrition content is printed on the bag or tag, making it easier to compute the daily ration. In most commercially available feeds the nutrient content may be adequate but the protein content is typically only ten to fourteen percent. Hard-working polo ponies require the additional protein intake and bulk of hay or other supplements. In fact, some manufactures of commercial feeds include hay in their pellets to slow the rate of consumption. Pellet density, rather than size, is more important. Hard crunchy pellets are consumed more slowly than soft, crumbly ones but both are often consumed more quickly than grain mixes.

Read the content labels of all commercial feeds. This word of caution is imperative for even single grains. Content can vary not only because of manufacturer's formulae, but also due to various methods of processing. Depending on type, processing only adds from a two- to ten-percent increase in nutrition. Local feed prices may make it easier and cheaper to feed whole grains even when greater weights (amount) are needed to achieve the same nutritional value. Obviously, a thirteen-percent higher cost in processed grain would not be economically prudent if all that were gained were a five-percent increase in nutrients.

Unlike hay, grain can spoil very quickly, even overnight. Most barns are continually open to outside air, and there is usually a dramatic change between the high and low temperatures on any given day. The contrasting temperatures cause airborne moisture to condense forming dew, frost or fog. This dampness collects on the underside of grain bags causing mold spores to burst into bloom.

Most horses will not eat moldy feed, but if they do, it can be, and usually is, toxic (see below). The best solutions are not to store grain on the ground and to let air circulate around the feed bags. A readily available and inexpensive remedy is to place grain on pallets.

Roughage/Hay

Hay is the horse's natural feed, because it contains sufficient amounts of all of the required nutrients on which a horse can subsist. While grains may be an option feed, roughage is a necessity to aid in digestion (peristaltic action) and, for the stabled horse, to reduce such vices as wood chewing and swaying. No matter how scientifically balanced a commercial feed may be, horses still need roughage. For the average polo pony being fed grain, the daily roughage intake should be *no less* than one percent of his body weight (ten pounds for a one-thousand-pound pony). If the horse is only fed roughage, the quantity should be increased to 2.5 percent of body weight.

Horses should be fed only good-quality hay containing a high proportion of green leaves and tender stems. Good quality is the same regardless of type and, when choosing roughage for your string, quality is more important than type. Good-quality hay means a high leaf-to-stem ratio, without weeds, debris or insects. The hay should be a rich green color with a sweet, some say "odorless" or "clean," aroma, and the stems should be small in diameter, soft and pliable. Some hays have a "sweet" smell while others have none. Blanched hay has little nutritional value. The most instrumental factor in making good hay is when it is harvested. Green crisp hay has been cut too early. Hay that is stemmy has been cut at a more mature stage of growth. It will have a lower nutrient content and will be less digestible than hay cut in the spring (first cutting). Finding good quality hays is a never-ending challenge for horse owners. A visit to the hay grower to learn about the date and method of harvest is well worth while.

Whether traditional bales, round or cubed (cubed hay is preferred by most horses), the type of hay determines the nutrient supply. There are two types of hay: legumes and grasses. Hays that draw nitrogen from the soil and convert it into protein in the form of pods are called legume hays. Because top-quality legume hay produces high lactic acid, it is more digestible than grass hay, but lower-quality legume hay is not. Almost any type of hay can be fed to horses, but all have the potential to be dangerous if it is improperly harvested, with toxins or other foreign matter, or improperly stored. Some weeds are highly toxic to horses. Yew, foxglove, rhododendron, and nightshade are poisonous to horses. Many horsemen are more suspicious of large round bales and often remove the weathered outer layer. Grass clippings should also not be fed to horses since they often contain harmful chemical and toxins.

The type of hay, when it was harvested, and humidity at time of cutting all factor into how long it takes hay to cure (ferment) after it has been cut and baled. Usually, it takes about ten days for hay to cure. The best way to tell if hay is okay to feed is to open a bale. It should be dry throughout the bale with no warm spots and no sign of mold. If any heat or moisture is detected don't feed the hay because it is still fermenting. A moist bale that eventually cures completely and doesn't develop mold is okay to feed, as well. If there are any signs of mold throw away the bale.

Chart No. 1b/Composition of Some Popular Hays

HAY TYPE	MATURITY	MEAL/lb	CRUDE PROTEIN	CALCIUM %	PHOSPHORUS
Alfalfa	early	1.02	18.0	1.28	.19
	middle	.94	17.0	1.24	.22
	mature	.89	15.5	1.08	.22
Bermuda	early	.87	10.6	.35	.24
	middle	.89	10.9	.30	.19
	mature	.79	7.3	.24	.17
Broom	middle	.85	12.6	.25	.25
	mature	.71	5.6	.24	.20
Timothy	middle	.80	8.6	.43	.20
	mature	.78	7.2	.38	.18
	late	.72	6.9	.34	.13

Grown in the cooler, wetter areas of the United States, alfalfa is an excellent hay for horses if not overfed, but is more prone to have blister beetles than other varieties (see "Getting the Pony Fit to Play," page 27). Like clover hays, alfalfa is a legume and should not be more than thirty percent of the horse's daily ration. Timothy grows particularly well in cool humid parts of the U.S. and other grass hays are safe with a low probability of mold or dust, but also have low protein. It is easy to understand why so many polo players prefer to feed a mixture of timothy and alfalfa. T & A, as it is called, provides the necessary bulk to aid digestion and keep the horse occupied, with the alfalfa providing the protein in small enough quantities to avoid any colic problems. Hybrid sorghum-Sudan hays may contain toxins that can cause muscle weakness and urinary tract failure. Liver damage has been linked to eating some grasses. Fescue grasses can become contaminated with endophyte that poses problems to mares and breeding stock. Lately, research has indicated that horses are less susceptible to problems with clover hays than other livestock. Clover hays require acidic soil with a high moisture content and grow well in winterlike conditions. However, mold can often be present in improperly harvested sweet clover hays.

The presence of mold in hay is usually due to rain during harvest. While dusty hay can be moistened with water to reduce dustiness, moldy or black hay should never be fed to horses. In addition to respiratory problems, mold causes digestive upset that can lead to colic. As if that were not a good enough reason, recent research indicates that moldy hay can lose as much as forty percent of its nutrient value. The only way to tell if hay is safe to feed is to open the bale. If there is no detectable heat it is okay to feed—whether it is new or months old.

There is a big advantage in buying large quantities of hay at one time and from one cutting because it then becomes cost-efficient to have the hay analyzed to know its exact nutritional value. Once the nutritional value is known, it then becomes easy to compute the remainder of a horse's daily ration to obtain a balance of all required nutrients.

Beet Pulp

Beet pulp is what remains after the sugar is extracted from the beet. The resulting vegetable matter is dried and sold in shredded, or pelleted form, often mixed with molasses. Beet pulp is an inexpensive but highly digestible fiber that is easy to feed and handle.

Although its protein level (>.10%) is less than grains and some hays, beet pulp can be used as a supplement to other feedstuffs. Beet pulp is usually soaked in water before feeding but, because of it has very little dust, it can be fed dry mixed with other rations. A pony's regular diet can be augmented with up to forty percent beet pulp adding roughage without adding protein.

There are many reasons horsemen feed beet pulp: it is light and easy to take on the road, it is more than just roughage but less "hot" than grains, when soaked in water it can make supplements more palatable or disguise medications. It can be stored for long period without fear of rodent or insect infestation. And, last but not least, it adds luster to a horse's coat.

Water

Water is a horse's most important nutrient. It is essential; a horse will die without water. It makes up almost sixty percent of his body weight. A 1982 study proved that horses could survive up to twenty-five days fed *only* water. Conversely, they could only last two to three days deprived of water but fed grains. There is no compromise. Horses must have free access to cool, clean water. Water aids in temperature control, digestion, sight and sound. It helps to lubricate joints and acts as a cushion for the central nervous system. It is worth repeating: horses must have free access to cool, clean water.

Horses whose water consumption is rapidly reduced are more prone to colic. Obviously, sweating and urination can cause water loss, but diarrhea is more often the cause of rapid dehydration. Sudden water losses should be replaced as quickly as possible. Pinching the skin in the area of the middle of the pony's neck and pulling it taut produces a pucker—the "pinch test." The length of time it takes for the pucker to disappear indicates the severity of dehydration. Ideally, the pucker should vanish instantly. Severe dehydration would be indicated by a lapse of fifteen seconds. Such a condition, if allowed to go uncorrected for even a short period of time, can cause the eyes to sink deeper in their sockets and the stomach to draw tight ("tuck up"). An equally good test is to measure capillary refill time (CRT). After curling back the lips to exposes the horse's gums, firmly press a finger against the gum and quickly remove it to produce a pale spot against a pink field. If it takes more than two seconds for the pink to return to the pressurized spot the horse is dehydrated.

The safest and quickest way to replace water lost after strenuous exercise is called "watering off". After the pony is unsaddled and bathed the horse is continuously walked (see "Getting the Pony Fit to Play," page 27) until breathing becomes regular, and then allowed to drink. After eight swallows the horse is led away and walked a few more minutes before being allowed another eight gulps. This practice is continued until the pony refuses to drink.

During periods of hot weather, strenuous exercise, illness (fever), loss of blood due to injury or stress, a horse's water intake should be increased. Diet also has an effect on a horse's water needs. Horses fed hay will require more water than those on grain, and a horse turned out on fresh grass will need less than both. For this reason, it is difficult to unequivocally state exactly how much water an individual horse needs in a day (see "Daily Ration," page 25). A recent study indicated that the same horse's daily water ration had varied over the course of a year from two to twenty gallons daily! (See "Electrolytes," page 25).

Minerals

Regardless of the amount of exercise, a horse needs minerals. Every horse requires calcium, phosphorus, potassium, sodium chloride, magnesium and sulfur. All are needed in relatively large quantities for normal cell function. Polo ponies require greater amounts of these so-called macro minerals. Trace minerals, such as iron, copper, zinc, iodine, selenium, fluorine, iodine and cobalt are required in lesser amounts. Potassium deficiency can lead to cribbing (see "Evaluating the Prospect," page 10).

Some minerals can ionize and carry positive or negative electrical charges (see "Electrolytes," page 25). While horses are generally tolerant of a wide range of mineral intake, content of both grains and forages must be carefully considered in order to avoid mineral imbalances that can lead to bone disorders and laminitis. Because horses have the ability to conserve minerals when needed and can excrete them at times of oversupply, over-supplementation is much more often the cause of problems than deficiencies.

One mineral that can and should be fed to polo ponies by free choice is sodium, and not only during hot weather. Sweat is seven percent salt; the foamier, the saltier. A horse can lose up to a fifth of a pound of salt a day through perspiration and urination. For a horse in moderate work, one percent of salt in the daily ration is sufficient. Salt content needs to be increased to 1.5% to 3% for a playing polo pony. Two ounces of salt per day is a bare minimum for a pony in very hot weather. If a horse doesn't eat enough salt, he won't drink enough water.

Available in blocks, it can be plain, iodized or trace mineralized. Consumption should be monitored to insure sufficient intake. If offered by free choice, it is more difficult to monitor. If an insufficiency is detected, granulated salt can be added to the feed to insure consumption. Trace mineralized is often preferred because it is an inexpensive method of providing the daily minimum requirements. Iodized salt is only indicated in special situations (injuries, deficient soil content) and should only be used on the advice of a veterinarian. Although somewhat less so than other animals, horses have a natural ability to regulate their bodily needs by using salt as a natural inhibitor to balance their intake. Salt, in moderation, will enhance palatability, but too much will limit the amount of feed eaten. Compared to other animals, this phenomenon is only mildly efficient in horses.

Supplements/Vitamins

All horses need vitamins for growth, muscle repair, and to aid digestion. Of the two types used in horse feeds, fat-soluble vitamins (A, D, E and K) are stored in the body. Water-soluble vitamins, (B1-6, B12, B complex and C) are metabolized.

Calcium is important for bone teeth and body function. The high feed intake of the average polo pony is usually sufficient to supply its need. Any boost in calcium must be offset by an equal boost in phosphorus. Phosphorus is vital to the large intestine for production of essential acids and protein. Always remember that it must be fed in a specific (50/50) relationship to calcium.

Potassium is a major factor in cellular acid base balance. A working polo pony requires seventy-five percent more potassium than a non-performance horse. Besides what is lost through sweat, polo ponies are susceptible to potassium deficiencies due to their high level of stress. A potassium-deficient pony can exhibit muscle weakness, which can seriously affect performance. A daily ration made up of fifty percent forage (hay, pasture) is usually sufficient to supply the required amount.

The conventional wisdom is to provide one supplement that balances all minerals and vitamins. Mineral balances can also be altered by mixing simple feedstuffs such as a commercial balanced feed (pellets) and oats.

Electrolytes

Every horse has electrolytes in his system without which he would be incapable of producing enough energy to trot, let alone play polo. Electrolytes are the salts (calcium, chloride, magnesium, potassium, sodium) of the body and are extremely important for the process of metabolizing (burning calories). They are second only to water in importance to the horse.

In normal conditions horses can recycle electrolytes efficiently. Except in the warmest and most humid climates, free access to a salt block provides enough electrolytes for the average horse. (Many packaged feeds also include salts.) Polo ponies usually require a greater and more controlled infusion of electrolytes. Strenuous polo activity can cause a pony to lose electrolytes faster than the body can reproduce them. That frothy white stuff that appears on some ponies after a chukker are salts—salts lost! High temperature and humidity can accelerate electrolyte loss. Often, when a pony lathers up prior to a chukker while still tied to the trailer, the reason is low electrolyte levels, which can be caused by sweating, urination and waste passage. Lack of sufficient electrolytes to carry oxygen to the muscles will result in extreme fatigue and weakness. That is why ponies should be given electrolytes *before* and after they become dehydrated. In some cases, an electrolyte-depleted pony will have no desire to rehydrate himself through drinking or eating. Insufficient electrolytes can cause muscle cramps ("tying up" see page 143), spasms and high temperature.

The two most popular methods of boosting a horse's electrolyte intake are by either adding supplements to the feed or to the water. Adding to the feed is preferred by most because it is more easily regulated. Water may often be left in the bucket resulting in unconsumed supplementation or less water may be consumed. Automatic waterers and "turn-out" further complicate the use of adding electrolytes to water. However, care must be taken that powdered electrolyte supplements do not fall through feed tub or remain uneaten on the bottom. Often horses reject feed that has been mixed with electrolyte supplements, so many manufactures now produce flavored supplements (apple, cherry, molasses) to make them more palatable. All electrolyte supplements are not equal. Varying the amounts of minerals can produce either a beneficial or detrimental effect on a horse. Some supplements are designed to replace sweat *after* exercise, while others are used to store up salts *prior* to exercise and yet others may be detrimental if used during exercise. So, check with your *local* veterinarian, who can factor in regional weather differences.

Determining the Daily Ration

It is not surprising to learn that a horse's diet is not only directly related to his performance, but also his temperament. With this universally accepted notion firmly implanted in the minds of polo players, it is shocking to find that polo ponies are rarely fed in a scientific manner. Just ask a player what he feeds, and you are likely to get an answer, "Two *quarts* of oats (or pellets, or sweet feed, etc.) and a couple of *flakes* of hay." Some more sophisticated players might even add that their feed is twelve percent protein, and they throw in a *coffee can* of such-and-such supplement. However, to precisely regulate a horse's daily ration it is necessary to speak in terms of weight not volume. For example, a measure of corn will hold the same volume if filled with oats but the corn will be 1.75 heavier than the oats. In fact, when you buy feed you pay for it by weight, yet it is rare to find a scale in a feed room. Often what a player feels is the most beneficial feeding program for a pony is not at all what Mother Nature had in mind.

The volume of a horse's ration stretches his stomach muscles (distention) telling him that he has eaten enough. The higher the temperature (atmospheric or body), the lower the intake. Conversely, colder weather stimulates appetite. This is largely related to blood sugar levels. When blood glucose level are high, appetite is diminished; when the glucose level is low, appetite is stimulated.

Horses have very weak stomachs and very inefficient digestive systems. The horse's stomach is unusually small for his size compared to other animals. (Two gallons compared to forty-four gallons for that of a cow.) Because food passes through the stomach very quickly, horses need the bulk of grass or hay to slow the passage through the intestinal canal. Bulk relates to volume rather than weight. Vague as most horsemen may be, they almost always talk in terms of volume, i.e., scoop, measure, coffee can, etc.

Without rationing a horse's diet by weight it is impossible to compute nutritional content. Total digestible nutrients (TDN) are the key to proper diet. While it may be commonly understood that corn delivers eighty percent TDN compared to only seventy percent of oats, this information is useless without factoring in weight. For example: ten pounds of corn delivers eight pounds of nutrients. The same volume of oats delivers only seven pounds of nutrients.

The recommended total daily food intake for the average horse is 2.5 to 3 percent of his body weight. If we assume the "average polo pony" to be 15.2 hands tall and to weigh one thousand pounds, that would mean twenty-five pounds of feed. During demanding tournament scheduling, finely tuned high goal ponies can consume double these averages, depending on amount of stress and temperature, etc. The total feed intake should be proportioned in accordance with his age and amount of exercise. The daily ration of a medium goal pony under an "average" amount of work should be divided evenly between bulk and concentrated feed. As work is increased, bulk should be decreased and concentrates increased accordingly, up to about sixty-five to thirty-five percent in favor of the concentrated feeds. Although it is possible for horses to get all of their daily requirements from roughage, it is more efficient to feed grain, because they will deliver the required nutrients without adding as much bulk.

Exercise, not work (see "The Daily Routine," page 29), is a major factor influencing a horse's appetite. Even in moderation, forced daily exercise programs such as those commonly practiced by the polo professionals burn calories and stimulate appetite. The more calories that are burned, the greater the consumption and weight gain. A delicate balance of diet and exercise combined with attention to environmental needs is required in order to reach a balance (homeostasis). In an effort to gain maximum performance, many players feed enriched diets and work their horse almost to the point of exhaustion. Care must be taken not to overwork a horse because, to the extent that he loses his appetite and refuses to eat, he will lose weight.

Horses are better adapted to the cold than heat but, whether Florida or the California desert in the winter or New England or Texas in the summer, most polo is played under the hottest conditions requiring players to take special precautions.

Because horses get hot quickly and it is difficult and time-consuming to cool them down, it is often hard to know when a horse is cool enough to safely feed. If time permits, most players prefer to wait at least two hours after playing or after a stressful haul before feeding. This is especially true of most polo ponies that are usually asked to work hardest in times of extreme heat only to be followed by a stressful trailer ride home. When in doubt, remember it is always better to miss a feeding than to feed a hot horse and risk colic. Another solution is to feed only hay, since it is the grain portion of the ration that is most critical. During hot periods horses will require more water and salt.

Some Helpful Feeding Hints
>   (1) Feed small amounts and often.
>   (2) Make feed changes gradually.
>   (3) Feed at regular times every day.
>   (4) Allow at least an hour after feeding before work.
>   (5) Always water before feeding.
>   (6) Feed abundant fiber.
>   (7) Keep mangers and buckets clean.
>   (8) Factor in age and amount of work to determine proper feedstuffs and amount.

Getting the Pony Fit to Play

"Wet saddle blankets make good horses."
Anonymous

We've all heard this adage and for the most part it is true. The best way to keep a polo pony in top physical condition and health is to get the horse fit and keep him that way. Except for an injured animal, the more you work a horse, the better he will become. But there is a fine line between getting a pony fit and exhausting one. Before conditioning begins, the ponies have to be shod, wormed, vaccinated and teeth "floated" (if necessary). The day after being shod the actual conditioning process begins by "ponying" (leading) the horse to make sure the fresh shoeing is well suited and to round off nail heads before working around other ponies.

The horse needs to know what is being required of him. By working the pony six days a week and resting one, the work/rest routine enables him to fully recoup before having his workload increased. By making Monday the day off, it most resembles a polo schedule, and when actual play begins he will be more able to take it in stride. Most players like to stable the string during conditioning periods. It not only enables them to more closely monitor dietary intake but also to keep them warmer. Again like humans, horses' muscles respond better when warm and, as a side benefit, their coats will improve quicker. A short ride in the trailer will also help a pony to psychologically adjust to competitive life.

In caring for "made" ponies, polo players are mostly concerned with two types of conditioning: (1) getting the pony fit, and (2) maintaining a high level of fitness without exhaustion ("souring a pony"). Renowned trainer and 10 goal player Tommy Wayman advises the following rule of thumb: "It takes one week of legging-up (conditioning) for each month that a pony has been turned out to reach playing condition again." Remember to ease ponies into work so as not to cause gall sores around their girth area. Conditioning is not playing polo. Conditioning requires a slow, steady progression of exercise levels in order to avoid injuries like pulled tendons and other strains.

At the end of one chukker of polo a horse has elevated heart and respiratory rates. The anaerobic lactate system makes a large contribution to the pony's energy supply, permitting the execution of many rapid accelerations, decelerations and changes of direction. The lactate values of polo ponies are greater than those reported after the speed and endurance phase in three-day eventers, but lower than those of racehorses after a race. (This is evidenced by the elevated amounts of blood lactates that accumulate during a chukker and remain high for about fifteen minutes after it is finished.) Perhaps this may be attributed to the preference of polo players to feed alfalfa.

Blood samples taken from polo ponies after a period of play also show increased levels of packed cell volume, hemoglobin, protein and sodium. After fifteen minutes of rest there are reductions in potassium and phosphate levels that were unchanged immediately after exercise. All of the above indicates that cardiovascular conditioning is of paramount importance in polo ponies.

The first part of conditioning is to establish a baseline level of fitness through long slow-distance work until the horse can work for a continuous hour. The exercise period should be done at alternating intervals of walk, trot, lope and canter in such a manner that the pony returns to the barn refreshed. Much like humans, horses become more fit by being subjected to stress (both anaerobic and aerobic) and then be given time to recover. Each time the pony recovers, his body becomes more capable of handling similar stress in the future. By *slightly* increasing the amount of stress, a horse can be conditioned to a point where he will play two or even three chukkers of high goal polo on even the hottest and most humid day.

The key to determining a horse's fitness, or ability to withstand stress, can be accurately measured by his recovery time. A horse at rest will have a pulse rate of 32 to 44 beats per minute while respiration rate (inhale/exhale) is 8 to 16 times per minute. By measuring the pulse and respiratory rate immediately after exercise and then noting the time it takes to recover to a normal rate, the extent of conditioning can be evaluated. It should take only a maximum of two minutes for a polo pony's vital signs to return to normal after a chukker. A less accurate method of determining fitness is by visual and tactile judgment. Visual signs of a horse's general condition include coat shine and definition of musculature.

Once a baseline level is achieved, specialized drills, such as rollbacks, wind sprints, abrupt stops, etc. can be worked into the routine to fine-tune a baseline level of conditioning into peak playing capability. Young ponies and those recovering from injuries may take more time than more mature veterans.

In addition to cardiovascular conditioning, a polo pony's training should include strength and suppleness exercises. Polo players are very resourceful in creating strength training exercises through ingenious use of available terrain. Running a horse up and down inclines or in deep sand, or swimming in water are some techniques used to increases muscle stress for horses that have achieved a high level of baseline conditioning. Circles and lateral movements performed at slow speed aid suppleness of back and spine. These exercises can be loaded by increasing the speed and decreasing the size of the circles.

Most polo players work in what they call "sets": riding one horse while leading several others. For the following example we will assume that we are working with a string of six made eight-year-old ponies that have been turned out for three months after competing in three straight months of high goal winter polo. We will further assume that the horses have been turned out on good pasture without grain and might be a little overweight and somewhat sluggish. It is assumed that each horse is ridden every third day and is led or "ponied" on the days not ridden. (It does not matter if the ponied horse trots or lopes during conditioning sessions.)

In the beginning the horse is predominantly walked. When a horse is "at the walk" it means that he picks up his feet and puts them down firmly and purposefully. His head doesn't droop or bob up and down. This is a very important indicator because, unlike the human collarbone, the horse uses his neck muscles to hold his forelegs onto his body and as a total balancing device. After the first few weeks of conditioning a pony's neck should lose its limp, spongy feel and become firm and solid. He is alert and attentive to his rider's commands. He should have an attitude that he could keep up this pace indefinitely. The pony is not asked to move up in pace until he performs at the walk and returns to the barn fully refreshed. With increased work, feed is increased proportionately (see "Nutrition, page 17). As the conditioning effort intensifies, the ration of bulk in the feed is decreased.

After the first week trotting is added. A horse's trot should be an extended stride rather than just plodding along. The longer the stride, the less potentially injurious it is to limbs and tendons. Not posting, or "sitting the trot," will force the horse's hocks under his body and engage them properly.

Finally, the horse is allowed to canter and/or gallop for short intervals before returning to the walk for the final twenty minutes of the session. A simple conditioning schedule would look something like this:

> *First week*: Begin with a 15-minute walk, 5-minute lope, followed by a 15-minute walk. By the end of the week times should have been gradually increased to a 2-minute walk, 10 minute lope, 20-minute walk.

> *Weeks 2 to 4*: Times continue to increase to a 25-minute walk, 15-minute canter, 20-minute walk.

> *Week 5*: The horses are worked individually and times are changed to include a 20-minute walk, 5-minute lope, 5-minute walk, 10-minute canter, schooling or stick and ball as necessary, followed by the obligatory 20-minute walk.

> *Note*: A lope is a slow canter, about the same speed as a trot. There is great debate in the polo community about the value of trotting. Those in favor cite the value of the trot for "legging-up" a pony and building endurance. Others argue that a polo pony should never trot. Since the first stride should be at a full gallop, they don't want their horse to even know how to trot. If you prefer, trotting can be substituted for canter work, especially after the pony is fit.

By the end of the fifth week, and during the sixth, slow practice, or "pony" games, can be undertaken. By the end of the sixth week the ponies should be fit and ready to play. At this point, the focus is on maintaining the level of fitness.

Once conditioned, a pony's fitness can be maintained with a schedule of a twenty-five-minute walk, fifteen-minute lope and ending with a twenty-minute walk. Still each horse should be ridden every third day and ponied on the off days. Wind sprints, short bursts at top speed, generally aren't necessary while the horses are being played.

The Daily Routine

Hardly ever in the competitive world of polo, with constantly changing tournament schedules to compensate for player scheduling conflicts and weather, can a day be called routine. However, for the purpose of this writing we will call a routine day any one other than a Monday (when most polo clubs are closed and grooms are given the day off). There is no polo today, but probably tomorrow or Wednesday, and all horses are sound and fit.

The day begins with the morning feeding. "Feed-up" is commonly between 6:30 and 7:30 A.M. The horses are usually left to quietly digest their feed for at least half an hour. Then the horses are removed from the stalls and "picketed" while the stalls are cleaned ("mucked out"). The water buckets are emptied, cleaned and refilled. The horses are "groomed" (brushed, curried, hoofs picked, etc.) and returned to the stalls to be made ready for the daily exercise.

Those to be ridden will be "tacked up" and those to be "ponied" will wear halters with lead shanks.

Photograph by David Lominska

A morning workout at Old Pueblo, John Hall's West Texas ranch. The front groom rides one and leads three in a four horse "set." Notice that each pony's lead shank is held individually. Many polo clubs limit the number of horses in a set and prohibit linking one horse to another.

After exercise the horses will be washed and "groomed" again and placed back in their stalls. Many players feed a small amount of hay at this time to reward the animal and help him relax. Finally, the stalls are "skipped" (surface-picked) and the floors are swept before a lunch break is taken.

At about 3:00 P.M., after lunch and a short siesta, the afternoon work begins by "turning out" the horses in the paddock. The stalls are cleaned again, and the evening feed, water and hay, is placed in the stalls ready for when the horses are brought in. Barn chores and tack cleaning are accomplished until the horses are brought in about 5:30 P.M. and "groomed" again before being returned to their stalls. Before leaving the stable for the evening, the floor is swept again and all doors, gates and bins are checked that they are secure.

The daily routine is often augmented with other, non-daily, frequent chores. How often the horses will need body or mane clipping ("roaching") will depend on the climate. Tails will need to be periodically thinned ("pulled") to make them easier to tie up. The horses will have to be readied for the farrier every four of five weeks. And let's not forget cleaning out the trailer after use, etc.

Grooming

Good grooming is important for any horse. Although its most noticeable effect is cosmetic, good grooming is important to a horse's health and wellbeing. But, because of polo's inherent hectic scheduling, grooming is often given short shrift.

Horses should be brushed regularly using the proper brushes, curries and wipes. Always brush downward and toward the tail using long, firm strokes. Short-bristled brushes are best for the body, while longer bristles are better around the face. In addition, horses should be washed regularly—not just when they come in from a muddy paddock. Mild soaps such as Orvis should be used, preferably with warm water, to loosen dirt and skin oils. Brushing will be more effective on a regularly washed horse.

To facilitate evaporation, (cooling), and to avoid entanglement with reins, etc., polo ponies manes are commonly "roached" or clipped. Manes should be clipped close to the skin and continuously *maintained* that way. Some players prefer to leave the shock of hair that falls forward between the horse's head unclipped to provide some fly protection when turned out. Other players leave a clump of mane on top of the withers for a visual guide to saddle placement.

Body Clipping

There are some grooming techniques that require a lot of practice and patience; one is body clipping. Most horsemen would rather not body clip a horse because the coat does not reflect the true color after clipping and is without sheen and dry. More often than not, a horse is body clipped after a long period of rest, usually winter months when a horse's hair grows quickest and fullest. Results will vary between horses that have been turned out for a while and those who have been regularly groomed and just have long hair. Dark bays and sorrels will usually turn a lighter shade. Unlike show horses, which are clipped for aesthetic reasons, polo ponies are clipped to facilitate cooling.

There are various clippers designed for different parts of the horse. Large standard clippers are used on the body while smaller and quieter clippers are used for the head, ears and other sensitive or intricate spots. Prior to clipping the clipper blades should be checked and replaced if necessary. Remember to oil the clipper blades frequently during the clipping process.

The best place to start is with a good bath using a mild soap and rubber curry to loosen the deeply imbedded dirt. Be sure to leave enough time for the coat to thoroughly dry before beginning to clip; if necessary, bathe the day before. The clipper will function more effectively and the blades will last longer if it doesn't have to shear through dirt and grime.

While the clipping process does not bother many horses, it isn't something that they look forward to. So, pick a place where the pony can be tied out of the way of any traffic, either human or otherwise, and a time when the area is quiet, usually mornings and evenings after feeding, when the horses are more settled. Ponies that are particularly skittish should be introduced to the clipping process gradually. Aside from not pinching or cutting the horse's skin, the most important concern when clipping is to not leave shaving lines.

Start by massaging the horse, gradually running your hands over every part of the body paying special attention to those areas that aren't usually touched—under the belly, the poll and ears, etc. Then turn on the clipper some distance from the horse. Leave the clipper running (on a cloth to minimize vibration) while stationary and move back to the horse and continue the massage. When the horse seems calm, pick up the clipper in one hand. Holding it away from the horse, continue massaging while gradually moving the clipper closer and closer to the horse's body, eventually replacing the massaging

Photograph by David Lominska

hand with the body of the clipper. When the horse realizes that the buzz is not an insect that needs to be swatted and relaxes, is the time to introduce the blade.

Hair should be cut against the grain. Start with the legs. It is an area that the horse is used to being handled frequently with various tools. Use light, even stokes where applicable and short strokes in tight or uneven places. Short strokes overlap the cut, which avoids creating lines. If a horse has very long hair it may be necessary to clip first using a coarse blade and then finishing the final cut with a finer one. Remember that it takes practice and patience to achieve a desirable result.

Insect Repellant

Insects are an important concern to the polo pony. The pony's natural defenses are impaired because he is often tied to a trailer or hitching post for long periods with its tail tied and fully tacked. No player wants his string stomping the ground and kicking out while tied in close quarters, so repellants are an important part of the grooming process.

There are a plethora of products on the market. Most contain natural ingredients, such as oil of citronella and pyrethrin. Some contain highly limited synthesized compounds. Those that are sold interstate are subject to FDA regulations. These products come in various forms. Wipes, sprays, aerosols, creams and ointments are available in various price ranges.

Water-based solutions are less likely to irritate or cause allergic reactions. However, they do not last as long as oil-based solutions. Many horses are allergic to oil-based products and can develop severe skin irritations and burns. Newer propylene glycol solutions last somewhat longer than water-based ones and seem to have less of an effect on the horse's skin.

While it is important to protect the horse, care must be taken not to get the repellant between the skin and tack or areas that come in contact with tack. It is for this reason that wipes are preferred over sprays and aerosols. Aside from the waste factor of spraying a horse out in the open, it is more difficult to insure that the repellant will go only where it is needed. Even if a spray product is preferred, it is best to spray it on a rag for application. If you must use a spray, be careful not to get it in the horse's eyes or nostrils...or you own.

Part Two:
The Player

"A person who plays polo is short-lived,
but polo players last."
Sue Sally Hale 4h. USA Goals (1938-2003)

Many will agree that polo players certainly are characters. True as it may be, it is certain that to be a good player takes classic character—the mental and spiritual traits marked by dedication to the game, moral excellence, good sportsmanship and, above all else, *love of horses*.

First and foremost, a polo player must *love and respect horses*. The highest-rated players show their respect by their almost compulsive concern for the well-being of their horses. Before they ever sit down for dinner they make certain that their ponies are fed. Polo ponies work hard to earn respect. They need to be shown it in such a way that they know they are appreciated. *Horsecare cannot be compromised*. Spending as much time as humanly possible with the ponies so as to learn their pecking order and how to perceive the subtle changes in their body language will aid the player in becoming "one with his horse." Know your horses' state of mind as well as physical condition...and let them know you. Many years before joining the English National Team, Alan Kent (7h. UK) was strongly rebuked when he defied a school proctor in order to bed down with one of his sick ponies—an act that many horse lovers can identify with. Horses have good and bad days and, just like people, react differently to the vicissitudes of life. The only way to know how they are feeling at any given time is to *maintain daily contact*. As Cecil Smith (10h. USA) says, "Even if they aren't the best ponies, you can make them better by going to the barn."

The second defining characteristic of a polo player is good *sportsmanship,* or at least it should be. Polo has always been a gentleman's game. If for no other reason, the high risk factor inherently involved in playing polo dictates adherence to a strict protocol. The player who runs half out of control, helter-skelter around the field without regard for his fellow player is never welcomed regardless of handicap. A polo player must be genuinely concerned for the safety of his fellow man, including opponents, and the animals. A selfish player who abuses his mount will never be held in esteem, nor will a constant fouler.

A dedicated player should be able to uphold his quarter of the game and should be *prepared for the level of polo* he has chosen to play. He should try his hardest every chukker. Rather than being "over-mounted," he must be able to control his mount in all situations and at all times. It is his obligation to keep himself and his horses in top physical condition. The good player is always striving to improve both his string as well as his ability.

Most polo players have a very intense competitive spirit. In Argentina they call it *garra*. Literally, *garra* means claw, but when spoken about another polo player it refers to *courage* regardless of the circumstance. The ability to keep a *cool head* and always fight to win distinguishes the great players from journeymen. Poloists that exhibit these qualities and a high level of moral character are the most revered, regardless of handicap.

Polo Equitation

> *"The polo field is the best method*
> *of training a rider."*
> E. Engle, *Polo Magazine*, 1932

Stewart Iglehart (10h. USA) wrote that it was improvement in his riding ability <u>alone</u> that caused his handicap to rise from eight to ten goals in 1938. While a good horseman does not necessarily make a good polo player, it is clear that as riding improves, so does playing ability. A poor rider is severely handicapped on the polo field. Therefore the best way to improve is to ride. There is no substitute. Any serious player rides every day. Even people with "day jobs" and hectic schedules find time to ride every day. Some rise early to ride before going off to work while others get in a little practice on the way home.

One shortcut to improved riding ability is to ride as many different horses as possible. Familiarity breeds complacency in both horse and rider. Unfamiliar mounts necessitate closer adherence to uniform fundamentals. A greater awareness of riding technique and its effect will translate to an overall increase of both horse and player performance.

Riding for Polo

> *"For the seven minutes (sc. of a chukker)*
> *you have to forget about the horse."*
> Alfonso Pieres (10h. ARG)

A lot has been said about *becoming one with the horse*. Whether called centered, balanced, natural, synchronized, harmony, united, or one, it is an obvious concept to embrace to the point that it happens *unconsciously*. If a basketball or football player had to keep up a running dialog with his legs, he wouldn't be able to focus on playing the game. The polo player's ability to transmit thoughts instantly to the horse and have those signals obeyed unfailingly, while desirable for all equestrian disciplines, is imperative for polo.

The human body's approximate center of gravity is located three inches behind the navel and four inches below that point. More than the center of gravity, it is the center of a person's physical being and the spot from which all energy emanates. The sense or feeling through which muscular motion is perceived must unite with the horse's physical center and move as one. "Thinking" from the physical center rather than head, body and legs, etc., facilitates this "kinesthesia." The two heads and six legs must act in unison.

The horse's design does not make instinctive control any easier. In his natural surrounding a horse will graze for most of his waking hours so his eyes are positioned to afford visual acuity with the head only a few inches off the ground. In a running position, or even worse, during a stop, when the horse's head naturally rises, the pony's vision is poor at best. Even the horses' naturally good acoustic discrimination is impaired on the polo field due to the hullabaloo of the event. And the speed of the game renders their acute sense of smell, which usually acts as a sort of radar to provide early warning of danger, next to useless.

In general, the regularly used rider aids are more pronounced and emphasized for the polo player. Polo demands greater use of hands and heels than other forms of riding, because it is necessary to communicate instantly and decisively with the horse. Contradictory and confused signals at high speed can result in an unseated rider and, if repeated frequently, will result in the un-training of the polo pony.

How then, does the horse put up with a rider subjecting him to the rigors of polo? The answer is that the *pony trusts the rider* to guide and protect him. It is unfortunate that an inferior mount that may engage his entire attention usually handicaps the beginning player.

Ill. #3: The polo player is hardly ever seated. By adopting a half-seat instead and with his body over the withers he enables his pony's athleticism and aggressiveness.

Enabling the Horse

When the rider is one with the horse he enables the horse to overcome his natural fear. This bonding will enable the horse to be brave, more willing and trusting of the rider's commands. In the horse world physically becoming one with the animal is defined as "having a good seat." When seated the player should move his weight slightly forward so that the fleshy muscles of the thigh are pushed outward and to the rear. Rotating the ankles inward will naturally force the inside of the legs (not the back of the calf) to maintain contact with the horse. This position may seem a bit awkward at first, but as the muscles become stronger it will become effortless and second nature.

The polo player must maintain his balance inside the parameters of the horse's balance. Just as it is easier to carry a dead weight than a live toddler who is leaning every which way, it would be easier for the horse to carry the poloist if he were glued to the saddle. Unfortunately, a polo player is not glued on and in fact, rarely seated, and often has to lean far outside the horse to make a play. Care must be taken not to shift weight suddenly while a pony is leaning into a turn or both horse and rider can go down and get seriously injured. The rider must make every attempt to remain centered and balanced. The faster the horse runs, the more his center of gravity moves forward. Therefore, the rider has to move forward to stay one with the horse, like a jockey moves up on the withers, so as not to interfere with the horse's manner of going. This is easier said than done in any horse discipline and especially difficult in polo because the body is often moving in a different direction to that of the horse when swinging a mallet.

Almost all modern players have adopted the basic principles of forward seat equitation, but polo's high-speed factor dictates an exaggerated forward lean more like a jockey with the rider's center of balance over the horse's withers. The upper body should be inclined forward from the hips. A polo player *is hardly ever seated*. His support comes from strong upper leg (thigh) and knee pressure and as little amount as possible of his weight in the stirrups. Even when not "rising in the irons" to swing, the rider is almost always in a "half seat" in an effort to keep an *eye on the ball*. A respectable rider on the show circuit, hunt field or trail may not necessarily have the particular balance and knowledge of the aids required for polo. The best riding school for polo is on the polo field. Polo forces the player to unthinkingly become "one" with the horse.

Polo players must develop a feel for the muscles of the horse under him in order to recognize extension and collection. It is important that he learn how to tell which lead the horse is on—not by looking down at the shoulders or legs, but by feel. Besides allowing the horse to use his athletic ability safely, it gives the player a good platform to address the ball, and allows the striker to add the horse's power to the stroke. Care must be taken to insure that the pony changes leads starting with the rear legs. It is easier for the horse to change his front feet first, but it causes him to be off balance in the process. This brief imbalance is not particularly critical in general riding situations, but in polo it can come at an inopportune moment and result in a bad spill.

The horse is said to be on the right or left lead depending on which foreleg is extended first. To make a right turn or to hit an off-side stroke, the horse should be on the right lead. That is, the right leg is locked straight, directly under the horse's body, to support the full weight of his pivot and/or the stroke. Obviously, the reverse is true for a left turn or a near-side shot.

Although the lead is called by the name of the leg that we perceive to be extended first, actually this is the last leg that the horse puts down in the canter sequence. For this reason, to change a horse from one lead to another, the hind legs must change first so that the horse has enough balance for his front feet to switch in front before setting down for the next step. An effortless lead change at speed can only be accomplished when all four legs are in the air.

To accomplish the high speed or "flying change," the first step is to collect the pony by slowing ever so slightly to let him know that a signal is coming. The rider shifts his weight to the opposite (new lead) side and forward just as the horse is about to raise his last leg. This simultaneous motion is accompanied by a *slight* tug on the bit (to set the head) and pressure from the rider's outside (opposite) leg. The overall effect is one of lifting the horse and transferring its weight through, from one of the rider's legs to the other, and placing the horse on the new lead.

The horse doesn't carry the rider to the ball. The pony must be ridden there and his stride rated so that the correct foot is fully extended and directly under the horse (collected) as the ball is being struck. Even a perfect polo pony has to be ridden into the play. This can be achieved by maintaining light leg pressure and contact with the bit. Running on a loose rein with the horse not balanced and traveling on his forelegs will result in hurried miss-hit shots.

Leg pressure enables the horse to go...and stop in a "collected" manner. While steady pressure urges the horse to go faster, intermittent pressure (kicking) will force the pony to "draw up" his legs under his belly (haunched). By "drawing up" rather than hyper-extending the hind legs behind, the pony is "collected" on his haunches and ready and able to move in any direction or stop. It is important to signal the horse to stop when his hind legs are under him. The horse's nose is lifted slightly as the rider's weight is forced into his seat. Stopping uses up a tremendous amount of the horse's energy, so it is not good practice to ask him to make quick stops unnecessarily.

A player executing an abrupt turn causing the opposition to be left in the proverbial dust has scored many a goal. A quick turn is made with the horse traveling on the correct lead and turning on his haunches (hocks). The player should lean into the turn, but care must be taken not to exaggerate the lean, because the pony has already calculated his balance to compensate for centrifugal force of his own weight and speed. Although the rider's upper body should lean into the turn, almost all of rider's weight should be in the outside stirrup (away from the turn). The rein hand is moved up and in the direction of the turn. This places the opposite rein against the horse's neck signaling direction and causing the horse to move away from the rein ("neck reining"). A gradual turn can be made at speed with the horse running fully extended and not on his haunches.

Stirrup Length

Everyone's "seat" on a horse varies according to his height and shape so stirrup length is adjusted to suit each rider. The polo player has to take into account not only his "seat," but also his ability to strike the ball. Unlike show riding, the stirrup can be positioned under the foot anywhere from the ball to against the heel. In fact, many players ride with their feet all the way through the stirrup ("shot home"), with their *toes* pointed down. Although this can be seen from time to time, surprisingly on even some of the best players, it should be avoided because keeping your *heels* down helps enable the rider to maintain a secure leg position.

Stirrup length has always been a matter of personal preference. Early polo artwork and photographs show extremely long stirrup lengths. The prevailing theory was that since a better stroke was achieved from a standing position, it was easier and quicker to stand if the leg was almost straight to start. The closer and tighter the rider was with his mount the greater the transference of the horse's power would be to the ball. (This style was re-inforced by the equally prevalent use of very whippy mallets.) Today, the theory is that the length of the leather should be adjusted to allow the most contact of the upper calf. Naturally, stirrup lengths should not inhibit the player's ability to rise from the irons easily. It should be noted that longer stirrups increase the possibility of injuring the "jockey" muscle while "riding short" necessitates a more inclined body, which compromises flexibility. Riding too short with the attendant accentuated body incline also means that the reins will have to be held shorter, which is not desirable in polo equitation. Most players ride so that when rising from the irons there are three or four fingers of space between top of the pommel and the bottom of their crotch.

Some players prefer leathers of uneven lengths. With the right longer, they explain, they have more reach on the most used off-side. Others like the left longer, saying that it enables them to make

Digital Image by R. D. Lubash

A player who is bothered by the extra thickness of the stirrup leather and buckle under his thigh can twist the end of the strap forward and then under the part attached to the iron. Depending on the player's physiology, the resulting bulge will be in front of the thigh rather than under it. The slit showing just below the strap end is to accommodate an overgirth.

the difficult near-side shots more easily. It stands to reason that even lengths would make it easier for the rider to be balanced and, therefore, make it easier for the horse to balance. It is all right to experiment to find the best length for you, but keep in mind that you want to make it easy for your legs to urge the horse on from behind the girth.

In polo equitation the horse show practice of turning the toes in is eschewed in favor of turning the hitting side toe out and the other leg toe in to facilitate greater upper body flexibility when addressing the ball. Turning the toes in constricts the body while the slightly-out Western style promotes greater upper-leg contact with the horse and enables the rider to maintain flexible knees and, to a lesser extent, enables the ankle joints to work as shock absorbers.

All of the player's movements should be fluid and as smooth as possible. Jerking the horse interrupts his concentration and may even scare him out of a move that he could have otherwise made. The horse is running the entire game even when the player doesn't have the ball. So don't use the pony up unnecessarily. Quick stops (starts, too) and hard turns and rollbacks take a lot out of a horse. Try to ride so as to conserve horsepower. Make gradual turns unless absolutely necessary (often players pull up their horses abruptly when the ball goes out or over the back line), trot or canter (in a half seat) back to throw-ins and foul shots. Let the pony stand still and rest for a few seconds before play resumes. "Breathing spells" are desirable and will be greatly appreciated by your mount.

The Other Leg

"In a thousand riders, 999 try to do too much with their hands and too little with their legs."
Gen. Guy V. Henry,
Chief of Cavalry, Ft. Riley, KN, 1926

Unless you are traveling on a straight line in a horse race with both legs squeezing the pony to urge him on, one leg is doing all the work. Whether serving as a pedestal for the striker to hit off or sending a signal to the horse to go one way or the other, one leg is busy all the time. What is the other leg doing?

Little attention is paid to the "other leg," even though it provides almost all of the rider's mobility in the saddle. By placing it behind the girth (for a forward stroke) it has the effect of stepping into the swing. For backhand shots, the reverse is true (see "Off-Side Backshots," page 52). By holding the knee in and the foot high, the stirrup leathers act like a sling to hold the rider into the saddle and enable him to lean out on the opposite side to reach the ball.

Most of all, it is the other half of the striker's platform. Sure, you may be mostly hitting off one foot, but you are standing on two. The act of hitting causes a transfer of weight from one foot to the other. So pay attention to where you place the other leg for the various strokes. Don't just concentrate on the leg holding you up.

Reins

Hands control the horse, and you must control the horse before you can control the ball. In polo, four reins are always attached to the bit. Even for bits that normally require only one rein, two are used. While this may sound like duplicity, the extra pair will come in handy should the primary rein break.

Photograph by David Lominska

South African eight-goal sensation, Stuart "Sugar" Erskine, puts the "other leg" to good use on this Off-Side forward cut shot. Note: the straight line connecting his right hand, head, left shoulder and ball. Also, the loose forefinger.
Equipment: Gag bridle with rope caveson and drop noseband. Polo wraps and Tackeria™ coronet boots. Fleece covered girth and breastplate. Sugar is wearing a Patey helmet, two strap Hipwood style knee guards and Franklin baseball gloves.

41

The Hands

"No hand; no horse."
Anonymous

The left hand should maintain continuous light contact with the horse's mouth, so the reins should be held fairly short. In polo context, fairly short means as long as possible while still maintaining constant control. This constant contact insures instant communication of your thoughts to the horse. However, constant contact does not mean a constant pull! Suppleness of the body by maintaining flexibility in the ankles, knees and hips enables the rider to have constant contact without inadvertent spasmodic tugs. Under no circumstances should the player use the reins to pull himself up or as an aid to balance. However, it is not only acceptable, but suggested that the rein hand be placed on the horse's neck for support.

The rein should be used "quietly". Too much "hand" puts backward pressure on the bit, causing loss of mobility in the horse's neck, which affects the shoulder down through the hocks. The hand should only work on the horse's jaw. Since a bitted horse's jaw can only open about four inches; the limit to the amount of rearward pull on the reins should ideally be just about the same. Pulling back more than that causes the horse to arch his neck resulting in loss of "collection." Muscular extension of the head, neck and back (extensor muscles) produce "collection." Improper use of the reins, affecting more than just the jaw, can interfere with the extensor muscles and ruin any possible chance of collecting the pony. Gradual interplay between the hand (preferable, affecting only the lower jaw) and legs are the proper way to control a horse.

It is imperative that the left hand be held low and disassociated from the rest of the body in order to maintain contact without tugging or using the reins for support. This is best accomplished by keeping a straight line from the bit through the reins to the elbow. The wrist should be loosely flexed, forcing the back of the hand to face forward. Straightening or flexing the wrist will act as a damper to minimize sudden jerks. In polo, the rein hand is held slightly higher than normal in hacking, because when a horse stops his head rises. The rider's hands should also rise accordingly in order to maintain the straight line between hands and jaw. (The rider should be careful to place his head to either side of the horse's neck so as to not catch a blow to the chin on ultra quick stop 'n'-go's.)

Suffice it to say that it is nearly impossible to have good hands with first attaining a good seat!

Holding the Reins

There are several popular methods of holding the reins. Although a matter of personal preference, which method used will depend, to a varying degree, on the following factors: type of bit, style and ability of the rider and, of course, the horse's manner of going.

Many top players prefer the over/under, or Argentine style. The back of the fist faces near-side (left) and the reins are carried in the palm with the thumb up. The first (index) finger is used to separate the top pair (snaffle) from the bottom (curb) pair. An advantage of this method is that it is easier to open the hand slightly and place it on the horse's neck to further aid balance, and it is easier to grab the reins after switching hands to use the whip. A variation is to divide the reins left and right rather than curb and snaffle. This method allows the rider to use the curb and snaffle independently and facilitates two-handed control. Which rein is placed on the outside will depend on the desired type of bit action required since the outside rein affords more leverage.

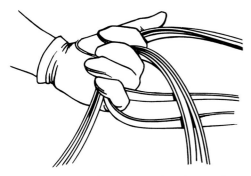

Ill. #4: Argentine 'over and under' style.

Equally popular is the four-in-hand or English style in which the back of the hand is facing up and each rein is separated by a finger, beginning with the pinkie, and the last rein over the index finger and held in place with the thumb. Usually the two outer reins are the snaffle and the curb. Proponents of this style like the added control obtained by laterally rotating the wrist to apply pressure to one side of the mouth or the other ("facing" the horse) without changing the overall tension on the bit. The English system will not be as advantageous on Argentine-trained ponies, because they usually don't use the direct reining method of training their ponies. Variations on the double rein method include: snaffle outside, curb in; snaffle between thumb and forefinger, curb between pinkie and middle finger. For the novice, the English system is beneficial because it reduces the chance of bit pressure being applied unevenly.

Still others hold all four reins in their palm thumb up and then held in place by the thumb and forefinger. The main advantage to this style is that it is not only easier to switch the reins to the right hand and back, but it facilitates lengthening and shortening when needed (near-side shots).

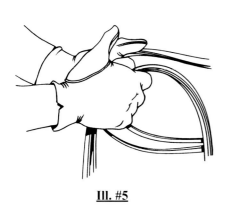

Ill. #5

Other variations include tying the reins in a knot, independently or together, with the knot either in front or behind the hand. This style is often employed when playing in the rain as insurance against the reins slipping.

Some players prefer open-ended reins to the more common closedloop style. Ten-goal brothers Benjamin and Santiago Araya (Argentina) point out that, should you take a spill, there is less chance of the horse stepping through the reins and breaking the bridle or, even worse, getting hurt. Regardless of which style is adopted, the looped or open ends of the reins past the hand should hang to left side of the horse. This is to keep them out of the way and from interfering with a stroke and away from the rider when using the whip.

Whenever possible, use two hands to hold the reins. At first it might seem awkward to place several fingers of your right hand over your left or around the one pair of reins while still holding a mallet. Not only are two hands more effective because it allows greater diversity of bit action (see bits), but it also helps keep the rider square to his mount. This position forces the shoulders and, therefore the upper body, to be centered over the horse's withers. It is easy to realize that two hands are always an advantage when you consider that in many equestrian disciplines it is a penalty or disqualification if the rider takes undue advantage by using two hands. You will never see a jockey riding one-handed unless he is using the whip. When using the right hand as a helper be mindful not to let the mallet-head swing over to the left. Not only can this cause injury to another player, but it is a foul.

It is often necessary to adjust the reins. Sometimes lengthening the reins is necessary to facilitate Near-Side shots, leaning out to hook or to whip with the left hand. Lengthening is easy enough. Just loosen the grip and let the reins slide through. To shorten up again, grab hold of the reins with the middle fingers of your mallet hand behind the left and slide the left hand forward. Here again, take care of your mallet angle.

Draw Reins

The name is derived from their ability to "draw" the horse's head in toward the body. Draw reins are long continuous reins that are attached to the saddle and through the bit into the rider's hands. This pulley-type configuration increases the pressure on the bit. By attaching the draw reins higher or lower on the saddle rigging, the angle or "action" of the "draw" can be fine-tuned.

Ostensibly used as a training device to "set" a horse's head to a desired position, draw reins have become commonplace on the polo field. Old-timers will say that they don't take the time to train horses the way they used to and that draw reins are a "cheatin' device" to keep a horse's head down. While this may be true, the vast majority of today's players feel that draw reins are softer on the mouth than double bridles or ported pelhams and more forgiving.

Once fitted, draw reins are held and used like any other set of reins.

Mallet Work

> *"No matter how sound a tactician a man may be it will avail him little unless he can hit the ball where he wishes and with reasonable consistency with regard to distance."*
> Devereux Milburn, (10h. USA)
> *Spur* Magazine, 1925

The Grip

The mallet is gripped mainly with the fingers. The handle of the mallet should be flat against the palm of the hand to better align the mallet-head with the biomechanical pendulum of the shoulder, elbow, and wrist. With the lip of the handle resting against the fleshy heel of the palm, use the pinkie finger to hold the mallet in place. The pinkie should rest against the widest part (lip) of the mallet handle. It is better to have the end of the handle below the heel of the palm than to choke up on the grip because it frees the wrist. Some players, however, like Tomás Fernadez Llorente (9h. ARG), prefer to choke up on the handle, saying that it increase mallet quickness especially when dribbling or attempting to control the ball during intricate maneuvers. The pinkie is the key to the grip for both accuracy and distance. If possible, it is desirable to hold the stick with just the pinkie, much like a hook and eye. Do not let the fingers separate (open) at the top of the backswing.

The thumb and forefinger wrap around the grip and almost touch, creating a V form where the two fingers meet when viewed from the top. This V should point directly at the center axis of the mallet shaft. The other two fingers are purely supportive and are wrapped loosely around the handle. A fist-like grip causes the lower arm to tighten up just enough to cause you to "top the ball."

Every stick-and-ball sport has its version of the polo axiom, "Let the mallet-head do the work." This cannot happen if the mallet is gripped excessively. A vise-like grip, handle thrust too deep into the palm and a fist-like wrapping of the fingers individually or collectively causes the joints of the hand, wrist and fingers to inhibit the desired biomechanical pendulum effect of the shoulder to the mallet-head.

Some players recommend switching the grip for a backhand stroke. Probably the most famous proponent of this theory was the great 10-goaler Devereux Milburn (USA), who was a perennial member of everybody's "Best Back Who Ever Played The Game List." In, "The Science of Hitting in Polo," published in *Spur* Magazine in 1925, he pointed out that rotating the mallet slightly in the hand so as to

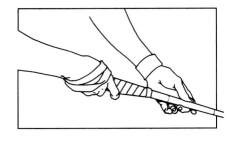

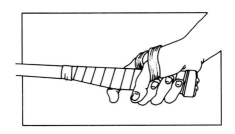

Ill. #6, #7, and #8

allow the thumb to be placed on the flat side of the handle to act as a "brace" made it easier to make the more difficult backshots (tail and away). Modern players, as well as players in Milburn's era, argue this point vehemently saying that while accuracy may be slightly improved, there was a tremendous loss of power. Obviously, it will be quicker to get off a shot without altering the grip each time. Don't tell that to Tommy Wayman (10h. USA): he changes his grip frequently.

There is a natural tendency for the fingers to loosen and the hand to open at the top of the swing. This is a very common fault and, other than timing, is probably the greatest reason for missed hits and lost accuracy. One reason why players do not constantly change their grip is because they feel that it contributes to "losing" the grip at the top of the swing.

Rotating the grip in the palm of the hand clockwise to open the club face and counter-clockwise to close the club face can be useful for making angled shots. By opening the face of the mallet before a tail shot will increase the angle. On an off-side forward shot it will enable a very acute cut-away stroke.

When not in the act of swinging, one should carry the mallet in an upright position at all times with the forearm horizontal. When the mallet is carried upright, its weight is balanced in the hand. At any other angle the mallet's weight is amplified by the length of the stick and can strain even a strong wrist. By carrying the mallet in a haphazard position it is more difficult to make a uniform (grooved) swing, which greatly reduces the ability to time the swing accurately. In addition, carrying the mallet "at the ready," or upright position, speeds up the swing. If a sudden situation develops, the stick does not have to be repositioned before striking.

The sling or thong is a safety device to keep the mallet from flying free of the hand. It does not figure in the grip and, therefore, is loosely looped over the back of the hand and around the thumb. Some players with large hands prefer an extra long sling so that it doesn't bind the hand and reduce wrist flexibility.

The Swing

Make sure the horse is going straight before beginning the swing. Almost all of the power comes from the shoulder, and the balance from the snap (whip) of the wrist. The arm and wrist are used to deliver the power-the-drive train. Consequently, getting the shoulder into the swing dictates the proper position to address the ball. The lower body adds very little dimension to the final outcome of the swing other than providing a good platform from which to address the ball. The less movement there is in the knee and the lower leg, the better the "platform" will be.

The "grooved" polo swing takes place from the knees to the shoulders. The torso and shoulders are isolated from the head and lower leg. During the swing, the torso and shoulders rotate (coil and uncoil) around the stationary axis between the knees and head, which must remain fixed directly over the ball. Ideally, the head should never move either forward or back, nor up and down.

Isolating body movement does not mean that the rest of the body is not involved, but rather that all of the body's muscles are used to aid movement of the isolated part. The action is similar to that of a golfer, a dancer or a boxer. A golfer rotates his body, shifts his weight as his hips move through the ball, without moving his head or feet. A dancer stands on one leg while raising the other leg (battement). A boxer "throws" a jab without moving the shoulders and keeping the other arm cocked. In all of these, as in polo playing, the non-isolated parts are not relaxed or uninvolved.

It is better to swing too early than too late. It is much easier to slow down a swing than to speed it up. Did you ever see a player mis-hit because he swung too early? Yet the number one error beginning polo players make is to swing late on forward shots and too soon on backhanders. If the pony is going at full speed and the ball standing still, the player should begin his swing about twenty feet from the ball. Some players prefer a pre-swing or preliminary wind-up, sometimes called the Argentinean twirl, before the actual swing to make contact. Generally this not a good habit to develop because it makes it much more difficult to time the swing and easier for an opponent to hook because a swing would have to be begun about twice as far away. Proponents of the pre-swing, however, argue that it enables the player to align his body more readily and develop greater mallet-head speed. Today, the pre-swing is mostly seen on strokes where there is no chance of being hooked (knock-ins, penalties, etc.) and on near-side strokes, where body alignment and follow-through are more compromised. Still other players begin their swing from the ground level, which is the worst starting spot because it delays timing, increases the chance of being hooked, and retards the swing.

Ill. #9

Not maintaining the vertical plane is a common impediment to a good swing. That is, the swing is begun away from the horse and ends up close to the horse. Not only does it disrupt the natural arc, but reduces distance and accuracy. It goes without saying that the player should always try to finish the swing without hitting the horse on the follow-through. (See "Follow-Through," page 48.)

The plane of the swing should be absolutely vertical. That is, the top of the swing should be at the same angle to the ground as the bottom. The plane of the mallet-head should be perpendicular to the direction the ball is to be hit and vertical to the ground throughout the swing—top and bottom. Addressing the ball as close to the horse as possible (without striking the horse's legs) will provide the easiest and best vertical plane. The farther the ball is away from the horse, the more a rider must lean out in order to maintain a vertical swing.

The swing should be timed to make contact with the ball at the exact bottom of the arc. It should not be hurried. Rather, it should gradually and evenly build momentum, reaching maximum speed a split second *before* contact is made. Peaking just prior to striking the ball brings the mallet's whippiness into play, adding to the mallet-head's velocity.

Ill. #10

Photograph by David Lominska

Adolfo Cambiaso (10h. ARG) follows through on an off-side neck shot. Note the flexibility of the mallet cane as it whips around his back. His pony is wearing "Pichiqueras" skid boots made of neoprene and hard plastic for added protection.

Follow-Through

Power may come from the shoulder, but precision comes from the follow-through. While the follow-through may have little effect on the distance of a stroke, it has a lot to do with aim, because the ball stays in contact with the mallet-head for a brief instant. It may sound elemental, but not hitting the horse with the mallet is another critical reason to develop a complete follow-through. It will also ease arm fatigue since it is the direction that the mallet will naturally follow. To cause the mallet to go in another direction uses extra energy.

In many instances where the stroke is in front of the horse or at opposing angles, there is a danger of striking your or your opponents mount with your stick. On a severe angled neck shot the mallet could even whip under the horse's neck and hit a player riding alongside.

On neck shots make sure to keep the elbow straight and extend the hand well under the neck. On tail shots take care not to bring the mallet back through the horse's hind legs. On forward shots, both near- and off-side, keep the mallet going straight and the hand going forward toward the horse's head.

Once the swing has become "grooved," distance becomes totally dependent on the mallet-head velocity and how cleanly the ball is struck. Greater speed is achieved by starting with the elbow straight and keeping it locked straight throughout the swing, thereby forcing the mallet to gain momentum as it circumscribes a greater arc than the arm. "Keep your eye on the ball" is an axiom heard in all ball sports. In polo the hitter should look at the spot where the ball meets the ground, not at the ball itself.

Ill. #11

Loft

Since the ball meets with less resistance in the air than it does on the ground, it is desirable to loft most shots. Loft is achieved when the mallet-head meets the ball below its equator and at the start of the upswing. If the ball is "topped," the resulting force drives the ball *into the ground*. If it is hit too far beneath the equator, there is a loss of distance and a tendency for the ball to pop up.

Slowing the swing, even imperceptibly, just before impact and allowing the cane to whip the mallet-head into the ball will insure a lofted drive. At the point of impact the ball should be in front (ahead) of the wrist.

More loft is gained by employing a twist of the wrist immediately prior to impact. This twist of the wrist, often referred to as a "hitch" or "flick," is actually a rolling over, from front to back (on an off-side forward stroke). The quicker the wrist is rolled over, or "snapped," the more loft will be attained. If the mallet handle is gripped too tightly, it is more difficult to "flick" the wrist.

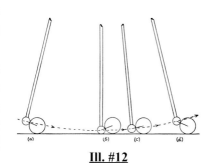

Ill. #12

Another way loft is added is to reverse the direction of a rolling ball. For example, when backing

Photograph by David Lominska

Mike Azarro (USA) shows his 10-goal form on this cut forehand stroke in front of his pony. Note the straight line from his hand through head to left shoulder. With right toe out and the "other leg" well behind the girth, it appears that all that is holding Mike onto his pony are the ball of his right foot and his left knee aided by hinged stirrups. Mike's pony wears a braided rawhide noseband. The flat braid makes the noseband less severe than regular round rope but still offers greater control than flat leather. The breastplate is fleece covered.

a ball that has been hit forward and is still rolling. The rotating ball has a tendency to roll over the mallet as you strike it, causing it to leave the mallet-head at a greater angle. For this reason, players often tap the ball forward prior to making a backshot, especially if there are a pack of riders in his line of aim, or in the goalmouth.

The Four Basic Strokes

While a ball can be hit from every conceivable angle imaginable, all strokes are basically variations of the four basic strokes. The angle may change slightly or the stroke's arc altered, usually by shortening in length, but the form should remain the same.

Exaggerated forward seat equitation, often called the "polo brace," as has been discussed in the "Riding for Polo" section forms the basic position for addressing every stroke, whether forward or back. The following assumes that the striker is already in the "brace" and out of the saddle. Any increased extension means further than the "brace" position.

Off-Side Forward

The off-side forward is the first stroke to master since it will account for up to eighty percent (ninety percent if you are a forward) of all shots. Most goals are scored with the off-side forehand, because it is both the most powerful and most accurate of strokes.

With the ball lying eighteen to thirty inches in front of the right stirrup, twist the body at the hips so that the left shoulder points down at the ball. It is imperative to be able to see the ball over the top of the shoulder. The upper body should be over the ball. The right hand is held high above the head, extending the shoulder muscle. The wrist is cocked at a forty-five-degree angle to keep the shaft (cane) of the mallet parallel to the ground, palm pointing away. The heel of the mallet head should be pointing up. Although it inhibits biomechanical motion, many players make the mistake of trying to hold the mallet-head horizontal to the ground throughout the swing.

In this position the player is coiled and ready to swing. Uncoiling begins the swing. With the elbow straight throughout the swing, the heel of the handle is brought down with as quick a start as possible in an effort to create a bend in the cane (the stiffer the cane the faster the start). Maximum speed should be reached as the wrist passes the belt line with the greatest thrust from hip to knee.

With the elbow still locked straight, the entire arm slows slightly, causing the cane to unbend and, combined with the snap or flick of the wrist, driving the mallet-head through the ball. The

III. #13

III. #14

Photograph by David Lominska

Adolfo Cambiaso (10h. ARG) prepares to hit an off-side shot. Notice how the line from "Dolfi's" right hand, elbow, right shoulder, head and left shoulder all lead straight to the ball. His right hand holds the mallet parallel to the ground with a classic grip as his left rests on the pony's neck. The White Birch pony sports a large ring gag with draw reins and a rope caveson with a drop rope noseband. Note the minimal contact with the horse's mouth.

velocity of the mallet-head is the single most important factor in determining distance. (In an average swing the mallet-head travels over one hundred miles per hour. at point of impact causing the ball to travel at speeds of over eighty miles per hour) The amount of transferred power depends on where and how "cleanly" (not striking the ground first) contact is made with the ball.

Off-Side Back Shot

The ball is addressed by rising up in the saddle (to increase the distance the shoulder travels) and out over the ball. Twist the body to the left so that, with a slight bend in the elbow, the ball can be seen over the right shoulder and the mallet is angled back over the left shoulder. Rising from the stirrups, the mallet-head should be horizontal to the ground and heel of the mallet head pointing up. Simultaneously untwisting and straightening the elbow starts the swing. The quicker the elbow straightens out, the greater the velocity of the mallet-head. Therefore, thrust the right arm forward and up—at least to eye level, with the stick horizontal to the ground or slightly rear.

Ill. #15

Bringing the handle of the mallet handle down continues the stroke, while keeping the elbow straight and close to the body. Take care to keep an eye on the ball over the right shoulder and not under the arm. The wrist may be held looser in the back shot than other strokes.

Many players do not cross the right hand over the left shoulder but keep the stroke entirely on the right side from beginning to end. This "hammer" type shot forces the body forward (not into the ball) and the head down. Although this stroke may sometimes be useful for quick cut shots, distance is greatly sacrificed.

The point of impact should be when the ball is behind the right heel. The distance behind and away from the foot depends on the angle desired for the shot. The further back, the greater the angle on shots made under the tail.

Ill. #16

Most beginners are advised to turn the horse away from the stroke. While it is safer to turn to the left to avoid a collision with an oncoming player, it rarely happens in an actual game situation. In match play, if an opponent is not able to ride you off the ball, he will anticipate your tail shot and turn to the left to take up the new (anticipated) line that will be created after the ball is hit. Rarely, if ever, will an opponent attempt to hook a backshot, since it is almost impossible, dangerous, and can result in a foul (see "Rules— Differences: Riding into a Shot," page 106).

Perhaps the proper name for this stroke should be tail shot since, more often than not, that is where the ball is hit—under the tail.

Photograph by David Lominska

Carlos Gracida (10h. USA) drops the "hammer" on a tail shot. Although Carlos' head is directly over the ball, his mallet is held outside the plane to gain angle to pass the ball under the pony's tail. Note that his mallet with an oversized head, is held parallel to the ground. His pony wears a large ring Barry gag and draw reins, leather caveson and drop noseband, polo wraps all around with tendon boots on the front legs and a fleece breastcollar protector.

Photograph by David Lominska

Sunny Hale (4h. USA) shows perfect near-side form. No wonder she is America's highest-rated woman player. Sunny's right elbow leads the swing as she uncoils her "V" with her head outside the arc of the swing. Notice how her "other leg" is well behind the girth as her left hand moves up the neck so that it doesn't interfere with the pony's manner of going. Sunny uses a Bell® helmet (no longer available), hinged irons and a breastcollar protector.

Near-Side Forward

Over-twisting the body to the left so that the ball is again visible over the right shoulder begins the near-side forward shot. The elbow is bent in the form of a V to address the ball, and the hand is faced inward and held at eye level. At the top of the swing the mallet should be inclined slightly ahead of vertical.

Start the swing by throwing the hand up and back, as the body is uncoiled. Try to extend the hand as far back as possible to increase the arc of the mallet and let the elbow lead the shot until the mallet is almost perpendicular. Then straighten the arm and exert as much wrist action as possible.

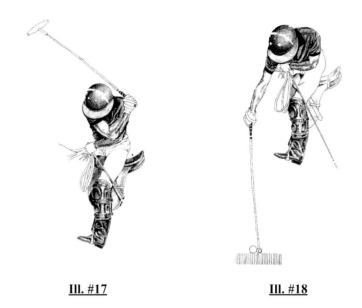

Ill. #17   **Ill. #18**

Keep the elbow close to the body, the toe end of the mallet-head pointed forward. Arm motion commences by bringing the mallet handle down with the follow-through passing to the left of the horse's head.

Near-Side Backhand

The near-side back shot is a useful tool for getting out of trouble quickly. While it is effective for quickly reversing the direction of the play, it is often not conducive to good polo because it forces the striker out of position for an excessive amount of time after the play has been turned. This is because he usually has to turn away from the ball to avoid fouling.

This spectacular shot is surprisingly similar to the off-side forward stroke. While rising in the stirrups to address the ball, extend the arm head high and allow the mallet-head to fall almost horizontally over the left shoulder. The ball should be visible *over the left shoulder*, which should be lower than the right due to the extended right arm. Extra effort must be exerted to lean out from the horse and over the ball while maintaining direction and tension to the reins. Throwing the mallet-head up and forward while straightening the elbow starts the swing.

Follow-through by severely twisting your body to the left. Follow-through is extremely important in this shot, for without it the left elbow will inhibit the right arm.

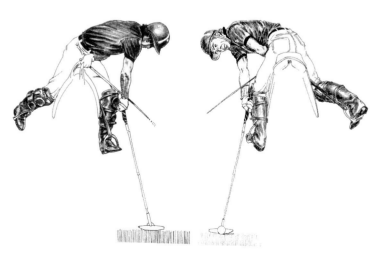

Ill. #19   **Ill. #20**

Neck Shot

The main difference between the neck shot and an off-side forehand is that, although the horse is "collected" in the same manner, the swing is not begun with the mallet overhead but out to the side and forward of the horse. This causes the swing to be horizontal to the direction that the horse is traveling. Therefore, the horse's speed has nothing to do with the outcome of the shot, so keeping the horse "collected" makes it easier to time the stroke.

Approaching the ball, the mallet hand should be outstretched to the right and forward of the horse. The mallet is held high up to start with the cane vertical. The elbow should be locked straight and the wrist should be cocked at about a ten-degree angle, causing the mallet-head to point over the horse's head.

Ill. #21

The point of impact should be directly under the horse's head, forward of the throatlatch and inside his right foreleg. The deeper the angle of the shot, the farther the ball should be inside the right leg, and the earlier the swing must begin. In fact, if able—and many are—it would be best to make contact with the ball inside the horse's left hoof.

The neck shot is a dangerous stroke because it can cause severe injury to the pony. If the horse gallops with high leg action and long strides—if he is a big mover—or has an uneven gait, it is very easy to hit the horse's legs with either the stroke or the follow-through.

Dribbling

Always try to dribble the ball as far forward of the horse as possible. Besides being able to avoid a hook more easily, it gives the player a second chance to swing at the ball should the first attempt be muffed.

There are three different dribbling strokes, the push or brush stroke, the wrist stroke and half (or quarter) swing. For the push stoke the mallet is dragged just above and parallel to the ground. With the wrist held somewhat more firmly than other strokes, the ball is pushed forward. The action is very much as if trying to

Ill. #22

sweep the ball forward—hence the name. The wrist stroke begins the same way but at moment of impact the wrist is flicked forward without much arm movement, much as if you were using a small whiskbroom. This stroke is sometimes useful in avoiding a hook and when lofting the ball to avoid a block by a horse or stick.

The half or quarter swing is the same as a regular stroke, except that it begins with the arm waist-high or lower. This is a very accurate shot and is often used for shots on goal within twenty yards. It is also a useful stroke to pass the ball to yourself while waiting for a teammate to get into position to receive a pass.

Photograph by David Lominska

Hector Galindo (9h. USA) sets for a neck shot with his head directly over the ball and a straight line from his hand and locked elbow through both shoulders, Hector's mallet hand is stretched out and the mallet is parallel to the ground but across the pony. His swing will move across the pony with the follow-through finishing on the pony's near-side.
EQUIPMENT: The pony has a large ring gag, draw reins, rope caveson and leather drop noseband. Note Hector's ungloved hands and the classic grip on the mallet with an oversized head. Hector wears a Patey helmet and his pony uses standard 'polo wraps' with Tackeria® coronet boots, large ring Balding gag, leather draw reins, drop caveson and the ever more popular braided noseband and breastcollar protector.

Photograph by David Lominska

Carlos Gracida (10h. USA) drags his mallet head close to the ground. By hitting the ball a little late he keeps the ball on the turf, making it easier to hit the next shot by allowing the ball to roll rather than bounce or create backspin.
Equipment: Large ring Balding gag bridle with rope-center draw reins, braided rawhide caveson a drop noseband and adjustable leather breastplate with sheepskin cover. The horse wears polo wraps all around with Italian tendon boots added to the front legs. Note: Carlos uses an equalizer girth and no saddle pad.

Stick 'n' Ball

The main advantage that professionals have over amateurs is that they spend a greater amount of time on the practice field stick 'n' balling. This form of polo practice is not about how far the ball can be hit. Many players practice only easy shots or tap the ball until they get a good lie and hit as hard as they can. But this doesn't approximate match-like conditions. In a game the ball rarely comes to rest allowing time to set up. Therefore, when stick-'n'-balling, it is better to limit yourself to a specific number of strokes, say a hundred, and take them as they naturally come up on the practice field without regard to lie.

Always try to aim at a target—a divot, a tree or, ideally, goal posts. Every stroke should have a definite objective. Trying to hit the ball a hundred or one hundred and fifty yards is not very important. It is better to develop accuracy within the fifty- to seventy-five-yard range. Other than hitting the pony with the stick, the worst habit to fall into is stopping when the ball is missed. *Keep going!* Even if it is necessary to circle the entire field in order to maintain pace it is preferable to giving the horse the idea to stop on every miss. Similarly, always try to turn away from the direction the backshot is hit.

When stick 'n' balling, use several balls so as not to have to pull up if a shot is missed. Hours of practice where the pony is stopped at each mis-hit will eventually teach the pony bad habits that will be hard to break, not to mention the player's bad game habits.

Practice

All too often, when players practice, ninety percent of their shots are off-side forwards. This is because it is the easiest shot to master, produces the most rewarding results and, therefore, is the most satisfying. Try and devote equal time practicing all of the strokes.

When stick 'n' balling concentrate on form to develop a "grooved" swing. Practice until it becomes second nature to swing the stick from any angle and still remain in the groove. More will be learned from miss-hitting a ball with good form than hitting the ball with incorrect form. During a match the player should concentrate on the game and not form. The goal of practice is to enable the player to hit the medium-difficult shots confidently and the easy shots more accurately. The more difficult shots will always be low-percentage conversions.

Practice at as fast a pace as field conditions and your pony will allow. Many players look like high-goalers on the practice field when traveling at a slow pace, only to revert to low-goal proficiency at game speed. A beneficial solution to approximate game-like conditions is to practice with another player. Combined stick 'n' balling not only provides a target, but also teaches how to pass advantageously to a teammate. In addition, it causes strokes to be made at varying angles under pressure that approaches game conditions.

Another useful routine for combined practice that develops hand eye coordination and a strong wrist is to play "take-away." One player dribbles the ball toward goal at a slow pace while another player tries to steal the ball. Control of the horse is the key of this exercise, and a full swing is never attempted. This training can come in very handy during goalmouth melees and throw-ins.

Care must be taken not to stick 'n' ball a playing pony too much. Most professionals do not stick 'n' ball their "made" ponies at all because of fear that the horse will become "stale." Look for signs of the pony becoming stale such as cross-cantering, frequent unasked-for lead changes, twitching of the tail, etc. Some horses do not appreciate stick 'n' ball practice and will exhibit vices that they don't show during the intensity of a match. Some players keep a stick 'n' ball pony in their string so as not to ruin a good tournament horse with endless hours on the practice field.

As ability increases so should the pace. Remember to practice horsemanship as well as stick work. Regardless of the pace of practice always maintain control of the pony and ride "collected" to the ball. Care must be taken to quit if the wrist tires. Repeated strains can do irreparable damage.

Mallet Drills

Foot Mallets

Anyone who has spent any time along the sidelines of a polo match has seen them. Kids of all ages and sizes hitting a ball around with a short, about thirty-two inches long, mallet. However, these mallets are not just for kids. They are useful in honing your swing, timing and form, not to mention, hand eye coordination and, when used with a partner, aim and distance.

It is easy to spot the up and coming young players. They are the ones who pick up the ball on one hop, bounce it in the air several times off the mallet head and then send a nice lofted shot to their partner across field.

Another useful variation is the hand mallet. About the same length as a foot mallet they are fashioned with a lead weight at the end instead of a traditional mallet head. The weight is added to the short cane to give a feel similar to a regular length stick. It is intended to be swung slowly to build strength and to 'groove' the swing. Making short strokes by utilizing only the wrist can strengthen the wrist and grip.

Sets of Balls

Another very effective way of increasing hand-eye coordination, as well as timing, is multiple-ball practice. Beginning with just two balls placed about fifteen yards apart, hit the first ball directly over the lie of the second ball and fifteen yards further. Then hit the second ball directly over the first in the same manner. Continuing to rotate balls, move around the ground at differing angles so as to work all strokes into the practice. Adding more balls and/or spacing them closer together will heighten the effectiveness of this exercise. This practice helps develop good timing, pinpoint accuracy and precise distance. After developing a measure of consistency, start varying and alternating the strokes: off-side, near-side, etc.

A variation of this exercise is to place a dozen or more balls in a row about ten yards apart. Working with an assistant or alternating with another player, gallop down the line of ball. As each ball is approached, the assistant should call for a desired shot, "Off-side forward, neck, near-side tail, leave it," etc. By not presupposing the type of stroke or which ball to hit and by delaying the call as late as possible, the player gets a chance to practice his strokes in a situation that approximates pressure similar to match play.

Push Away/Inside-Out Drills

This basic stick 'n ball variation is begun while maintaining a circle. Instead of hitting directly forward, the ball is pushed outward from the horse at a ninety-degree angle. The size of the circle is gradually decreased to the point where the ball travels only a short distance as the player keeps tapping the ball to the opposite side of the circle. By enlarging the circle, the required strength to reach the opposite side of the circle is increased. This exercise is a prerequisite to turning the ball.

Golf Balls

Stick-'n-ball practice with golf balls is another very effective method of heightening hand-eye coordination and of perfecting timing of the swing. Because a golf ball is much smaller than a regulation polo ball, even the tiniest flaw in a swing will be greatly magnified. Unless the ball is met exactly at the correct point of the swing and at the optimum angle, it will hardly move. On the other hand, when met correctly, watch out! A golf ball will travel further and faster than a polo ball, so be mindful if there are other players on the practice field.

Dribbling with a golf ball is one of the most difficult exercises to master. Anyone who can dribble a golf ball around a greensward at will should have no trouble doing it with a polo ball through a pack of defenders.

2-E Handicap

After returning from England, where he had first witnessed polo being played, James Gordon Bennett introduced polo in the United States in 1876. It didn't take long before some players and their teams had become much more proficient than others and were winning all the tournaments. In 1888, H.L. Herbert devised a handicap system based on a number of goals (American System) to allow players and teams of varying ability to play against each other. Actually, a system for recognizing players who were not playing up to "recent form" was used by Col. Sanders Darly in 1887 at Bagatelle. The United States Polo Association (USPA) adopted the American System rule at its formation in 1890. The American handicap system had a profound effect on the world of polo forever more. The idea was so successful that the HPA (Hurlingham Polo Committee, UK) adopted a similar system in 1910 for the 1911 playing season. Today the American handicap system is in use in virtually every polo playing country, albeit with some discrepancies. In 1910 it also indirectly led to the abolishment of the English off-side rule.

Prior to 1910, the HPA used the "Recent Form List" which, de facto, served to ban the best English players from all but a few competitions. The majority of players of the day tried not to make the list. Initially, the American system assigned each player a number based on the number of goals he could be expected to score during one game (sixty minutes of play). By then totaling the aggregate team handicap, players of differing abilities could compete together. If there was a disparity in total team's handicaps, it put pressure on the higher-handicapped players to make up the differential. Handicapping players, along with the abolishment of the Field Off-side Rule (see "Strategy and History," page 85) led to higher scoring and to modern polo as we now know it.

Each player is assigned a handicap rating from –2 to 10 goals based upon comparative evaluation of horsemanship, hitting and game sense, (knowledge of position, rules, defense, team play, quality of horses (horse power) and "overall value to the team." "Overall value to a team" usually translates to *garra*, organization skills and positive attitude.

In the infancy of polo handicapping, often two different handicaps were assigned to one player. One handicap represented his handicap when he played individually, and another when he played with his regular team, where he was not only used to his teammates' moves, but also had a better choice of mounts. Obviously, a 1-goal player with twenty excellent ponies is worth more to a team than a similarly rated player with four aged ponies of questionable soundness and athletic ability.

Handicap Evaluation Criteria

Mongol Emperor Akbar the Great (1542-1605) may have been the world's first ten-goal player. He was famous for hitting the ball in the air and is credited with carrying the ball from one end of the field to the other without the ball touching the ground and then scoring. The most recent (July 2002) *USPA Bulletin*® codified its handicap evaluation criteria for the five most populated brackets (Novice to 2-goal) as follows:

Novice: A person who is in the introductory stages of active participation in polo and is a true beginner with little or no experience in polo. A beginning rider who has had no previous riding experience at speed and has no technical understanding of the game. This person could also be a player who is an expert rider but is just learning to hit the ball and learning game strategy. A novice is not eligible to play in any scrimmages until he is able to ride his horse under control and he is not endangering himself or other players on the field. Once the player is determined to be safe, he or she would be allowed to play in non-USPA games under the direct control of the club.

C or –2: This player has a very basic understanding of "game strategy," and should play, under club guidance, in practice games only. They have the following skills:
- RULES: Limited knowledge of the USPA rules.
- HORSEMANSHIP: Beginner of basic riding skills at speed.
- HITITNG ABILITY: Can exercise offside shot some of the time, but not necessarily a good striker of the ball.
- TEAMWORK: Assist with offensive plays some of the time, can finish some plays, but has a hard time initiating new plays. Possesses the ability to execute "hooks" some of the time.
- STRATEGY: Minimal position experience. Requires direction in order to be positioned for "throw-ins," "knock-ins" and "penalties" in accordance with the team plan.

B or –1: These players have limited experience and can take plays away from teammates. The player can play under tournament conditions without constant coaching and is able to create a limited number of plays for their teammates. This player would play as a –1 and be certified to play in up to 8-goal tournament matches.
- RULES: Basic understanding of the USPA rules of the game.
- HORSEMANSHIP: Beginner or intermediate riding skills and be capable of playing in a relatively safe manner.
- HITTING ABILITY: Execute some of the shots most of the time.
- KNOWLEDGE: Assist in offensive plays from the "end line," "throw-ins," "turnovers" and "passing."
- TEAMWORK: Possesses the ability to execute legal "ride-offs," "bumps" and "hooks" some of the time.
- STRATEGY: Minimum understanding of some game strategies and plays.

A or 0: This player is an asset to the team. This player produces more positive than negative plays. This player can adapt with little coaching to new situations. This player can ride at speed, make plays and hit the ball more than twice at a fast gallop down the field under pressure.
- RULES: Has a good understanding of the USPA rules.

◆ HORSEMANSHIP: Intermediate or better riding skills and be capable of playing safely and under control most of the time.
◆ HITTIG ABILITY: Execute most of the strokes the majority of the time in a satisfactory manner and occasionally be able to "turn" and or "dribble" the ball without fouling.
◆ KNOWLEDGE: Possesses a clear understanding of his/her position played.
◆ TEAMWORK: Survey the field visually with the intent to pass to an open player, to defend an uncovered offensive player, to assist a teammate in trouble or to anticipate advantageous positioning.
◆ STRATEGY: Have minimal experience in planning and implementation of various game strategies, including the ability to position teammates, schedule ponies and select plays in the most effective manner.

1 Goal This player shall have:
◆ RULES: Clear understanding of the game and shall be able to verbally explain and demonstrate the rules of play to others.
◆ HORSEMANSHIP: Shall have intermediate or better riding skills and be capable of playing in a safe manner.
◆ HITTING ABILITY: Execute most of the shots, a majority of the time in a satisfactory manner including the ability to "turn the ball" and dribble in a 30-meter circle most of the time.
◆ TEAMWORK: Player shall possess the ability to initiate offensive plays from the "end-line," "throw-ins," "turnovers" and "passing."
◆ STRATEGY: Minimal experience in planning and in the implementation of various game strategies, including the ability to position teammates, schedule ponies and select plays in the most effective manner.

2 Goal: This player shall have:
◆ RULES: Clear understanding of the USPA rules and shall be able to verbally explain and physically demonstrate the rule of play to others.
◆ HORSEMANSHIP: Advanced riding skills and capability of playing in a safe manner and under control.
◆ HITTING ABILITY: Ability to execute all shots, at will, in a satisfactory manner, including the ability to "turn the ball" and "dribble" in a 30-meter circle. Offensive: Possess the ability to initiate offensive plays from the "end-line," "throw-ins, "turnovers," "passing" and be counted upon to successfully convert 50 percent of #2, 3 and 4 penalties. Defense: Possess the ability to execute legal "ride-offs," "bumps," hooks" and "blocks" and shall be able to turn the play from defense to offense without incurring a penalty.
◆ TEAMWORK: Shall routinely survey the field visually with the intent to pass to the open player, to defend an uncovered offensive player, to assist a teammate in trouble or to anticipate advantageous positioning. Shall be properly positioned at all times in accordance with the team plan.
◆ STRATEGY: Shall possess moderate understanding and have minimal experience in planning and implementation of various game strategies, including the ability to position teammates, schedule ponies and select plays in the most effective manner.

Each year every player's handicap is reviewed by the Circuit Handicap Committee and as proficiency increases or decreases, ratings are adjusted. A 10-goal rating represents the very best of these attributes. Although the ratings are assigned by the USPA, the actual ratings are first awarded at the club level, then affirmed by the Circuit Handicap Committee, and only then awarded by the USPA. While many feel that this system is flawed (especially for low-goal players who only play at local club level), it has proven to be an effective method of "leveling the playing field" and enables players of differing abilities to play together with equanimity. Most players who attain a 3 goal or higher rating are professionals. When the aggregate handicap differs between two teams, a commensurate number of goals is awarded to the lower rated team.

The present USPA Rule 2c states that a C or (–2)-rated player or N (Novice) cannot participate in any USPA events. A player with a handicap of B (–1) may not participate in play above the eight-goal level in a USPA-sanctioned tournament. Likewise, Rule 2c also states that in no case may a player's individual handicap exceed the upper limit of a tournament with a limit of 4 goals, and in events over 4 goals may not exceed 3/4 of the upper limit. This so-called "3/4 or Bachman Rule" means, e.g, that in an 8-goal tournament, the highest-rated player on the field could not be greater than 6.

The following is a breakdown of outdoor handicap ratings for the 2,893 players registered with the U.S.P.A. in 1998, 2,516 players in 2000 and the 3,014 players in 2002:

HANDICAP	10	9	8	7	6	5	4	3	TOTAL	%
No. of Players:										
'98	10	7	8	17	22	52	72	139	327	.10
'00	11	9	9	19	20	41	66	129	304	.10
'02	11	9	20	22	29	49	77	157	378	.125

As the above numbers indicate, 87.5% of all players are rated at 2 goals or less. "High-goalers" rated 6 or above account for only 2% of the playing populace. In 1933, "high-goalers" also accounted for only 2% of all players, but 17% were rated 3 or higher. Today only 12.5% rated over 3 goals.

One hundred years ago there were only three 10-goal players in the world—today there are eleven. During the past hundred years there have been only 240 players ranked 7-goal or higher by the USPA. That same period has produced a total of 42 10-goal players.

Theoretically, polo players should desire a low rating, because an underrated player is a benefit to his or her team. Additionally, a lower handicap allows the team more flexibility in choosing teammates to best answer a specific opponent. Invariably gripes can be heard about so-and-so being underrated or a ringer. Sure, it happens. But discrepancies are quickly adjusted. The viability of the handicap system is born out by the unusually high number of games decided in overtime or by just one goal, usually scored with only seconds remaining on the clock.

Photograph by David Lominska

Grant's Farm *patrón* Andy Bush, one of America's highest-rated amateurs, at 5h stretches before a Federation of International Polo (FIP) match in Santa Barbara, CA where he represented USA.

Physical Training

"If every player were as fit and as gallant
as his ponies, imagine the standards."
Adam Snow (10h. USA)

It has often been written that because of polo's relatively high cost and the amount of time necessary to play the sport, most novices come to take up the game fairly late in life. A 2002 USPA study revealed that most players take up the sport between the ages of 35-40. The median age for all male players was 48 and 35 for females. Certainly amateurs who have to devote time to work, family and other pursuits are rarely in the superb shape that a high-speed, full-contact sport requires. But a close look at photographs of polo players going back a hundred years shows that almost all were superbly conditioned athletes.

Physical conditioning is an integral part of a polo player's routine and cross training is very popular. Back in the '20s, Tommy Hitchcock used to rise especially early to box three rounds with a trainer before going off to Wall Street. He chose boxing because, he said, "I think it brings a fellow to the point of exhaustion quicker than any other exercise." As if there were any doubt, imagine a 10-goal player (America's first at age twenty) who could stay with Mike Tyson in the ring, beat Sampras at Wimbledon, drive the Indianapolis 500, ride both steeplechase (in 1887 he won 79 races out of 101 that he entered—a record that stands to this day) and flat race winners, beat the U.S. Open Champ on the golf links and defeat all comers at skeet and pool. Such a man was Foxhall P. Keen (1870–1941), whose father had a standing offer of $100,000 (more like a half million dollars today) to anyone who could beat his son in any of ten sports. No one ever took up the challenge.

The leg and lower back muscles are used extensively in riding. So far, the best way known to man to exercise these muscles efficiently is to ride, ride, and ride. However, pleasure riding still won't give the legs anywhere near the amount of stress encountered when playing polo. One way to increase the intensity of exercise to the "riding muscles" is not to use stirrups at the trot. Posting and maintaining balance, even for short distances, is the best and quickest way to strengthen the crucial muscles.

In addition to building muscle strength, it is important to increase bone density. Needless to say, bone mass is very important in case of a fall, and free weight lifting is an excellent method of maintaining bone mass.

Seeing a polo player arrive fieldside just before the start of a game, it is easy to assume that they do not warm up prior to mounting. But that is rarely the case. Most players consider stretching before a game extremely important, and those that don't do it fieldside usually do so in private. Stretching is especially important after sitting in a car for a long drive to a match. Yoga and pilates are two disciplines that are popular with polo players.

Most polo players who work out tend to concentrate on their upper body because of its importance in long ball hitting often at the expense of working on the legs. "After all," goes the refrain, "I ride a bunch of ponies every day." True as that may be, there are some muscles that don't get enough work. The most infamous of these is the "jockey muscle," but back pain, joint pain and spasms can all have their origins in poor leg muscles and tendons.

Wall Squats

Wall squats are a great way to strengthen legs for riding and rising out of the saddle. Stand with head, back and hips against a flat wall while your feet should be same distance from the wall as the length of your thigh (@18 inches) and shoulder width wide. While maintaining head and back contact slide down the wall until the knees are bent at a 90° angle. Make sure to keep your ankles directly under your knees, shins perpendicular; thighs parallel. Hold this position for fifteen to thirty seconds.

This isometric exercise builds slow twitch (Type 1) muscles and will increase leg muscle endurance. The difficulty of this exercise can be increased by placing a ball between your legs and holding it in place while executing the exercise. Start with a larger ball and work you way down to a tennis ball.

Weight Wheel

Another useful exercise that strengthens the wrist and forearms is to curl a weight around a stick while holding the arms parallel to the ground. Use only a two-to-three-pound weight at first and rotate the stick both clockwise and counterclockwise.

Ill. #23

Part Three:
The Game

Polo is believed to have originated in Persia prior to A.D. 1000. In ancient Persian writings the game was called *chaugán,* which refers to a polo stick. By the fifteenth century the game had become the rage in the Himalayas, where it was called *kan-jai-bazéé* (*sagol kangjei*). In his most famous work, "Book of Kings," (1010) based on actual events of the Persian Court, Firdausi (935-1020) referred to the game as *chaugán-gui* or stick and ball. *Pulu,* the Tibetan word for "knot of wood" (po-long) from which the first polo balls were fashioned has long been accepted as the origin of the word polo. However, modern etymologists now agree that *balti,* the Tibeto-Burman word for ball is more likely correct. The game attained popularity in Manipur, a small state between Assam and Burma, and then spread throughout the peninsular region. The name polo was not used until the nineteenth century, when British soldiers and civilians encountered the game during service in India and *Pulu* became Anglicized to "polo."

Why Play Polo?

"It takes hot blood and a cool head to play polo."
Juan Carlos Harriott (10h. ARG)

Like all games that have endured for centuries, polo mirrors life: it is thrilling, dangerous and enlightening. But polo is more than a game, it is a way of life. Not necessarily a life of champagne, caviar and black tie balls; polo demands a tremendous commitment of time and resources. Polo is considered the second most dangerous sport, having a mortality rate second only to that of auto racing. A polo player's dedication to the sport usually involves the whole family and may impact on place of residence, schooling of the children, family vacations, and employment. The total devotion that the sport demands melds polo players into a world-wide fraternal brotherhood that few outside the sport can understand. It is not surprising then that without introspection, polo can take on unexpected importance. It is a selfish, expensive game that few can play and fewer can master. So, why would otherwise rational people take up the sport?

Perhaps the best answer was given by the often-quoted J. Moray Brown in the 1891 edition of *Badminton Library of Sports and Pastimes*:

> "Angling teaches a man patience and self control; (fox) hunting improves not only good horsemanship, but pluck and observation; whilst shooting inculcates quickness of hand and eye coupled with endurance and the power of bearing fatigue, football, cricket, rowing, rackets, tennis all bring to the front and encourage qualities that are essentially manly; and perhaps no sport tends to combine all these lessons so much as polo, none makes a man more a man than this entrancing game, none fits him more for the sterner joys of war or enables him better to bear his part in the battle of life."

If you substitute the combat of modern big business for "war," this is still an apt description.

In ancient Arabic writings dating as far back as 600 B.C. there are references to the sport of polo. According to Sir Richard Burton's translation of *Tale of the Wazir and Sage Buban*, one is led to believe that the game was a viable "elixir for ill health and effeminacy arising from a soft life and want of exercise." Some believe that it is this theory that gave rise to polo's social panache, since in those days only kings and princes were likely to lead a soft life. Rather than an "elixir," most of today's players are likely to agree that polo is an addiction that can only be broken by poverty or death.

Polo is the fastest team sport in the world. As Julian Hipwood (9h. UK) emotionally phrases it, "The thrill of sitting on a horse, hitting a ball, galloping flat out round the field is unbeatable. The wind in my face, the speed." It might be added that it is the only full-contact team sport that can be played after school years and well into later life. The element of danger is real and part of what bonds all polo players. The concentration required to ride fast and safely is intense and requires complete focus. Many players find this aspect of the sport almost therapeutic because it cleanses the mind of the everyday worries brought on by the normal vicissitudes of daily life. In most other adult sports each individual is concerned with his "personal best" score; in other words, he is always trying to beat himself.

The famous American humorist and 2-goal player Will Rogers, speaking of polo said, "They call it a gentleman's game for the same reason they call a tall man shorty." Even though polo is a rough-and-tumble sport involving high speed, full body contact and many serious accidents, it is a scientific game requiring good horsemanship, discipline, unselfishness, quick judgment and decision, as well as faith in your teammates.

Knowing when to go fast, when to rate your horse, when and which way to turn, when to attack and when to take up the defense can only be learned by playing and watching polo for a period of time, if not eternally. Every player must strive to improve his own skills as well as his effectiveness as a team member. Fortunately, television, videotapes and slow motion have brought the high-goal superstars into every living room. This gives modern players an advantage over their predecessors, most of whom never saw high-goal polo. Repeated viewing can be an invaluable training aid, but there is no substitute for playing as much polo as possible.

Students of the game agree that it is the most scientific outdoor team sport because it combines athletics and hand-eye coordination with strategy and discipline at very high speed. The prerequisite traits for a polo player are physical fitness, quick thinking, team spirit, nerve, anticipation, and skill coupled with an intrinsic desire to overcome adversity and win. Polo players are highly competitive, aggressive, fit, quick-thinkers with nerve, team spirit and a healthy respect for the opposition. With such a strong desire to succeed and work under pressure, is it any wonder why so many successful people from such diverse fields enjoy the sport of polo? In addition, they have a strong desire to succeed, and yet can withstand criticism and work well under pressure.

Before a player steps onto the polo field for the first time he should, at the very least, be fully cognizant of the two fundamental concepts of polo—The Line (USPA Rule 23) and The Right-of-Way (USPA Rule 24).

Individual Play

Individual brilliance rarely wins the game. However, there are many individual characteristics that enhance team effectiveness. Grace under pressure is often cited as the most desired trait. Always try to play within your ability and be sure to concentrate on the game and free your mind of other considerations.

The Line and Right-of-Way

"The Line" is the line of the path that the ball has traveled and the line of its path should it continue to infinity. The Line remains intact until it is changed, *even if the ball is at rest*! No other player may cross that line or give cause for worry that he might. In addition to the Line, a right-of-way (ROW) exists to the immediate left and right of the Line and in both directions. Each side of the right-of-way or path is wide enough to comfortably accommodate a horse and rider. If a player correctly enters the ROW along the line, he is said to possess or "have" the Line.

Common sense dictates that two players coming at the ball from opposite directions attempting to execute an off-side forehand shot must pass one another in the left side right-of-way or the horses will collide head to head (see ill. #29, page 104). However, easy as it is to explain or understand, it is the most commonly committed foul at every level of the game.

Let's examine some of the finer points of the rule to see why it gives players so much trouble. To enter the ROW correctly, the player must do so at a safe distance.

What constitutes safe is a somewhat subjective matter to the umpire, who must take the relative speeds of both players into consideration. The basic criterion is that the entry must be made in such a way that another player, also on the Line but further away from the ball, does not have to slow his speed or adjust his play in any way. In fact, the player shouldn't even be concerned that he *might* have to execute a maneuver in order to avoid an accident. The faster the speed of play, the greater distance required to safely enter the Line. Theoretically, a player who has the ROW could shut his eyes and continue the play without fear that another player will cross the Line or his right-of-way, or that anything will impede his progress.

Once a player has successfully established himself on the Line, the only way to wrest possession of the line is to execute a ride-off, which can be thought of as pushing the opponent out of his right-of-way. Crossing another player's right-of-way, or infringing in any manner, constitutes a foul. This includes placing a mallet-head in the path of a horse's hoof or not leaving sufficient space for the player to continue on his path without trepidation. The most common crossing foul is committed by a player executing an off-side back shot (see ill. #16, page 52) and does not involve crossing the Line but, rather, the right-of-way. Many fouls occur when a player misjudges when he will make contact. Invariably, being late causes the bump to happen after the opponent has established his ROW to swing. Even if only the horse's nostrils or tail are in the ROW, it is still a foul.

As shown in the sidebar on page 103, two primary right-of-ways exist at all times, one in each direction. The path to the left side of the ball is called the primary right-of-way; the secondary right-of-way is the path immediately to the right of the ball. In other words, two players can "have" the Line simultaneously while traveling in the same direction, but from different sides of the Line. Neither may cross into the other's ROW. Both players are entitled to a play on the ball, but the player in the secondary ROW is forced to use the near-side to avoid crossing the Line and riding into the other player's ROW.

Any two players traveling in the same direction, having correctly established themselves on the Line, have the right-of-way over any single player even if that single player is on a primary right-of-way. Always! If the player on the secondary ROW pulls out of the play, both players on the primary ROW (each to the left of the ball) may claim equal right to play the ball. When one player is following the ball and another one is meeting it, the one following the ball has the ROW regardless of the two players' respective angles (Rule 24f).

The rules of ROW and crossing the Line should be ingrained in a polo player as deeply as the rules of automobile driving. (This may be somewhat easier for those players used to driving in the United Kingdom.) Sometimes it is difficult to see all of the players at once and who is entitled to the Line. If a player who has a better vantage point notices that a teammate is about to commit a foul, he should call out to warn him to pull out.

USPA Rule 25 states that that if the ball should happen to pass a player's stirrup directly parallel to his horse, he has the Line. This occurs so rarely that the point is all but moot. Consequently, "owning" the ROW becomes all-important. The quicker a player can get to the Line and establish his ROW, the better. Often, because of a smaller angle, it is possible to get on the Line before a player who is closer to the ball, thereby placing him in a position to foul.

"Man, Line and Ball"

"First, take out the man, then look for the Line and, lastly, go for the ball." This advice is heard *ad nauseam* throughout the polo community. While innocent enough and basically a sound admonition for the beginner, it is the harbinger of trouble at a later date. It would be far wiser for the tyro to learn to recognize the Line (and ROW) first. After all, how will he know in which direction to ride-out his man? Therefore, the admonition might be more accurately said, "Line, man and ball."

The above not withstanding, always "take out the man." Even if you are in possession of the ball, go to the man first and maintain contact with him. If you don't, he can time his "bump" better and make it more effective. You can always move back to the ball to keep your man in check and control the Line.

If you cannot get to the man to "mark" him, get on the Line of the ball. If you are on the Line, your opponent must spend his effort to move you off the Line. Once you have taken your man out of the play and assumed the Line, then you can go for the ball without worry of fouling.

The "man, line, ball," concept is important for all players, but it is especially critical for the Back. A defensive foul in his own territory usually results in a goal for the opposition.

Ride Hard

Always ride as fast as you can when on the attack. Hanging back to make certain of hitting the ball slows down your entire team and forces it out of position. In addition, it allows the opposition to set up a defense. Don't wait for the ball to settle to get a good "lie." It is comparatively easy to be sure of hitting the ball when going slowly, but of little use in a game. It is accuracy at speed that counts and should be practiced (see "Stick 'n' Ball," page 59). Conversely, don't dribble the ball unnecessarily. The faster the polo, the less opportunity there is for dribbling. If you plan to play high-goal polo, learn to hit hard and fast. You will probably be so well marked that you won't have a second chance.

Always try to take the ball on the *off-side* as much as possible and hit toward goal, if not to goal, then to a teammate headed to goal. However flashy other shots may look, none are as accurate or can travel as far as the off-side forehand. This so-called "natural" side uses up less horsepower too. By hitting longer shots, the team can spread out further, thereby stretching the defense.

Never play an opponent or teammate for a miss. You must expect and trust your teammates and opponents to perform their duties well. When in doubt of where to go, turn toward the center of the field.

Players ahead of the ball should always be looking backward. Whenever you see your teammate take possession of the ball you must turn your horse in the direction you think the ball will be hit before it is struck.

Try never to be caught out of position. During the time you are racing to get back into position, your team is playing with only three players.

Stopping the Ball

Though polo should be played at a full gallop there are many times when it is useful to slow down the pace of play—even stopping completely.

A player who has successfully entered the ROW and has the Line, has the right to slow down or come to a full stop, providing that he has allowed for following players to go around. This should not be confused with missing the ball at a full gallop and abruptly coming to a stop. Such stopping on the Line is a foul (USPA Rule 25b). Legally slowing down the ball is a useful tactic allowing the player with the ball to wait while his teammates get into position to receive a pass.

Anticipation

*"The most basic rule is to win the play
before the ball comes to you."*
Pite Merlos (10h. ARG)

Like chess, polo is played with the mind. Moves must be planned. Anything that happens on the polo field can be anticipated. Good anticipation means not only knowing where the ball is going before it is hit, but recognizing the probable new Line. Anticipation, often called "polo sense," can help compensate for lack of horsepower by saving your pony from unnecessary runs, stops and turns. Good anticipation is a product of hard work and practice. Poor anticipation is evidenced by the inability to keep up with an opponent. Thorough team discussion of strategy well ahead of game time will further efforts to improve anticipation.

Working on the polo field means perpetual motion, always trying to position oneself so as to best help the team. The best position is not always where the ball is, but marking your man, watching the ball, conserving your horse, etc. Concentration must never falter. In order to neutralize your opposite before he gets to the ball, you must develop total field recognition and know where everyone is at all times. Know the strengths and weaknesses of your teammates and their horses. Also try to learn the same about your opponents' capabilities.

A major key to developing good anticipation is to always try to be in the right place at the right time. The easiest way to accomplish this seemingly unattainable feat is to always try to place yourself slightly ahead ("knee-up") of your opponent. Controlling the off-side is tantamount to winning the match. Turn quickly to present an easy angle for your teammate to aim a pass. By noticing how an opponent is holding his mallet and the position of his horse as he lines up to make a play, you can often determine the new Line that the ball will take after it is hit.

Mental practice aids anticipation. Try and rethink actual games in your mind. It is absolutely crucial that we do not mentally practice mistakes but rather visualize ourselves making perfect plays. This mental picture is carried over onto the playing field. Quickness is mental—the faster you think, the faster you are.

During the three and a half years that Bob Skene (10h. USA) was held captive in a Singapore prison, he replayed past matches over and over in his mind. When he was released, he returned to polo maintaining his handicap as though there had been no hiatus. Many said that he had actually improved!

Backing Up

If you are in the next position and on the Line, you should always follow a teammate "carrying" the ball in case he should miss or be ridden off the ball. "Backing up" requires precision and timing. If you ride too close, you won't have time to swing. Too great a distance; your opponent will get there first. Depending on the relative speed, fifteen to twenty feet is as close as you should ever get to the player you are backing up.

If you are being ridden off, don't allow your opponent to take you too close to the player you are "backing up." Disengage and pull up slightly. Chances are that your opponent will charge on and be too close to hit the ball or cause a foul. In either case you (or your team) will get the shot.

The call to "leave it" is most commonly heard when players are in a backing-up situation and should always be obeyed. A player should yell for another player to "leave it" when he has an easier shot than the player with the ball does or when he is unopposed and the player with the ball is being ridden off. Another instance when the "leave it" play is called for is when there is no teammate to pass to in front of the player with the ball. Upon hearing the call to 'leave it', the player with the ball should not hit it but ride ahead as fast as possible to receive a pass from the player for whom he has just left the ball. Never leave the ball without being called to do so, and when you hear the "leave it" call, get out of the way quickly and take the man, if applicable. It only stands to reason that a player should never call "leave it" unless he is certain he has a better play on the ball. There is no worse feeling than leaving the ball for a teammate only to see him getting hooked or ridden off the ball by an opponent he didn't see.

When a player gets the ball and begins a run, his teammates should attempt to get on the Line behind him to back him up should he miss, be hooked or be ridden over the ball. When backing up another player, it is important to keep a distance of three to five strides so as to be able to see the ball clearly and to react if the ball is kicked or slightly mis-hit. Similarly, if you have the ball and mis-hit, get hooked, or ride over the play, you should circle back to get into back-up rotation unless you know that you are being backed up by a teammate who has a legal play on the ball, affording you to go out for a pass.

While circling back may not seem as effective as hitting forward to an open man, in certain situations it is often the only play available (as when nearing the back line). Obviously, if there is an open teammate within range and on-line, the most aggressive offensive play is to try to pass ahead to the open man.

Marking the Man

Marking the man means riding close to your opponent. It is a mistake to think that you've got your man covered if you are a horse-length ahead or behind. Only the most experienced player can afford to be even a yard away from his man. It is equally mistaken to think that keeping yourself between him and the ball marks your opponent.

The inexperienced player should ride next to his man and preferably on his "offside." If nothing else, this may serve to put a superior player off his game. It is mentally consuming and disconcerting to be constantly trying to shake an adversary who is marking closely.

If you miss or lose your man, it is generally futile to chase after him. Let a teammate pick him up while you go to the open man. Remember, *not marking someone is wrong!*

The Ride-Off

There is probably no play in polo where experience is more important than in a ride-off because it requires not only rating the relative factors of speed, distance, and angle, but the relative size and strength of the horses. The ride-off is the maneuver used for gaining undisputed possession of the ball. It is also useful for attaining an advantageous position over an opponent, for creating an opening for a pass, challenging a player on the line, or rendering a player unable to hit the ball. Overzealous or continuous riding-off of an opponent is counterproductive to good polo, because it is very tiresome to horses, de-emphasizes offensive strategy, and reduces the positive effects of combining with teammates (see "Teamwork," page 88).

Photograph by David Lominska

Red Number 2, Adam Snow (10h.USA), maneuvers his pony to get his right knee in front of Hector Galindo's (9h.USA) while blocking his advance. Hector's pony wears a breastcollar protector, polo wraps and Tackeria® coronet boots. Both men are wearing two-strap Hipwood knee guards but Hector wears Argentine style polo boots while Adam sports Western style.

If you have any choice in the matter, you should always try to ride your man off on his stick or "off" side. Winning the ride-off depends on placing your horse slightly ahead of your opponent. But he knows that as well which is where experience counts. The approach must be deliberate, and the timing of the contact is critical. If you are too fast, you will slip ahead of your opponent and cause a foul. Being too slow will result in a late hit and also cause a foul. Executed correctly, both players should come together, "saddle to saddle."

Being on the correct lead, i.e., with your horse's foreleg extended on the same side as the opponent, is desirable, but often there isn't enough time to execute a "flying change" under the pressure of game conditions. A well-trained pony can throw his weight into a "bump" on either lead, however; he will do so more effectively when he is on the lead nearest to his opponent. It has been said that a good pony will anticipate the "bump" and change to the correct lead without the rider's aid. Lots of luck! In case not, guide your pony ahead of your opponent first (about a neck-length, or three feet) and then use vigorous outside (opposed) leg pressure together with neck reining to close contact. A pony that hasn't learned to move away from the leg will be of little value in a ride-off.

The ideal contact position is for your leg to be just ahead of your opponent's knee and lying against his horse's shoulder. Some players lean into a bump, and some lean away. Either action is based on a theory that the pony will react to the rider's weight and produce a more forceful bump. A rider's weight adds little to the final outcome of a ride-off. More often than not, a quick weight shift interferes with the horse's athletic ability and concentration. A centered or evenly balanced position offers the most control and gives the pony a greater sense of security.

Whenever possible, you should try to ride your opponent off on his mallet side to take away his ability to swing at the ball if the ride-off is not completely successful. Care must be taken not to ride a man off who is in the act of swinging, as this constitutes a foul (see the discussion of fouls in the chapter "Rules," page 105).

Once contact has been made, immediately move over the line to establish your right-of-way on your off-side. The quicker contact is made, the more time there is to gain the line. Control your speed to maintain the advantage until the end of the play. When you have gained the advantage and the Line, then, and only then, concentrate on the ball. Adhere to the rule "Man, line, ball."

When the object of the ride-off is not to gain the Line (and ball) yourself, but to stop your opponent from hitting, a hard, quick ride-off or "bump" is required. This is accomplished by closing contact at a greater angle. You have to be especially careful to make contact saddle to saddle and not to bump so hard that you cause your opponent's pony to stumble or mis-step, thereby creating a foul. Watch the elbows, too. It is permissible to make body contact with your opponent with the upper shoulder, but an extended elbow is a foul.

Often veteran players will feign a ride-off. An opponent expecting a bump will urge his pony on and lean into the ride-off. The experienced pony will lean into the play as well. Knowing this, the wily veteran will pull up his horse so that the other player, receiving no resistance, will cross over the Line, creating a foul.

The offensive ride-off occurs when the player carrying the ball sees his opponent closing in to make contact. Instead of maintaining the line to the ball, he will veer from the line, sometimes as much as a few feet, to initiate contact off the line. Then, if he loses the ride-off he can 'allow' himself to be moved over to the line in time to re-hit the ball. While this can be a tricky play to execute, it is far safer than trying to speed up your pony to 'scoot out' of a bump. This usually results in timing being thrown off and horses coming together too late to avoid a bad accident.

Care must be take to avoid riding-off an opponent into the ROW or Line of the Ball of other players. Not only because it is a foul to do so, but because it can be extremely dangerous. The danger factor is exacerbated by the fact that more horses are involved and it is usually unexpected and often coming from a blind spot. It is also a foul to attempt a ride-off while an opponent is in the act of swinging at the ball. However, it is legal to ride-off a player on his mallet side while he is dribbling. Dribbling is defined as the mallet head not rising higher than the knees or hocks of the horse.

Hooking

All too often a player will be too late getting to his man in order to execute an effective ride-off, but there still may be a good chance to hook the opponent's mallet. If you can't get to the ball to strike it and are not close enough to effect a ride-off, the next best thing to do is hook your opponent's mallet. Very often a chance to hook is missed because the player was only concentrating on hitting the ball. The hook can be a very viable alternative. It can be such a devastating tactic that the first USPA rules formulated in 1890 prohibited hooking an opponent's mallet under any conditions. Although permissible in England, it remained prohibited in America until 1911.

A legal hook can only be attempted when all of the following apply:

1. An opponent is in the act of swinging at the ball. (A pre-swing is not considered part of swinging at the ball.)
2. A player is on the same side of the opponent as the ball or *directly* behind.
3. A player does not reach over, under, in front of, or behind another player's horse.
4. A player does not hit his own or another player's horse.
5. A player's mallet remains below the opponent's shoulder.
6. A player is responsible for his mallet at all times and cannot slash at or otherwise recklessly use his stick.

When attempting to hook, ride with the mallet at the ready (upright) position until the actual moment of the hook. Riding with the mallet extended slows down the horse and makes it easier for an opponent to avoid the hook. Likewise, swing the mallet to make the hook. This makes it easier to aim the stick and, by bouncing the opponent's stick out of the way, gives the hooker an opportunity to hit the ball (see ""Hook and Hit" in the chapter "Advanced Plays," page 95) after the hook had been completed. Remember: a violent or "slash" hook is a foul.

Conversely, when trying to avoid an opponent's hook, lean as far forward as possible and try to make contact with the ball in front of the horse's head. It is almost impossible to swing through an opponent's hook, and the resulting shot would be highly inaccurate anyway. Another alternative is to pre-swing backwards into the opponent's mallet to knock it out of the way just prior to your own stroke. This is more easily accomplished if the opponent is carrying his stick extended rather than at "the ready"—which is another reason to always carry your own mallet at the ready.

Hooking an opponent's mallet while he is not in the act of swinging or while the stick is above the shoulder is a foul. In keeping with rules promulgated to protect the horse from injury, it is also a foul to reach across, in front of, or through a horse's legs in order to hook an opponent. Likewise, it is a foul to use excessive force or to swing in an "intimidating" manner. Remember Bob Skene's admonition, "A shot spoiled is equal to a stroke made."

Photograph by David Lominska

Talk about cane flexibility! Rick Hartnett (2h. USA) gets some help from teammate Andres Weisz (6h. ARG) hooking blue number three, Martin Estrada (6h. USA). Martin's horse is bitted with a double bridle using a gag bridoon, direct reins and breastcollar protector. All three ponies are wearing polo wraps on all fours and Italian tendon boots on the fronts with Professional Choice® coronet boots. Andres' pony is the only one without coronet boots.

Scoring

Regardless of your regular position or number, if you should find yourself ahead of the pack with possession of the ball, it is your obligation to try and score. The sooner you can get the ball to the center of the field, the better, because it makes the difficult approach shot that much easier. Your first shot should center the ball on goal. The aim of your next shot, the approach shot, should be to place the ball for an easy tap-in. This is easier said than done! It is especially difficult because the approach shot usually demands a long, hard straight shot. In any event, it is important that you aim for a spot about seventy yards in front of the goal mouth. The approach shot is critical. Although distance may be required, accuracy is always absolutely necessary. Aim for a spot inside of twenty-five yards from the goal center. Ideally, you want an easy tap in for your final goal shot.

Even if you are unopposed and have a clear shot from the seventy-yard line, it is better to plan to hit a forty-five-yard approach shot. Not only will this insure an easy goal but, should you miss, it will leave the ball for a teammate.

As evidenced by the proportionately high number of knock-ins in a typical game, more balls go over the back line wide of goal (due to acute angle shots) than goals are scored. Obviously, the approach shot is the key for the setup of the goal shot.

When making the actual goal shot, try not to "rate" (change the speed of) your horse, but rather concentrate on the easy tap. All you should have to do is maintain a firm grip and make contact with the ball. Shoot at the goal as soon as you are within range and have a high-percentage angle. If you are on an oblique angle, aim for the farther goal post to compensate for the horse traveling in a direction different than that in which the ball will be struck.

Once, while watching a game beside veteran 10-goaler Bob Skene, a seventy-yard neck shot miraculously found its way through the goal posts, and the crowd yelled enthusiastically. Mr. Skene responded, "It would have been a prettier goal if it had gone in beside his horse."

Position Play

"For, our number one's a dandy,
Number two is fast and handy,
Number three is the hardest hitter of them all;
But nothing can be grander
Than that solid old back-hander
When our back is being hustled, on the ball."
H. L. Herbert, First Chairman, The Polo Association (USPA),
The Book of Sport (1901)

Playing your assigned position or always maintaining the proper position is crucial to successful teamwork. Just one player out of position can have an immense negative impact on the entire team and make an otherwise strong team weak.

Because polo is an always changing game, requiring players to be ready at all times to temporarily assume another player's vacated position, each player should be familiar with all four roles and be prepared to assume them. Once there has been a natural rotation of position, no attempt to return to assigned positions should be forced. Remain in the assumed position until another natural rotation takes place or play is halted. Under no circumstances should a player leave an opponent unmarked.

The Number One is considered an attack or offensive position. He should be an "eternal optimist," always expecting the ball to come to him. The Number Two is the workhorse and scrappiest player. He is the offensive link between the One and Three and must restrict the opposing Three. The Number Three is the pivot and controls the team's tactics. The Back supports the Three and is always ready to defend and keep the proverbial back door closed. The opposite of the Number One, he is the "eternal pessimist" and is very cautious. The Numbers One and Two should be as readily interchangeable as the Number Three and the Back. Remember that it isn't the number pasted on the back of the jersey that determines your position.

Being out of position gives the opposition a huge advantage. It is difficult, time-consuming and horsepower-exhausting to try to regain proper positioning once it has been lost. While it is important for all four players to maintain proper position at all times, it is most important for the Number Ones and Fours, because the game is contained between them. Each player must evaluate where he is: his relationship to his teammates, where his opponent is, which half of the field he is on, whether he is on offense or defense, and the direction of the ball, to determine his proper position. A player riding to the boards to back the ball in his opponent's half of the field automatically becomes the Back.

Although polo is a sport of combination and teamwork, each player has specific duties within his assigned position. Before a player can contribute to team play he must know his own position and what his teammates will expect of him.

Number One (The Optimist)

No position is more important to a team than the Number One because he is usually in the best position to score. Yet, because the Number One's role is more easily defined and the strokes required are easier to master, most beginners are initially placed at this position. At the very least, the Number One should be able to advance the ball from both sides of his horse. Devereux Milburn (10h. USA), arguably the greatest Back to ever play the game, called a good Number One "the greatest asset a team can have." The Number One has two clearly definable objectives: for defense and offense.

Defense had always been a mainstay of the Number One's game, especially prior to the abolishment of the English off-side rule, but in modern polo a strong offense is considered the best defense. The Number One should be as aggressive as possible. He must possess an optimistic attitude and believe that the ball will come up to him. Whenever his team is on offense, the One should press the attack with abandon, giving little thought to the opposing Back except to gain the upper hand in positioning himself for a pass. The One's only thought should be scoring and, when failing to score himself, to advance the ball to a position for his teammates to have an easy shot at goal.

The secondary objective is, when on defense, to keep the opposing back from hitting the ball, thus leaving the way open for his teammates to score. For the most part, the Number One will be marked by a higher-rated and more experienced Back. This is especially true in low- and medium-goal polo. If a zero-rated Number One is able to keep a three- or four-goal Back from ruining the play and feeding his forwards, he has effectively negated his handicap deficiency. The ability to mark an opponent is the quickest and surest way for a player to raise his own handicap!

There are four strategies for playing Number One and neutralizing the opposing Back. One is to play "outside" the Back (between the Back and the goal) and make him chase to mark the One. When on the attack, if the One is always between the Back and his goal ("in position"), the Back is forced to gallop to you and is not otherwise engaged in helping his team. The second method is for the One to position himself "inside" the Back. This is less effective, because on long outlet passes the Back will be in a position to reach the ball first and better able to protect his goal. The third possibility is for the One to concentrate on marking the Back. This strategy is often employed when the Back is a vastly superior player than the One, and can be greatly enhanced if the One and Two rotate position more frequently. This can also be effective against a Back who marks his man too closely. By continually exchanging positions, the Back will have to hesitate in order to know whom to try to mark, thus being in danger of leaving himself out of position. The fourth and most effective strategy is also the most difficult to execute. It requires the One to play in the same area as the Back, neither ahead nor behind. It demands that the One pay very close attention to the Back in order for the One to place himself advantageously to receive a pass and, at the same time, try to keep the Back on his near-side. In the "same zone" strategy there is constant jousting between the Back and One to insure that the One doesn't get blocked by the Back when play turns. The one drawback of the same-zone strategy is the Back "coming through" with the ball. (When the back is let loose, it turns the play into three against four.)

If you are always bothering the Back by being on his off-side (again, "in position"), thereby neutralizing his effectiveness, your team will have the upper hand in the match. However, if the opposition has particularly effective near-side backshots, it may become necessary to switch strategies. It is the obligation of the Number One to immediately recognize when his team is on offense or defense and act accordingly.

Unfortunately, the Number One is the easiest player to be drawn out of position because he is usually galloping well ahead of the pack (or at least, should be). When play turns, he is the furthest away and traveling the fastest (again, or should be) in the opposite direction. It takes immediate awareness that the play has turned and quick reaction to avoid getting "left back."

Regardless of the circumstances, after the throw-in (see "The Throw-In," page 90), the Number One should never leave the Back alone to position himself at will. A strong effective Back allows his team to concentrate on offense. On the other hand, a compromised Back will cause his teammates to keep one eye on the "back door," thereby decreasing the effectiveness of their offense.

Beginning Number Ones have a tendency to play "off the Back" and a little closer to their opponent's goal when on attack. Their often-heard excuse is that they were "waiting for a pass." This should be avoided because, if the play turns from offense to defense, the Number One is then forced to chase after the Back to get back "into the game." Invariably, he will be late. Aside from allowing the Back too much of a free hand, it uses up the One's horse unnecessarily as he chases to get back into position. If, for some reason, the One should "lose" the opposing Back, he should find the nearest unmarked man and mark him, continuing that coverage until that play is over or reversed.

If the Number One (or Two) has an unopposed clear run at goal, he should forget about the opposition and try to score. If, on the other hand, the Back is between him and the goal, he should *always* go to the Back to try and ride him out of the on-coming play leaving the ball for his Number Two. This play should be second nature, and he should "leave it and take the man" even if he doesn't hear "Leave it" yelled from behind.

Finally, the Number One has an obligation to keep the ball in play at all costs. This means not taking wild shots at the goal. When presented with an acute angle or otherwise difficult shot, the proficient One will attempt to circle or make a backshot to center the ball to a teammate. Of the two, the backshot is preferred because it is easier to master and presents a faster solution. Remember, it is better to miss the ball and leave it in front of the goal than to knock it over the back line. Even if the opposition gets possession of the ball, probably by a backshot, the result is better than to give the opposing team a free hit knock-in and time to set up their attack.

Number Two (The Opportunist)

The Number Two is an opportunist. His overriding characteristic should be getting to the ball quickly. The Number Two must have sufficient courage to challenge the opposing Number Three for the ball. Number Two is probably the most difficult position to master, because it requires greater role latitude than any other position and faster thinking. In addition to the Two's main offensive role, responsibility for helping the Number One score–he must mark the opposing Number Three, who is usually the opposing team's best player. Because of the duality of the Number Two's role, he will generally use up more horsepower than any other position. Therefore, it is extremely important that the Number Two be well mounted. It helps if he is a good striker too who is particularly adept at difficult angle shots. The longer he can hit, the more the One can stay out in front to receive a pass.

More than any other position, the Number Two must be capable of quickly rotating positions with the Number One and Three when the need arises. The Number Two must be constantly aware of the ball while trying to keep the opposing Three from setting up his teammates. And, when on offense, the Two must vigorously press the attack without regard to defense. Due to this "free-roaming" opportunistic quality of the Number Two, there is more of a natural tendency to commit the cardinal sin of polo—being a ball hog—than any other position. Nothing is more disruptive to the effectiveness of team strategy (see "Strategy and History," page 85) than a selfish Number Two.

It takes a great deal of playing experience for the Two to avoid being "suckered" out of position. Often the Number Two allows himself to go too far into the rear of the game to help on defense. This negates the Number Two's primary offensive role when his Back or Number Three should back the ball. The Number Two is said to be "out of position" when a well-backed ball falls to the opposition. If the Number Three backs the ball and it falls to the opposition, it is usually the Two's fault. The Two must not forget that the Number Three is counting on having two players with whom to set up the attack. The Number Two is not concerned with defending the goal, unless he has rotated position with the Three. From a defensive standpoint, the Two can best help his team's defensive strategy by foiling the opposing Number Three.

The Numbers One and Two should be in constant communication, ready at any moment to interchange positions. The Two should always try to pass the ball to the Number One so that the One can receive the pass clear of the opposing Back and, preferably, on his off-side.

Number Three (The Catalyst)

Number Three is the team's pivot for their transition from offense to defense, he is in the most advantageous position to set the all-important pace of play and create opportunities. Although he is his team's first line of defense, he does not react but rather initiates. He is the resourceful playmaker and must possess a knack for passing. He must be able to set up his team's attack with quick, sure passes to his two forwards. Consequently, he should possess a reliable back shot. Accuracy, not distance, is important. Next to the Number Two, the Three must be capable of covering more ground than anyone. The Number Three doesn't get as many opportunities to show off his individual brilliance, but if he plays his position well, he will make his Number Two look like the best player on the team.

More important than his hitting ability is that the Number Three possess the most polo know-how on his team. Since he is often the most proficient player on the team, he is best suited to be the team's field captain. However, his hitting ability should be accurate and versatile enough to enable him to quickly place the ball advantageously for his forwards. The quicker, the better. The back shot, from any position and at any angle, is the Three's weapon of choice. It is much faster to change defense into offense with one stroke than a series of cut shots "taking it around."

The Number Three is neither an offensive nor a defensive player. Rather, he is the link between the Back and the forwards. Often he must rotate with his Back and convert his Number Four's backshots into offensive plays and feed his forwards accordingly. However, the Number Three should not try to do the work of the Back. Not quite as frequently, the Three must also exchange positions with his Two while marking the opposing Number Two.

In sixty percent of a typical match the ball is in the hands of the Two and Three. If the Back "comes through" with the ball, the Three must then assume the Back position. The ability to freely exchange position with the Back takes considerable experience and is the basis for good team "combination." Fortunately, the Numbers Three and Four usually have more interchangeable abilities than the Three and any other position. As a rule, the Three is the only player who should try to meet the ball if it is coming at him. When the ball is near the opponent's goal, the Number Three should play more aggressively and take chances. The Three will usually have more easy shots on goal than the Number Two.

Back, Number Four (The Pessimist)

The Back, or Number Four, carries the greatest responsibility on the team because his reliability allows the Number Three to join in the attack. Usually, the Back is the most experienced player on the team and, ideally, is best capable of maintaining his cool when under attack. Maintaining proper position is more important for the Back than for any other player in the line-up. Even though there is no teammate to back him up, the Number Four's action should be deliberate, not desperate. The aggressiveness of the rest of the team is directly affected by the degree of help they are forced to lend to the Back. The Back must anticipate the *next* new line better than any other player on the team. If the Back plays in such a way that his teammates are certain of his ability to "keep the back door closed," then they can concentrate on offense. When on offense, The Back must block the opposing Number One so that, when play turns, he is in an advantageous position to turn on the new line quicker than his opponent.

Because the Back can see the entire play in front of him, he has more time to think and not just react to the play as it unfolds. This added time factor should give him the advantage of never allowing the opposing Number One between him and his team's goal. The exception to this rule is when the opposing Number One is such a weaker player that you can play him mostly on the off-side to make the hook and hit play (see "Hook and Hit," page 97). Otherwise, the Back should always try to ride the opposing Number One into the boards (side of field), keeping the Number One out of an easy scoring position. The better the opposing Number One, the more the defensive Back should control his half of the field. Not knowing the location of the man you are supposed to cover ("mark") *at all times* is the first sin of polo.

A Back should try to, and be capable of, directly feeding his forwards without having to "outlet" the ball to his Three. While hitting the long ball can be a virtue for the Back, it is far more important that he change the line of the ball. A short shot that establishes a new Line is always preferable to a ball hit straight back up the old Line, no matter how far. Always tail an off-side back shot to the side farthest from your goal. (A player to right of the goal should execute an "open" shot to clear the goal mouth.) The Back should rarely try to meet the ball head-on. A muffed shot while meeting the ball all too often leads to an unopposed goal by the attacking team.

The back must be acutely aware of the flow of play as well as on which side his teammates are being marked. Whether clockwise or counterclockwise, he must make his decision to turn the ball, "take it around," or make a back shot, depending on how best to advantage his teammates. It is useless to back the ball if the opposition is in the best position to receive the pass. The Back must be able to execute an accurate backhand shot because he is often required to "thread the needle," i.e., place the ball perfectly for his teammate while avoiding the defensive player.

If the Number Three makes a backshot, the aggressive Back will immediately interchange and turn upfield to take up the attack, and the Number Three will become the Back.

If the attacking team executes a break-away and the Back finds himself caught between the Number One ahead of him with the Number Two carrying the ball, he should go for the man with the ball only if he is in scoring position (usually about sixty yards from goal). Otherwise, he should ride to the opponent closest to the goal, and a teammate will come up to cover the Two.

An important facet of the Number Four's game are his team's "knock-ins." In addition to the desirable accurate long hits, the Back should be capable of lofting the ball over the opposition. The "knock-in" is the only time the responsibility of passing the ball to a teammate falls on the striker. In all other instances, the onus is on the player looking to receive a pass. If the "knock-in" hit is properly executed, it is almost impossible for the opposition to defend without fouling or to meet head-on (see "Strategy and History," page 85.)

General Guidelines

Keep your eye on the ball at all times even while engaged in a ride-off. An experienced player knows where the ball is and where it is going. Aside from avoiding obvious mistakes, knowing where the ball and the line are is the only way not to foul.

The nearer you are to your own goal, the closer you should mark your opponent.

Never ride between the goal posts unless you are trying to defend your own goal from attack by blocking the ball with your horse's or your own body. Always endeavor to give your teammates a clear shot.

Always assume that your teammates will hit a perfect shot, even though this may only occur in high-goal polo. Occasionally, a high-goal player can get away with making an exception to this rule when marking a very inexperienced player.

Never stop on the ball. If you swing at a stationary ball and miss, keep on galloping, or you will commit a foul. Similarly, do not stop or turn immediately after executing a back shot. Not only does it constitute a foul, but will quickly teach a pony a bad habit that will ultimately inhibit the game's flow.

When your side is on defense and backs the ball, turn to the boards. When on offense, turn to the center.

The ball should always be hit as quickly and as hard as possible so as not to give the opponents time to set up a defense. Never dribble the ball when you are marked and a teammate is free. If you must "take the ball around," turn as sharply as possible and always take the shortest line to the goal.

Don't attempt to "take the ball around" by hitting an under-the-neck shot. Aside from being a difficult shot to master, if missed, the defense is in a better position to pick up the ball, as it is already on line to goal. According to the great Hall of Fame 10-goaler Tommy Hitchcock, "There is no exception to this rule."

Always try to take the shortest route to get on the Line, regardless of the distance to the ball: *get to the line first*. Even if you don't get the ball, this may allow you to take the Line away from the opposition.

Never ride toward your own goal without marking an opposing player. When on offense, try to ride clear of your opponent. When on defense, close the gap and attempt to get on the opponent's off-side and "knee-up."

Hit straight up and down the field, except when on defense, when angled shots to the sides of the field are most effective.

Hit under the pony's neck (neck shot) when trying to center the ball, except when near the back line, in which case you should use a backhander.

If there are two or more opponents in front of you, ride to the furthest one. If the numbers are equal, ride to the man beside or behind you.

General Guidelines for Forwards

When the Number Three gets the ball, the Numbers One and Two must support him by endeavoring to position themselves advantageously to receive a pass.

When on attack, if you are ahead of the ball and see that your teammate is being backed up, try to run onto to the anticipated new Line. Don't gallop down the center of the field waiting for a pass while your teammate is running along the side. When nearing goal, ride outside the left goalpost so as to be able to safely ride onto the line.

Once the defense has turned the play by feeding the Forwards, it is more important not to mis-hit the ball than to hit long, lofted drives. By putting together a series of hits and "carrying the ball," you have done your job even if you aren't the one who puts the ball in the goal.

Strategy and History

Polo is a tactically sophisticated game. Because of the large field size, continual high speed and varying horse and player abilities, it is difficult to formulate hard-and-fast team tactics. To add to the difficulty, play never stops, and often players have to assume a position other than their natural or assigned position. Still, there is probably no sport with an inherent fast pace in which team strategy is more important than modern polo. Lack of a pre-designed strategy forces a team to play a strictly orthodox game that is predictable and, therefore, easily defended.

It is useful to take a quick look at how polo tactics evolved. Early polo was more like war than sport. To the Persians polo, like archery, swordsmanship and falconry, were considered preparation for war. In fact, the horse was thought to be a weapon of war and underclasses were forbidden horse ownership. By the Middle Ages polo was played from Constantinople to Japan. The game lasted for about one hour, split into two 30 minute chukkers. Players used only one horse and the game was stopped only for serious injury. If a player was knocked out of the game, his equal opposite on the other team also had to sit down. When the ball went out of play it was immediately thrown back by one of the spectators. These rules and stone goalposts, as might be expected, resulted in many serious injuries and even deaths.

In Manipur, where it was called *kan-jai-bazéé*, polo became the national sport and Manipuriis were the high-goalers of their day. The first club was formed in 1859 as Silchar Kangjai Club. [In China and Japan a similar game was played with a net basket suspended between the goalposts on a board.] Initial tactics consisted of extremely rough riding and long hitting. In the sixteenth century players rode very small, 12- to 13-hand, ponies. There was no evidence of combination (teamwork), and dribbling the ball was unthinkable especially around the solid stone goalposts. For the next two hundred years written history of the game is practically nonexistent. The British military stationed in

India re-introduced to the game to India in the days of The Raj (1870s), and it immediately became a happy feature of army life. The first European polo club was formed in Manipur's Cacher valley by Bengal Lancer Lt. Joseph Sherer (Major-General), later to be known as "the father of Modern Polo."

True as that may be, polo as we know it today was started by men who never played, or even saw the game played. We owe it all to a guy with an odd nickname. One day in 1869, a certain Captain Edward "Chicken" Hartopp (1845–1882) of the 10th Hussars read a news account in *The Field* of a game between local plantation owners and a Manipuri team in Northern India. It sounded like "a good game that they have in India," so he and a few fellow officers in England began to play the game. It was Chicken, at the age of twenty-four, who drew up the first rules for the game of polo and formed the first polo club. From its nascent beginnings in England it spread to Ireland in 1872; to Australia 1874; the United States and Argentina in 1876 (the same year as "Custer's Last Stand"); and Canada in 1883.

Players used the military-type or hunting saddles of the period, rode seated far back, and long in the stirrups. Most used long whippy sticks with seven-ounce heads. Play was on a very small field (three hundred by six hundred feet!), and was begun by two opposing players, usually the best player of each team or the one on the fastest pony, who charged to a ball placed on the centerline from behind their respective goals. The first man to the ball then tried to score by himself. The off-side forward stroke was the only one in use.

In 1873, due to its growing popularity, the Hurlingham Club of England adopted the game. In 1874 the English introduced the *field* off-side rule, which relegated the Number One to a blocking back. Because he could not ride forward of the Back to receive a pass, his main objective was to ride out the opposing Back. The One was usually a newcomer to the game and a poor striker, since ball-hitting wasn't required. It was almost unheard-of for a One to attempt a shot on goal from the field. In fact, the off-side rule's effect on polo was such that most of the scoring was done from melees about twenty yards in front of goal, where all players were allowed to congregate. Almost every player was capable of making a shot from that distance. Teams consisted of eight men on a side until 1874, when teams were limited to five players. Penalty points were added to the score at the end of three twenty-minute chukkers, s foul-shooting was nonexistent. Hooking was against the rules until 1907.

The style of play was for the strongest player to try to get the ball himself. Once in possession of the ball, he would then attempt a run up the field toward goal. "Checking" (slowing down) to almost a full stop before striking the ball and then galloping off to the next shot, he tried to score by himself. The opposing Back defended the goal like a goalie from between the posts as the attacker tried to get past him. (Hence the admonition for a Back not to meet the ball head-on, for if missed, the attacker would invariably score.) More often than not, he would leave the ball inside the twenty-yard line, where all the players would converge on the ball in the famous melees. Since most goals were scored from this position, many players used fifty-nine-inch mallets even on such short mounts. This picture leaves little doubt to the origin of calling those furious efforts in front of goal "pig sticking." The hero of the day was the player who scored the most goals regardless of his team's overall performance. Tactical defense was the word of the day, and the game was rough-and-tumble, with a lot of blocking and few goals scored. In one recorded match it took sixty minutes before the first goal was scored, and the entire game was played without changing mounts!

In 1886 Captain John Watson's English International Team soundly defeated (10–4, 14–2) the Americans (Foxhall Keene, Raymond Belmont, Thomas Hitchcock, Winthrop K. Thorn) because they employed a new weapon called the back shot. This one simple act almost instantaneously sped up the transition from offense to defense and completely dumbfounded the Americans, who used the slower and more defensible method of dribbling the ball around to turn play. In fact, there was a sign posted at the Westchester Club (Newport, Rhode Island), to wit, "Any player making a backhand shot will be asked to leave the grounds." When the Americans developed their back shots later that same year, they were thrilled at their success at being able to back the ball twenty feet! Even after the turn of the century most players were still unable to play the ball on the near-side at all.

As proficiency increased, so did the speed of the game. In 1899 the height limit for ponies was raised from 13.2 to 14.2 hands. 1909–10 saw the abolishment of the field off-side rule. In 1916 the United States abolished height limits altogether, and England followed suit in 1919. Both of these changes served to speed up the game even further. The greenswards became better maintained, and sideboards became the standard in an effort to keep the ball in continual play. Saddles were designed to allow players to ride more like jockeys. Mallet design and manufacture was improved. Players became capable of hitting the ball relatively long distances, and accuracy improved to the point where any accomplished player could score from the field. Even though the game got faster, play still centered around the best player getting the ball and trying to score.

As handicaps came into universal adoption, in 1910–11, which enabled less accomplished players to compete with better teammates, the "ball hog" style of play became even more prevalent. After pony size became unrestricted, the pace of the game increased accordingly. But it wasn't until the British Army began to apply their tactical training to the sport that modern theory began to evolve, with specific duties assigned to each player.

1920 saw a change in the way in which penalties were awarded, which also enhanced and sped up the game. Prior to that time in the United States, penalties were not awarded or taken at the moment of the offense, but at the end of the chukker (a quarter point for a safety, half a point for crossing, etc.). Often players were not aware of their offense or the actual team score until after the game. In addition,

James Gordon Bennett pictured about twenty years after he, "imported polo to America." At the time horses were limited in height to Large Pony Size (14.2h). Mr. Bennett's long stirrups and relative short mallet fit the style of polo equitation of the era. Most players swung while seated and made contact with the ball behind the saddle. Feet were shot home and extended forward. (The Glorious Sport of Polo, Mumsey's Magazine Vol.24, No1, 1900)

the '20s rule change provided for stricter enforcement and a free hit at goal from the forty- and sixty-yard line.

It soon became apparent that the best defense was strong offense. Scoring became the watchword. Meanwhile in Argentina, cross-breeding programs began to bear fruit. The country's worldwide supremacy began with the 1924 Olympic Gold Medal. Then, in the 1930s, soccer tactics were applied to polo, and passing between teammates became the new weapon—once again! The "ball hog" teams were easily defeated by the dazzling passing of their opponents. Passing accelerated the pace of the game even more and, with greater proficiency and interchange of position, high-goal polo arrived, as evidenced by the more than twofold increase in total goals scored per game. Pace, more than any other factor, differentiates the professional high-goal game from club polo. As Brigadier General R. L. Ricketts, captain of the famously successful Alwar (India) teams of the early 1900s, put it, "Pace singles out the class player." The faster the pace, the more difficult it is to execute physical skills and to think about the game. The Argentines further added to the speed of the game not only through interchange of position but constant rotation of position, thereby adding a "run-and-shoot" offense to polo, which has enabled them to dominate high-goal polo ever since.

Today, the amount and level of international high-goal polo is greater than at any other time in the history of the game. Both man and mount have benefited from greater understanding of nutrition and conditioning, which produced bigger, stronger and faster polo than ever. Due to the ever-increasing demand for higher-quality polo ponies, trainers have less time to spend "making" their product. Today's ponies are hardly more than racing thoroughbreds and, even with the increased use of more severe bitting (gags, draw reins, etc.), short stops, fast turns, rollbacks and other finesse movements have given way to the "run-and-shoot" offense.

The run-and-shoot style of play magnifies the emphasis on player rotation and retaining possession by turning with the ball. Whoever is free works to get into the open to receive a pass on the run and automatically becomes the Number One, regardless of the number on his jersey. If he should miss or no longer be able to carry the ball, the trailing player takes over. Teammates will endeavor to ride ahead or to the flank to receive a pass and assume the Number One position. Should the rotation fail and the opposition gain possession of the ball, whoever is the closest player defending his own goal becomes the Number Four (Back).

The rotated positions are maintained until the play is over, repulsed, or stopped and there is sufficient time to realign the players in their assigned positions without the rotating player having to unnecessarily chase his mount. This basic concept dominates today's modern polo strategy. However, it can be weighted to favor unevenly handicapped foursomes, team parity, or horsepower.

Teamwork (Combination)

> *"The art of team play is to create a situation that*
> *results in a score and the obligation to create a*
> *situation falls upon the players without the ball."*
> Thomas J. Hitchcock, Jr., 1930

The cardinal rule of effective team combination is for each player to play the position in which he finds himself at any given time. In fact, it is the only way that players who have never played together before can be effective. Fluid interchange of player and positions is essential to good team play.

While that may be the rule, the secret of team play is free and fluid rotation of position when circumstance or opportunity warrants. Each player should know the duties of every position and be responsible to uphold it should he find himself temporarily in that position. Ideally this works best for a team with even handicap distribution. But even for teams with unequal distribution it is the best strategy, albeit with a little extra care on the part of the higher-rated players. The famous left-handed 10-goaler James Watson Webb states, "The strongest game for a team is when the Numbers Two and Three change position constantly."

No player should ride closer than five or six lengths from his teammate and never parallel. In the excitement of a game, spacing is difficult to maintain and often teams become "bunched up." Nothing is more disruptive to effective team play. The urge to constantly seek the ball ("ball chaser") tends to draw players together. If one teammate goes to make a play, the three others must immediately turn to either receive a pass, block an opponent, or get into position to backup.

Easily interchanged positions and frequent, accurate passing destroys the opposition's defense. It challenges one's opponent to devise a defensive strategy, thereby negating any preset game plan they may have intended. An intra-team system should be devised so that teammates know in which direction to turn and where to hit so as to reach their own side. One popular method is for players to align themselves in an imaginary Vee emanating from the center of the goal and widening out to the corners of the field at the opposite end. The players attempt to position themselves checkerboard-fashion within the confines of the Vee. Short, wide-angled passes are more effective than long distance passes, because they are easier for teammates to pick up the new line and it is more difficult for the opposition to intercept. *Passing is contagious!*

The most effective team combination occurs when handicaps are evenly distributed between all four players. Building a team around one star player is detrimental to good team play and promotes "ball hogging." How can teammates be expected to place themselves for a pass if experience tells them it will never come? In polo, as Grove Cullum pointed out in his famous 1934 treatise on polo teamwork, "There is a tendency to play against an opponent rather than with a teammate."

After assessing the opponent's strengths, peculiarities, and horsepower, a plan of attack for how to best the other team should be developed. Perhaps an especially dangerous player will require extra attention. If the opponents are better mounted, an effort to slow down the pace will help. Maybe some preset plays can be devised to unexpectedly take advantage of a teammate's particular strength such as the ability to hit the long ball or make an accurate neck shot. Since horsepower represents seventy-five percent of a team's ability, most teams' strategic plans center around matching up horses chukker by chukker. A player on a fast but not very handy pony may ask a teammate to pay closer than normal attention to cover him in case he is unable to make an expected play.

An important aspect of team strategy is to utilize the team's horses in such a manner that each player is aware of when his teammates are riding their best or worst mounts.

Each player's string is comprised of ponies of varying abilities, strengths and weaknesses. Perhaps one player will have an especially handy pony that can make up for the shortcomings of a teammate who is mounted on a faster but less maneuverable pony, etc. By judiciously choosing which pony to play and in what rotation, it may be possible to gain an advantage or reduce the effect of a weaker string of horses.

If you are lucky enough to have a large string comprising thirty or more horses, you have the added advantage of being able to align not only one string but several strings so that you play the strongest horses in the most difficult tournaments.

Set Plays

In a game that boasts such a fast pace as polo, with long-ball hitting and instantaneous transition from offense to defense, it is difficult to formulate set plays and even harder to execute them. Consequently, there are only four situations that could be classified as set plays: throw-ins, knock-ins, safeties, and penalty shots.

The Throw-In (Rule # 20)

Although the throw-in is one of the most important plays of the game, it is the least practiced. At most polo clubs, throw-ins are eschewed in favor of knock-ins to save time. So it is not surprising that the lower-goal players tend to wait until the ball comes to them or a teammate, especially when playing with higher-rated players.

If possession is nine-tenths of the law, it is one hundred percent of polo—you cannot score without the ball. On the throw-in the main objective is to gain possession of the ball. Failing to gain control of the ball, the alternative object is to see to it that your opponent cannot get the ball. The best way to insure that your team gains possession is to make sure that your immediate opposition doesn't. As in all polo, take the man first. Once he is on your hip, presumably where he can't get a mallet on the ball, look for the ball. Instead of taking a 12.5 percent chance of getting the ball, take the fifty-fifty chance of taking out your man. If the ball happens to come to you, there is a better chance of mounting a sustained run if your man is already on your hip.

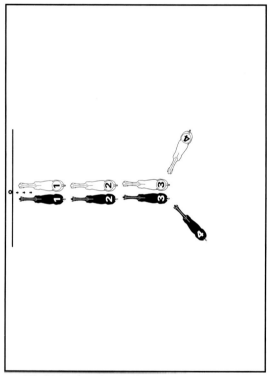

Ill. #24: The classic line-up for a throw-in.

Knowing that winning the throw-in is the key to ball control, and that without the ball you can't score, is one thing; gaining possession is an entirely different matter. Obviously, it is a lot easier job if you are lined up on the left side, because the ball will be on your off side. Positioned on the right of the ball forces use of the usually less agile near side. One interesting answer to this dilemma is for the Number One to line up facing his Number Two, so that he can run on the line of the ball and use his off side. This play takes increased communication with the Number Three, because he has to hold or block his opposite from being in position to hook.

The Number One should position himself five yards from the umpire and at a slight angle facing inward. Since both teams have to remain on their proper side of the centerline until the ball is bowled in, it is advisable for players to place themselves three-quarters of a horse length away from the line. Begin moving to the line as the ball is bowled. This will gain the advantage over a player who is standing still. The Numbers Two and Three should position themselves similarly, taking care to leave enough space between them so that they can maintain visual contact with the ball. The Back's position is often dictated by the position adopted by his opposite number. Ideally, he should position himself farther apart from line of the ball than the other three players and further away from the line. This will give him room to maneuver and to go in the opposite direction if the ball should come all the way through and the opposition gain possession. Remember that when an opponent has the ball, the whole team is on defense. If the ball passes through both Number Ones and falls to the opposition, the opposing Number One should ride his opposite out of the play so that his teammates do not have an open receiver.

If the Number One can get the ball, he should immediately try to take it to the goal. Often the ball is hit forward, forcing a neck shot and a run along the boards. When the Number One takes possession of the ball, the Number Two should immediately head to goal to receive a pass. If the Two gets the ball, he should try to score himself, and the One should fall into line to back him up. On those occasions when the One or Two takes the ball out of the throw-in, the Number Three should ride behind, but closer to the center of the field, to back them up. If the ball passes through the Ones and Twos, they should ride to an advantageous position (on a line between ball and goal) to receive a pass. If the Three gains possession, he should immediately try to feed his forwards rather than to score himself. If the ball comes all the way through to the Back, he becomes the Number One and should try to score or feed his forwards if they are closer to the goal than he is. In this scenario the Number Three becomes the Back.

If the opposing Number One gains possession of the ball on the throw-in, continue to mark him rather than seek out the player you would normally cover, even if you are at a handicap disadvantage.

The back usually positions himself slightly behind the Number Three, but two yards nearer his own goal. He should canter toward the ball as it is thrown in but be prepared to turn to defense if the opposition gains possession. The worst thing that the Back can do is go after the ball only to have the opposition gain possession and not be able to get back into position to defend the goal.

The Knock-In

There are two basic knock-in strategies based on whether the Number Three or Back is doing the hitting-in. The stronger offensive play occurs when the Back knocks in, but often, especially in low-goal polo, it isn't practical for the Back to take the hit in, because he is not a consistent striker or long enough hitter. In either scenario, the Forwards endeavor to elude their opponents and work themselves into the open for a clear pass. The One starts from about twenty yards ahead of the Number Two directly in front or slightly to the inside of the hitter (between the striker and the sidelines). The Number Two starts at a point that he knows the hitter can realistically reach and nearer to the sideboards than the Number One.

When the Number Three is forced to take the knock-in, it leaves the team's strongest player on the back line as the attack begins. Often any advantage gained by the Number Three taking the hit is lost by the opposition's stronger defensive alignment. If the Back takes the hit the Number Three would begin the play from a position in line with the closer goal post and slightly closer than the Number Two. If the Number Three receives the knock-in, he becomes the One and goes directly to goal, Two and Back backing him up. If the forwards receive the knock-in, the Three assumes his normal role. If the Three knocks in, the Back changes position with the Three but waits for the Three to come through (with or without the ball) and stays at Back.

Lining up to defend against the knock-in becomes self-evident, except for the Number One. While the other three players are trying to mark their opponents and block them from receiving a pass, it is the One's job to try to meet the ball if his teammates do such an excellent job of covering their men that the hitter decides to dribble the ball. This can only be accomplished if the defending Number One places himself no closer than thirty yards (USPA Rule 22a) in front and to the left of the expected line of the ball. Since the ball is placed according to where it went over the back line, it is often difficult and seemingly awkward to stay to the left, but it is imperative. Once the Number One is to the right side of the hitter, he has effectively taken himself out of the play—or, worse yet, caused a foul. If the One fails to intercept the dribble, he should try to cover his opposing Number Four.

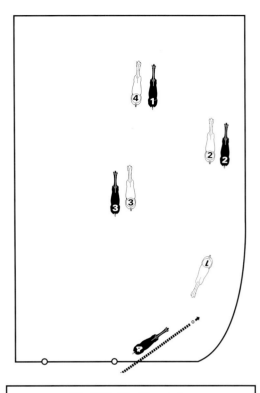

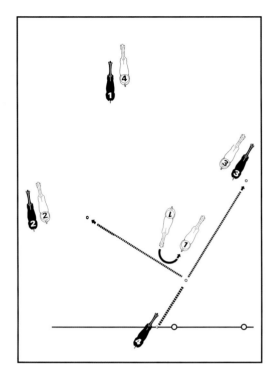

Ill. #25: The Knock-in
In this classic set-up, White No.1 has correctly positioned himself opposite and slightly to the right (on the off-side) of the hitter. This placement obligates the Black No.4 to either dribble to the right to get around the White No.1, or to hit a long drive up to his well covered forwards, usually the No.2. The one remaining route, across the goal mouth, is the worst choice because it can lead to disaster if there is any mistake. (Note: often the defensive match-ups of the No.2's and No.3's are reversed.

Ill. #26: The Knock-in #2
While this option gives the striker more options, it is also more dangerous. In this instance the White No.2, by positioning himself left of hitter, is trying to make the play go across the goalmouth. If, on the other hand he faces up-field, the striker can opt to hit a neck-shot to his No.2.

All offensive players should have their ponies moving at the time of the knock-in in an effort to receive a pass in the clear and at full speed. Defensive players, on the other hand, should wait to commit their position and direction until the last possible split second. Rather than being on the move, it is more effective to try to gain a position that is between the routes one's opponent can be expected to take, much like a defensive lineman in football might try to take the passing lane away from the opposing quarterback. The offensive players must stay aware of the opposition's position at all times during the knock-in, because a quicker, more skillful opponent might need to be ridden out of the play if it appears that he is poised to sneak in and intercept the ball.

Remember, the defending Number One should always be on the hitter-in's off-side. If he is not, the striker, with a simple short tap of the ball to his right, renders the Number One useless and out of the play or, worse yet, causes a foul. On the off-side, however, the Number One is free to move to his right and get on the line to defend should the hitter dribble the ball. This reasoning is also true of penalty attempts, especially Number Fives.

Penalties

Penalty shots typically account for approximately forty percent of total goals scored! So, clearly, they can be critical to the outcome of a match. And, never more so than today with the 1999 USPA rule change, which allows only one pass at the ball and open goals.

Usually the best striker on the team hits the penalties and often knock-ins, too. This is especially true in lower-goal polo, where only one player on a team has the consistent accuracy and distance required. In those situations it is obvious who will attempt the team's conversions. On teams that are more equally aligned, however, and even on some that aren't, dividing up the penalty shots has been shown to increase a team's percentage of conversions. It is theorized that by spreading the responsibility, individual pressures are eased.

Accuracy is more easily achieved on a steady mount, so very often the horse will dictate who will hit a penalty. The same horse that may be fantastic in the open field can be fidgety when approaching the ball slowly, especially after just finishing a sustained hard run. Horses that shy or jerk their heads also inhibit accuracy and timing. Another way of increasing accuracy is to take the shots at a walk. Most players, regardless of handicap, can convert Penalty 2, and 3s.

Penalties are assessed according to the following:
  a) Location of the foul
  b) Position of the two teams on the field
  c) Effect of the foul on the outcome of play
  d) Frequency of reoccurrence

Penalty 2

Penalty 2 is a free hit from the thirty-yard line opposite the goal mouth or, if preferred by the Captain of team fouled, from the point where the foul occurred. All members of the fouling team must position themselves behind the back line and not closer than thirty yards from the placement of the ball. The fouling team may not defend a Penalty 2 and the team fouled may only hit the ball once.

Penalty 3

Penalty 3 is a free hit from the forty-yard line opposite the goal mouth. All the members of the fouling team must position themselves behind the end line and remain there until the Umpire calls, "Play!" and the ball is hit or hit at. Defending players may not come onto the playing field through the goal mouth.

Penalty 4 and Safety

Penalty 4 is a free hit from the sixty-yard line opposite the goal mouth. A Safety is also a sixty-yard shot, but the ball is placed on the field at a position exactly opposite to where it was hit out. A safety occurs when a defending player hits or causes the ball to go over his own end line without touching an opposing player or mount.

Photograph by David Lominska

Eugene "Tiger" Kneece (7h. USA) concentrates on an off-side penalty shot. Note hand-head-shoulder-foot to ball line. Tiger braces with his left hand as he drops his left shoulder lower than the right while holding the mallet high overhead and parallel to the ground with the heel of the mallet-head pointing skyward.
HORSE EQUIPMENT: Small rounds gag bit with drop noseband and bit guards; draw reins (knotted at the ends). Suede Tackeria polo saddle with regular girth covered with sheepskin and hinged stirrups. English padded breast collar and standing martingale. Polo wraps all around with the front feet covered with Italian tendon boots and Professional Choice coronet boots.
PLAYER EQUIPMENT: Tiger sports short (2 strap) Hipwood style knee guards over Argentine zippered boots. Traditional Locke style helmet

The position of the players on a team taking a penalty shot is very important. The Forwards, Numbers One and Two should, position themselves just outside of and facing the goal posts at a forty-five-degree angle. This is done so that in the event the penalty shot goes slightly wide, it will hit a horse and roll on line toward the goal for an easy off-side tap in. Depending on differing team strategy, the player not taking the penalty shot will either follow the hitter if he intends to dribble to get closer or position himself midway between the goal and the strike. From this position he can either work to get open for a pass or take out the opposing Number Three, who is attempting to defend.

Penalty 5

Penalty 5 is a free hit from the center of the field, but in the case of minor infractions without danger, such as an inadvertent foul hook, the penalty may be awarded from the spot the foul occurred. Penalty #5 defense is similar to that of a #4 with exception being that the Forwards do not place themselves at the sides of the goal. Instead they mark the usual defensive assignments.

Advanced Plays

It should be evident that advanced plays should only be undertaken by players who can consistently execute them without compromising their team's overall level of play.

Turning the Ball

Although the backshot is the quickest and most effective method of reversing the direction of play, sometimes turning on the ball to set up a stronger and more accurate shot is advantageous. Before opting to turn the ball, it is necessary to determine if there is enough space to execute the play without being too closely "marked" so as not to foul and if your teammates are aware of your action and will move accordingly. As Rege Ludwig, renowned polo coach and instructor states, "If your teammates are as surprised as the opposition by your clever move, it's not likely to help the cause."

The turn is executed by simultaneously checking your pony and tapping the ball outward. Often this stroke is made with the backside of the mallet-head to gain a more acute angle. The ball should travel at least two horse-widths. While the ball is still traveling, the player executes a hard, sharp turn or "roll back" in the same direction as the ball, thus regaining control of the off-side and going forward. The sharper the turn, the later (farther back) the ball should be tapped. For example: for a forty-five-degree turn the ball should be addressed at the horse's shoulder; for a one-hundred-sixty degree turn the ball should be tapped from a position close to the horse's hind quarters.

If space permits, it may be desirable to turn the ball by using several taps instead of one. In this case it is most important to change the line that the ball travels with each tap.

Feigning a backshot just prior to turning the ball increases the amount of deception but the split-second timing required makes the shot much more difficult. In this instance the ball is not tapped outward but left in place. As the backshot is aborted, the player executes a quick turn (keyhole turn), making sure to return to the ball in the opposite right-of-way so as to not foul an oncoming player. It is within the USPA rules to slow down in the right-of-way as long as the slowing player is not marked closely. Usually, the faked backshot will cause the marking player to pull up and turn, leaving the turning player free to slow in the right-of-way and execute a rollback.

In recent years turning with the ball has become exceedingly prevalent. It is more evident in low and medium goal polo, where teams usually have one player with superior skill than the others.

Photograph by David Lominska

Jeff Blake (7h. USA) turns the play for Outback. Note: Jeff makes contact with the ball well behind the leg to make a more acute turn; the perfect line between head, hand, mallet to ball with the mallet head kept close to the ground. Jeff holds his rein the traditional English way and knots the ends to prevent entanglement. Even though he is almost standing he chokes up on the grip for the dribble.

HORSE EQUIPMENT: Once again we see the ever popular medium sized loose ring gag bridle with leather caveson and drop noseband. The pony wears leather draw lines and center-adjust breast collar, an equalizer girth with surcingle. Polo wraps on all four legs and tendon boots on the fronts with Professional Choice® coronet boots. "Chrome" leathers on a suede Tackeria® saddle and large platform stirrups.

PLAYER EQUIPMENT: Jeff wears Western style boots, two-strap Hipwood style knee guards and Locke style helmet.

Realizing that the other players are not in position to receive a backhand pass, and faced with the option of hitting to the opposition, the superior player will retain possession by turning the ball. Two recent rule changes have served to increase the difficulty factor in turning the ball. The first allows a player who is turning the ball to be ridden-off when his mallet head is below the hock or knee; the second does not allow a player to tap the ball more than once without moving forward.

Turning the ball is a difficult play for even the gifted. If the play is not executed properly it can lead to disaster because the ball will usually be left in a position for the opposing player to pick it up and make a run to goal without being marked. Many proponents of the game believe that turning the ball is vastly overused, to the detriment of good polo. George Oliver (9h. USA) likes to tell the story of when he watched a game with an old friend, Stewart Iglehart (10h. USA), who had been away from polo for some years and asked, "Have they changed the rules? Is it now a foul to back the ball?"

Sarcasm aside, this play is greatly overused, and when it is rarely helps the team. Alec Harper, former secretary of the HPA, claims that turning on the ball has become a "virus." He notes that "instead of going to the ball as fast as he can and hitting a big onc the first time, (slowing down) so as to let his team get into position gives the other team time to get into position too, so no one ever gets free except by chance." Harper adds, "It is terribly frustrating for a man who has slipped his man and gone for a pass and the No. 3 (turner) takes so long that the forward is closely marked by the time the ball arrives."

Hook-and-Hit

Hooking is a good defensive maneuver that usually is used when a player arrives at the play too late to make the better play of riding out the opponent and backing the ball to turn the play. The hook-and-hit is another aggressive play that requires forethought.

The play must be timed according to the hit portion of the move, not the hook. Therefore, the player must decide on the hook-and-hit before he gets into hooking position.

The player must hook his opponent's mallet sooner, about thirty to forty degrees from the bottom of the swing, as close to the head as possible so that the mallet shafts do not become entwined. The mallet should be gripped firmly and with a stiff arm so that the mallet-head is not moved far from the ball by the striker's force.

With the condensed amount of time for the hit, there isn't sufficient time remaining to take a backswing in the normal manner, but it isn't really necessary. All that is needed to make the hook-and-hit an outstanding play is to make contact with the ball and change its line. Just a slight raising of the mallet will impart sufficient energy to stop the offense, turn the play, and pass to a teammate all in one.

The King's Shot

Generally this shot is not recommended; most players frown on it, especially when mounting themselves. The reason for this is the high risk of injury to the pony, but also to the rider and other players. It is assumed that the term was coined because only a player with abundant resources, rich as a king, could afford to lose ponies by attempting the "King's Shot."

Nevertheless, it is often a useful shot when close to the goal mouth and any other maneuver might cause a foul or a lost opportunity to score.

In this shot, the mallet arm is extended perpendicular to the body, and the hand should begin the stroke from above the shoulder. The ball is addressed directly between the horse's legs. The downward stroke is a forehand, and the ball is struck with the face of the mallet-head. Rather than swing, punch at

Photograph by David Lominska

"The Kings Shot"–so called because only a king can *afford* to replace a pony who was tripped by a mallet on an errant attempt and had to be put down. Also know as a 'belly shot' for the obvious reason shown by Andy Smith (4h. USA). [The ball is visible on the end of the mallet.] Note that Andy, an early proponent of hinged stirrups uses a pair here of his own design and only wears a glove on his rein hand preferring the, "better feel," for control of the stick. He wears early style small knee guards and Western style 'stovetop' boots. His mount uses traditional polo wraps and Nylon center draw reins.

the ball in such a manner that the mallet-head will hit the ground under the ball instantly after making contact.

The ball will travel under the horse's belly out to the opposite side at a right angle to the direction the striker is traveling. Even if the pony steps on the mallet, at least he won't be bashed in the vulnerable ankle area, and there is little chance of tripping.

Tournaments

There are more than 230 club members of the United States Polo Association (USPA) with 3,522 members (2002). The Board of Governors of the USPA, upon recommendation of the Tournament Committee, awards various tournaments to host clubs. The host clubs are announced each Spring prior to the year of the tournament and are listed in the Association's *Year Book*. Each tournament has a specific goal level: 8, 12, 20, etc. The USPA receives a fee for sanctioning the event, but the host club is responsible for running the tournament. It is part of the host club's duties to set up a tournament committee whose members, in turn, set eligibility rules, fees, entries, draw, and scheduling.

As per USPA Rule 17, Round Robbins are not recommended, and the "American System," as opposed to a single elimination system, is most commonly used throughout the world. When the turnout of teams is small, however, a single elimination system is preferred.

The American System

The total number of teams is divided by lot into divisions of no less than two teams each. The divisions should be of equal numbers; never can one division have two teams less than any other division. Seeding is permissible to equalize the handicaps between divisions, and any byes go to the higher-ranking teams. The single elimination protocol does not allow seeding, and all unfilled positions receive a bye.

Each team in a division plays one game against each other team. The team with the best record in each division advances to a single elimination round to determine the winner.

The Captain

> *"The first necessary thing for the formation of a polo team is a*
> *Captain," and his most important qualification is leadership."*
> Gen. Robt. L. Ricketts, *First Class Polo*, 1928

The field captain must project a winning attitude and be a natural leader who can teach and inspire the rest of the team. Therefore he is usually the player around which the team is built. Being the best player or having the ability to do it all by himself does not imply a good choice for team captain. The field leader should be capable of relaxing and maintaining perspective during play so that he can effectively coordinate his team into combined opportunism.

As stated earlier, the Number Three is in the most suitable position to be an effective on-the-field team captain, because he is in the center of play. The captain usually assigns who will mark who and may design specific assignments for knock-ins and other dead ball plays. As Tommy Biddle, (8h. USA) advises, "If the captain doesn't organize and give instructions, he isn't making you part of the team."

The captain is responsible for team morale and, more than any other player, must possess a winning attitude. No matter how far behind his team may be, he must never allow his team to feel that they cannot stage a comeback. If the game is going against him, he must take constructive action. He must be aware of such variables as weather, wind direction, condition of the turf, etc.

The Coach

"All horsemen—horse breakers, gauchos, Cossacks, cowboys, grooms and
polo players—are unmanageable... (Coaching is) not a job for just anybody."
Alberto P. Heguy (10h. ARG),
Coach of Argentina's IPF World Cup Team

A coach can harness the power of individual emotions and fine-tune them to the team's best advantage. The coach's total team focus allows each player to concentrate on his own technical game without distraction. A coach has to manage four free spirits very carefully, respecting their idiosyncrasies yet blending their talents. From his off-field perspective it is easier to recognize and exploit mismatches in talent and horses.

The coach should be respected by his team and, in turn, be able to motivate and inspire his players to perform at a level that can maximize their individual abilities. If there are individual weaknesses, the coach should be able to work with that player so as to negate the effect of that weakness on the entire team's play.

Unfortunately, formal team coaches are usually employed only by high-goal teams with large organizations or in collegiate and scholastic polo. Often a coach will perform many of the field captain's off-field duties, such as punctuality, and logistics in addition to his regular duties. He should make sure that handicaps, team eligibility and entry fees are verified and paid. Often a coach will randomly check the size and weight of balls (3-3 1/2 dia., 3-3 1/2 oz. —USPA Rule 13) and make sure that the timekeeper and scorer, often the same person, are current with the rules.

A team coach should have a keen understanding of polo and insight in gamesmanship. The coach need not be a high-goal player or even an active one, but he should know how to diplomatically teach and communicate. He should develop a set of easily communicable signals so that the players can let their teammates know their intentions. The coach is the catalyst of four individuals and must be able to defuse any personal friction. He is in a unique position because he can view the entire breadth of the game from the fieldside perspective. He must be free to constructively criticize players in such a way that their individual abilities are preserved while at the same time bad habits are eradicated and self-sacrifice promoted for the good of the team.

Unlike the field captain, the coach is most effectively used prior to match time in practice chukkers where there is time to experiment and interrupt play. Shouting from the sidelines or hurried between-chukker advice is seldom heard or followed. It can disrupt a player's concentration and negatively effect a team's cohesiveness. From the ground the coach is most able to fine-tune specific field positions on set plays based on the player's individual hitting ability.

Rules

"In the majority of cases, accidents on the polo
field are the result of violation of the rules."
Capt. Wesley J. White,
Guide for Polo Umpires, 1929

Photograph by David Lominska

Dale Schwetz (5h. USA) [blue] crosses Marcelo Caset's (7h. ARG) line as he attemps a near-side backshot. Note the stress on the fetlock joint of Dale's pony.
HORSE EQUIPMENT: Dale's horse is bitted (notice how the force of impact has pulled the bit out of the left side of the mouth) with a Barry gag, nylon cord draw reins and both a rope caveson and drop nose band. Judging by the tack, it just might be that the pony caused the foul because it was hard to stop.

101

Photograph by David Lominska

Is this a foul? Here Lucas Criado (9h. ARG) is on the receiving end of Adam Snow's (10h. USA) elbow. It could be called a violation of Dangerous Riding Rule #26e "Lack of consideration for another player," or Rough or Abusive Play Rule #27. In many instances enforcement of the rules is left to the discretion of the umpire. In this case, if the umpire thought that the blow was accidental, he probably would not call a foul. On the other hand, if he felt the blow to the face was intentional, he could eject the offending player for the rest of the game without substitution (Rule 27c). Adam's pony wears Australian Protekta® neoprene wraps while Lucas' uses traditional polo wraps with coronet boots. Notice the stress on Lucas' pony's rear right fetlock.

Every player should know the rules well and not just be familiar with them. The three organizations that govern the world of polo are the United States Polo Association (USA); the Hurlingham Polo Association (United Kingdom, with approximately twenty countries); and the Association Argentina de Polo (Argentina and most of South America). In addition, the Federation of International Polo (FIP), formed in 1981, has established a set of rules extrapolated from the three associations to serve as a basis for possible future Olympic play and to promote international discipline. Each organization publishes an updated set of rules annually. The USPA® and HPA both publish their rules in their annual yearbooks called *The Blue Book*, so there is no excuse not to intimately know the rules. The USPA® also publishes an *Umpire Interpretation Manual* that explains various different play scenarios, how the rules should be interpreted, and which fouls should apply.

An infraction of the rules constitute a foul. The fact that there are as many fouls called in a 30-goal match as in 8-goal polo indicates that they are as much a part of the sport as any facet of the game. (If the opposition has a good striker, causing a foul is tantamount to giving up a goal.)

When penalties are exacted for dangerous and/or unfair play, the location of the foul on the field, the relative positions of the two teams on the field, and the effect the foul had on the outcome of the play are all taken into consideration. Therefore an inadvertent foul hook could result in a Penalty 5 (a free hit from the spot of the infraction or from the center of the field) or a Penalty 2 if the foul occurred in the goal-mouth and the team fouled would have scored on the play.

Polo is played in over forty countries. While the rules are not exactly uniform, they are alike in their attempt to refine the game from the ancient *chaugán*, where it was sometimes played to the death, to a game safe for the horse...and the player. Yes, in that order!

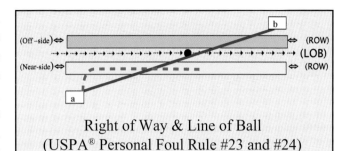

Right of Way & Line of Ball
(USPA® Personal Foul Rule #23 and #24)

Of all the rules of polo, the most crucial to understand are those governing the Right of Way (ROW) and the line of the Ball (LOB) often referred to as just "the line." A line exists at any time the ball is in play.

The LOB is that imaginary line that exists from where the ball was last struck through where it is at any one time and continues on to infinity even if the ball is at rest. A new line is created any time the ball changes direction regardless of the cause. No one may cross the LOB in front of another player in such a way that causes a player to pull up or for his pony to alter stride. The act of almost crossing the LOB, but then abruptly altering course at the last moment, is also a foul– intimidation.

The ROW is an imaginary lane wide enough to accommodate a horse and rider. The ROW exists on both sides of the ball and can be traveled in either direction and at all times. Once a player has legally entered the ROW and is closest to the ball he is said to "have the line." No player may impede or obstruct the progress of a player who has the line.

Players may enter the line at any time as long as it is deemed to be at a "safe distance." Relative speed and degree of angle are key factors in determining a legal ROW entry, but the final the decision is left up to the discretion of the umpire. In the above diagram any player riding on a line from [a] to [b] would constitute a foul even though he is taking the ball on the near-side. If there was no player coming along the Near-side ROW it would still be a foul because at the time the shot is made by the player riding from [a] to [b] his pony's head would obstruct the player on the Off-side ROW with the head of his pony. The correct way to enter the ROW is shown in red.

Two players riding in the same direction and on their respective ROWs take precedence over any one player meeting the two. There are no mitigating circumstances!

While the above sounds simple enough, lack of understanding of these two basic precepts accounts for seventy percent of fouls (crossing fouls) and an even higher number of crashes. When players respect the LOB and ROW it speeds up the game and "opens" the field to more spectacular play.

Location and degree of danger are the two factors that determine how fouls are imposed. The closer to the goal, the more severe the penalty. An inadvertent foul hook at mid-field would incur a less

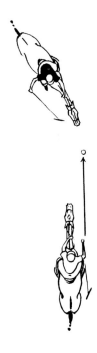

Even though the angle
may be slight and the
distance shorter, Black
may not cross the line of
the ball.

Ill. #27

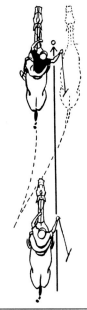

If the relative speed and
distance permit, Black may
enter the ROW parallel to
the LOB, as indicated, if he
does not interfere with
White's mount. If he should
cross the LOB to the dotted
position, it would be a foul.

Ill. #28

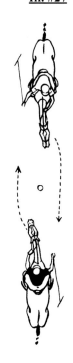

Two players riding at the ball
from opposite directions must
both give way to the left and
take the ball on the off-side

Ill. #29

In a bump or ride-off
Black would commit a
foul if, at the instant
of contact, Black's
mount's shoulders were
ahead of the White
player's.

Ill. #30

severe penalty than the same transgression in the mouth of the goal, possibly negating a score. Likewise, crossing in front of a player who has correctly established himself on the right-of-way would warrant a more severe penalty than a foul hook, because of the higher danger factor. One player meeting two players head-on would carry an even more severe penalty than either the hook or the simple line-cross, because it poses greater danger to a greater number.

Rule Differences

Many players are less effective when they go to play in another country because of the variations in the structure and implementation of the rules. If you plan to travel and play, here are some of the more pronounced differences among rules.

Penalty Five (Free Hit from the Spot)

In the United Kingdom and Argentina, a free hit from the spot is often used. With the USPA's greater emphasis on safety, a similar infraction might warrant a Penalty 4 (sixty-yard free hit).

The effect of this difference is that in the USPA version, even a minor foul can be extremely costly if the attacking team is just over mid-field and is awarded a Penalty 4. The difference could be as much as ninety yards! Obviously, the higher the cost, the less the reward for being aggressive.

Line Cross

Although the USPA has a more severe interpretation of what constitutes a cross or illegal entry of the Line, all three countries allow for personal interpretation of what is a "safe" distance or "relative speed." This has evolved into a variation of "When in Rome..."

The Argentines have the most liberal interpretation, especially on the off-side where, basically, if you can get there first, it is legal. To a lesser extent this is true in the United Kingdom.

Ride-Off

Both Australia and New Zealand consider "bumping" more than just an integral part of the game and take to it enthusiastically. By contrast, England and America enforce the "saddle-to-saddle" rule, with the USPA being slightly more stringent by calling it a foul if a bump causes a horse to break stride or stumble.

Hook

While the usually stricter USPA rules allow a player to ride perpendicular (ninety degrees) up to the line to place a hook, the HPA and AAP do not.

Meeting the Knock-In

Again, although you can do it in America if the ROW is correctly entered, neither Hurlingham nor Argentine rules allow meeting the knock-in under any circumstances.

Penalty Shot

As is often practiced in Argentina and the United States, a player can ride to the ball, not swing, and circle to make another approach as many times as he wants until he feels that everything is right before taking a shot. Under Hurlingham rule you have one attempt, so you better swing.

The Thirty-Second Rule

When the bell rings to signal the end a chukker (except for the last chukker) with the ball still in play, the USPA, Hurlingham and the IPF rules add thirty seconds to the clock, and the ball remains in play until a foul occurs or the ball goes out of bounds (or hits the sideboards), or until the thirty seconds have elapsed, whichever comes first. In Argentina there is no thirty-second time limit, so you keep on playing until the ball goes out of bounds or is dead.

Time-Out

The USPA allows the umpire to stop the game at any time for broken tack or a fallen rider. In Argentina no time-out is given under any circumstances, and in the United Kingdom a time-out is blown only if the broken tack or fallen rider constitute a "hazard" to the other players and horses, but not if the fallen rider himself is in harm's way. So if you are not playing under USPA or IPF rules, don't get off your horse on the field to fix tack. It is quicker to get a new mount.

Riding into a Shot

Under USPA Rule 26(h), if you ride into another player's shot (even if the ball does not hit your horse) you have fouled. Unfortunately, this does not hold for Argentine or United Kingdom rules, where the emphasis is on speeding up the game and making it more exciting for spectators, but more dangerous for horse and rider.

Teeing Up the Ball

HPA Field Rule 27a allows for a player to place the ball "advantageously" for a penalty shot. However, only a brief second or two is allowed for this purpose, and unlike the USA, under no conditions can one player tee up the ball for a teammate.

Part Four:
Equipment

Polo horsewear is different from other equestrian equipment in that it is made from heavier material and more durable construction in order to withstand strenuous use. In addition to heavier and generally wider leather goods, extra strong stainless steel buckles, keepers and reinforced stitching are necessary to withstand the rigors of polo. A player's life is literally often hanging by a thin leather strap. To make matters worse, a demanding polo schedule can subject equipment to adverse conditions and may not allow for immediate maintenance.

Basic Materials

Leather goods are only as good as the quality of the hides from which they are cut, and then, and only then, does workmanship become important. All leather is tanned (marinated) in either tannin (hemlock/oak tree bark) or chemicals. Bark-tanned leather is more porous and absorbs lubricating oils easily. Chemically tanned leather is durable, but usually thicker and darker, and does not become more supple with repeated use and dressing. "Chrome" tanning is usually used to make especially tough hides (Buffalo) pliable. Bark tanning is preferable.

Tanning can also hide the flaws somewhat inherent in all hides. Check leather by folding it tightly in both directions. It should not split, ripple, crack or flake on either side. The leather should be hard and not soft and spongy. If possible, place your hands on both sides of the leather simultaneously. Any variance of thickness could indicate heavy tanning and polishing to hide flaws. Likewise, rough spots and uneven stitching can indicate poor workmanship.

Saddles

A polo saddle is basically an all-purpose, close-contact, English-type, forward-seat (girth set back) saddle with a deep flat seat and long straight flaps without knee rolls. It is designed to provide maximum comfort, balance and mobility. Here again the overriding concept is to get as close to the horse as possible and not to interfere with his athleticism. There are dozens of manufactures in as many countries that sell saddles costing from $300 to $1,500 specifically designed for polo. Since the tree and interior workmanship are hidden from view, it is necessary to rely on the manufacturer's reputation. English and German craftsmanship are considered best.

Most popular polo saddles of today fall into three types. The standard design features a high pommel, deep seat (typically three and one half inches), a medium-high cantle that is either square or rounded, and short panels. The second type is virtually the same but with longer panels. The main advantage to the long panel is that it gives the effect of a "slight knee roll" to hold the knee into the saddle. A third type is called the Whippy saddle, named after the now defunct famous English saddle maker. Many manufacturers make a Whippy-type saddle that features a flat, broader seat and lower cantle similar to Argentine polo saddles.

All saddles come in seat sizes from seventeen to nineteen inches. Polo saddles, like all English saddles, are measured from the nailhead (on the side of the pommel) to the center of the top of the cantle. Most manufacturers market their saddles in three widths—narrow, regular, and wide—to accommodate varying withers' sizes.

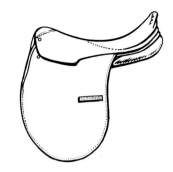

Many saddles are endorsed by top-rated professionals and incorporate *their* preferences. Your personal requirements may not be the same, but some prerequisites that are universally appreciated are: deeply recessed stirrup hangers with spring-loaded safety releases, a light but strong reinforced tree, high cantle, billet straps sewn with nylon thread to resist sweat rot, and linen or nylon webbing wrapped around the tree rather than just tacked.

Ill. #31: A typical Argentine close contact or "Baja" Saddle

Taken care of properly, a good polo saddle should last a lifetime even though it is subjected to hard wear and tear and often left wet in the sun. The key is the quality of the materials and workmanship. The most important part of the saddle is the tree (frame), which is reinforced with steel over the pommel and cantle to keep it from spreading. Most trees are made of wood or fiberglass with steel bars (springs) running the length of the saddle—hence the name, spring tree. Wood, even lowly plywood, is preferable to plastic and some of the new space-age polymers, because it will better hold the tacks used for attaching the binding. Regardless of the material, a broken tree is almost impossible to repair.

As for panels, some players prefer wool, felt or horsehair stuffing, because these can be reshaped periodically if they become compressed. Others like foam rubber or other synthetics because they retain shape better and are waterproof. Highly grained or embossed pigskin is preferred over smooth leathers for the seat because they are less slippery. Cowhide is the most popular, but some players go so far as to prefer suede or roughout leather for the seat.

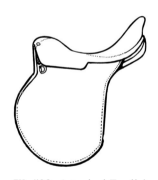

Most high-goal polo players prefer a very flat seat to allow them better movement on the horse and closer contact. Less competent riders may find the confinement of a deeper seat and higher cantle—-even knee rolls—reassuring. Either way, check to make sure that the deepest part of the seat is halfway between the pommel and cantle. If the deepest part of the seat is too far toward the cantle, the rider will be tilted back and his legs will be pushed forward. A flat, centered seat with stirrup hangers set slightly back will allow the rider the advantage of striking the ball off the front of the saddle. Make sure that the stirrup position allows the legs to naturally hang in the middle of the flaps. The twist of the tree should enable the rider to keep his knees and legs against the horse effortlessly while supporting the pelvis evenly.

Ill. #32: A typical English Polo Saddle

Some of the best and most popular saddles made today are manufactured by English saddle maker Keith Bryan (KB) and sold under the name of Tackeria, Lodsworth and Texas Polo. KB also sells its own brand. All of the KB saddles are preferred by today's top players because they offer a more modern design, allowing the rider greater movement and more forward positioning. Both Gracidas (10h) and Alfonso Pierses (10h) took their KB when they played in the Argentine Open. Enough said!

The Barnsby polo saddle is well made and still very popular as well, but its design is somewhat outdated, placing the rider further back and more upright. Other fine saddles are manufactured in Australia and New Zealand. For the cost-is-no-object set, Hermés makes a wonderful polo saddle with unique placement of the overgirth under the seat. Some saddles, like the Argosy, are made with a fiberglass tree that is not recommended for polo. Argentine saddles are generally less expensive, but the quality of workmanship and materials leave a lot to be desired, especially since their cost is rising

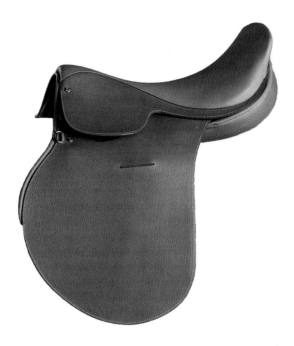

The Texas Polo Saddle® in London Tan leather is handcrafted in England. Designed in 1982 by award winning saddler Michael Pegg, this model features a "narrow twist" tree with hand forged pommel and wrap-over 'safety' hanger bars. This saddle also comes in Havana and suede options.

to the point of only minor savings. A $450 saddle will probably only last four or five years, whereas a $1,000 saddle, given proper care, can last a lifetime.

While it is desirable for the saddle to suit the rider, it is imperative that it fit the horse perfectly. An ill-fitting saddle can affect a pony's manner of going and cause physical damage. If a poor-fitting saddle is used for a prolonged period of time, it can permanently cripple a horse. Sometimes once is enough to render a horse unplayable. Conversely, a proper fit will allow the horse to carry a rider effortlessly. A proper-fitting saddle requires no saddle pad (see "Saddle Pads," page 111). Fortunately, the thoroughbred-type horse mostly used for polo has high withers and smooth muscles, rendering it relatively easy to achieve a good saddle fit.

Good tack shops will allow a saddle to be taken home to see if it fits properly. If they don't, shop elsewhere. Test the saddle for fit without a saddle pad. First make sure that the saddle rides high on the withers. The shape of the tree's bars should follow the contour of the back. The rigging or billets to attach the girth should be more forward than conventional saddles but not so far as to interfere with the horse's elbows. If the rigging is too far forward or the tree improperly designed, it may cause the back of the saddle to ride up in the air, placing undue pressure on the horse's withers.

The leading edge of the saddle should fit right behind the horse's shoulder. Daylight should be visible when looking down the gullet from either end. There should be a minimum of two to three fingers of space between the pommel and the withers *with a rider in the irons*. Have a friend run his hands under the saddle when you are mounted. There should be no folds, ripples or bunching up of the panels. The panels should make even contact from the fleshy part of the withers onto the kidneys.

The saddle should leave a distinct sweat mark that faithfully follows the outline of the saddle's panels. Dry spots within the outline of the panels on the horse's back indicate uneven and improper fit. Contrary to popular thought, a dry spot usually indicates a saddle that is too tight.

New saddles need to be thoroughly oiled once before their first use to prevent drying and cracking. Natural oils like neat's-foot or vegetable are best for this purpose. Do not use hydrocarbon-based oil on a saddle, because it will rot the stitching. A saddle should be cleaned after each use because the horse's sweat has a high acid content that can ruin stitching and canvas parts. Take care not to leave a wet saddle in the sun, because it will undo the original tanning and stretching of the leather.

There are several new saddles that do not use any leather at all but rather washable cloth. One manufacturer boasts an easily adjustable tree. Although these saddles have failed to gain widespread acceptance in polo as of this writing, the advantages they offer, light weight, durability, and ease of cleaning have made them popular with grooms for exercise use.

Girths and Surcingles

Most players, or more importantly, horses, prefer shaped girths (cinches) such as the Atherstone, Balding, or Humane variety to maintain proper saddle position. These girths are contoured at the elbows to facilitate leg action without rubbing (galling) and creating sores on the horse. Girths come in sizes from forty to fifty-four inches to accommodate various size horses. A low-withered horse requires a tighter fitting cinch than one with high withers.

Girths are made out of many kinds of leather and/or cloth webbing. Even though they are easy to wash and comfortable, cord string and webbed girths are not popular for polo. One reason might be that with an active polo schedule it may be difficult to keep them clean, and unless properly cleaned, they are more prone to chafe than leather. Recently, soft bag leather girths reinforced with strong saddle leather or Nylon backing have become popular. Fleece girth covers can be placed over any girth if a horse has thin sensitive skin that is prone to gall.

The Balding girth divides into three plaited strips at the elbow to afford maximum forearm mobility. The Humane girths (Argentine "equalizer") ends in one strap that passes through an O-ring. This attachment allows the tension on the billets to be equally distributed. Regardless of your choice, the girth should be without elastic spacers and have heavy-duty buckles. Nickel-plated iron is stronger than plain nickel. Nylon-lined buckle turns are a nice touch.

Many players like the extra insurance of an overgirth or surcingle. Made of leather or nylon webbing, it fits over the entire saddle and girth. Some surcingles have elastic ends for a more comfortable fit. They will hold the saddle in place even if the girth or billets break. An overgirth is a necessity if an Argentine "equalizer"-type girth is used, because the saddle can easily turn if even one buckle breaks.

Because of the highly athletic acrobatics often required of polo ponies, irrespective of the type of girth used, girths should be fitted to the horse so that the buckles lie well above the horse's elbows.

Fittings

Saddles are usually sold "without fittings" (stirrup leathers and irons). Most players prefer an inch and a quarter wide and fifty-four-inch-long leathers. However, there is a great divergence of opinion on material. Each of the three popular leather types has its respective devotees.

"Red chrome" tanned buffalo grain leather is extremely strong. Stirrup leathers of this type will probably never break but stretch a great deal. Some players like the leathers to stretch because this makes them very thin and easy to adjust. Others argue that as the fittings all stretch differently, it makes it more difficult to adjust the stirrup length by counting the holes. For this reason, regular leather and latigo leathers are also popular. Although usually double-stitched and sometimes reinforced, they will not stretch but are more prone to break, which detractors argue is potentially more dangerous than a little stretching now and then.

Tackeria® Hinged Stirrups

Stainless-steel stirrup irons are almost universally used in polo today. They come in four-and-one-half to five-and-one-half-inch widths. Larger widths are preferred because they are less likely to lock the foot into the stirrup in case of a fall. There are several quick-release or safety-type stirrups made, but they have not proved popular because they can catch on an opponent's equipment or, even worse, release unexpectedly. One recent innovation gaining popularity is the hinged iron. The bottom half of the stirrup pivots forward and back. This design enables the floor of the iron to remain in flat contact with the sole of the boot regardless of the rider's leg position, and facilitates quick release as well.

For the most part, rubber stirrup iron pads are not used because they frequently become dislodged during hard riding and rough use and can be an impediment to a boot sliding out of the iron when necessary.

Saddle Pads

As mentioned earlier, a proper-fitting saddle does not require a saddle pad and many players don't use them in an effort to stay as close to the horse as possible. An improper-fitting or dirty saddle pad can cause more problems than a properly fitted saddle without a pad. A narrow saddle used with heavy padding will put undue pressure on the withers, especially if the horse has a broad back.

While many players like to use saddle pads because they can carry team colors and give a more "professional look" that can be color-coordinated to match leg wraps, saddle pads are mostly used to keep the saddle clean. Other players like some of the modern composite pads for their sweat-dissipating and shock absorption qualities.

Although they come in a variety of materials and thicknesses, tests clearly indicate that wool offers the best wicking (cooling action). Crocheted types provide superior airflow. Modern science has given us composition "high density" pads and some filled with ski-boot cushioning material, but they are relatively thick and somewhat heavy. While they might be useful for a horse with back problems, they have the unwanted side effect of raising the rider's center of gravity.

Polo players prefer thin and small-sized pads, either thirty-by-thirty or thirty-by-sixty inches. Overpadding raises the saddle, causing instability and the need to cinch too tightly.

Bridles

Like all polo tack, the main difference that sets polo bridles apart from ordinary ones is that they are heavy-duty to stand up to hard use. The most common types are Pelhams and gags, although many more esoteric contraptions can be found on the polo field. Usually of fairly large size, the bridle should allow for variable adjustment of the cheeks on both sides to accommodate various types of bits.

Regardless of the style of bit, two reins of varying thickness should be used. The most common width is five-eighth or three-quarter inch, but some players prefer the three-quarter and one inch combination. The two different thicknesses make for a smaller handful and allow a rider to pick out one pair from another more readily during pressure of a match.

Bitting

"A bit for a horse's mouth is like a key to a door...
you've got to find the bit that fits."
Harold "Chico" Barry (9h. USA)

Improper bitting can render a top-quality pony useless and its rider ineffective on the field. Horses often require a change of bitting with a new owner who has different riding abilities. Bits should be mild enough to allow the horse to extend his head and neck into (against) the rein hand. A bit should be chosen that best suits the horse and the rider's ability to use it properly. It is strongly recommended that polo players study bitting more extensively, because proper bit selection can improve the performance of a horse and rider. But the right bit in the wrong hands is as bad as the wrong bit.

No horse has ever chosen to bit himself. Regardless of how well the device is made, a bit is a heavy, cold piece of metal that may pinch, interfere with swallowing, grind against the teeth, or put uncomfortable pressure on the palate and bars. All of these sensations are foreign to the horse and can affect his manner of going. The wrong bit or an improper fitting one can cause irreparable damage. Coversely, "A golden bit does not make the horse go any better," as the old proverb rightly asserts.

To correctly fit the bit to the horse it is necessary to understand the rudiments of how a bit works. A bit can apply pressure to any and/or all parts of a horse's mouth, lips, jaw, teeth, bars, tongue and palate, as well as the poll and chin.

A bit comes in contact with the lips at the corners of the mouth. The lips are covered with thin skin and are very sensitive. There should be one small wrinkle at the corner of the lips when the bit is properly fitted to the bridle.

The bit's mouthpiece rests on the fleshy toothless space called the bars between the front teeth (incisors and canines) and the molars. The bars can vary in shape and condition. They can be indented, usually from improper bitting, or of irregular thickness. The mouthpiece should be wide enough to easily accommodate the breadth of the two bars without the top of the cheeks (purchase) chaffing through the outside of the lips. A thinner diameter mouthpiece is more severe than a thicker one. So-called "sweet mouth" mouthpieces made of soft corrosive metals such as copper or alloys that encourage salivation are not as common because they are soft and wear out quickly.

Behind the bars are the premolars and molars that also interact with the bit. These teeth are the ones that require periodic dental care to make sure that they are flat and even, and do not adversely affect the action of the bit or cause irritation. Often a so-called "wolf tooth" is present just before the premolars. This is exactly where the bit lies and can cause serious bitting problems without proper dental treatment.

The horse's tongue also comes into contact with the bit. Although a horse's tongue is very strong, it is also very sensitive, and no two are the same. Tongues vary in both thickness and width. Before choosing a bit, lift the side of the horse's lip to visually gauge the size of the tongue. Is it sticking out of the side of the bars or is there a lot of room for a bit?

The hard flesh and skin above the tongue is the palate. The average palate is about two inches high, but can vary considerably from horse to horse. If you use a ported bit, it is wise to check the palate height in order to select the proper size port. Many ports do not touch the palate and are used only to facilitate swallowing. If the port is too high, it can put undue pressure on the palate causing a horse to overflex at the poll.

Although not part of the mouth, a bit can also affect the horse's poll and the chin (curb). The poll is located at the second vertebra at the top of the horse's neck. Downward pressure is applied to the poll through the crown of the bridle. The chin is affected by the curb chain, which applies pressure to the groove behind the horse's lower lip.

A bit can be assumed to properly fit the horse when he carries his head so that the poll is the highest point when the horse is relaxed.

All bits consist of two parts—the mouthpiece and the cheeks. There are two types of cheeks—shanks and rings. Mouthpieces vary as to length, thickness or metal and may be solid or "broken" (jointed). Snaffles, mullens, rollers, and spoons are popular ported mouthpieces. Shanks vary in length and angle. The amount of pressure and response time varies according to the length of the shank. The straighter the shank, the quicker the action. The longer the shank, the more pressure. In polo, where quick response is desired, straight shanks are most common. An inexperienced rider or one with "heavy" hands should avoid using longer shanked bits.

Rings come in many shapes, sizes and diameters. They may be fixed or loose so that the mouthpiece can rotate around the rings. They can also slide up and down freely on the cheeks. Most of the bits used in today's polo are combination bits—Pelhams, gags and full bridles (curb and snaffle)—because they affect all of the areas of a horse's sensitivity. With two reins attached, one to the center of the bit and the other to the bottom ring (curb), direct pressure to the mouth and leverage to the chin and poll can be applied simultaneously with one hand.

Bits

A golden bit does not make the horse go any better.
Old Proverb

The bits that the English poloists first encountered in India were common devices. Neck-reining was unheard of, and the only thing that kept players from careening into one another was the slow pace and small size of the ponies. Curbs were a nonentity. Polo demands immediate and unflinching response to the rider's

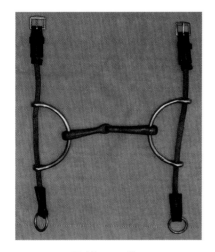

command, so military personnel returning to England advised new recruits shipping out to bring bits from home. The British introduced field bits like the snaffle, and military ones like the double bridle (bridoon and curb) and Weymouth. When the game crossed the Atlantic to America, the same bits continued to be used, albeit with longer shanks. After all, it was an English game, wasn't it?

Of the three basic bit categories—snaffle, curb and hackamore—the snaffle and curb are the two most commonly used on the polo field. Hackamores, bitless devices that apply pressure to the bridge of the nose, are only used as training devices and in Cowboy polo, although not specifically outlawed by the USPA. Some horsemen like to "sweeten or freshen" a horse's mouth that has become insensitive by switching from its normal bit to a hackamore periodically to allow the horse's mouth to heal from continual hard use.

Halfmoon Gag

The Snaffle

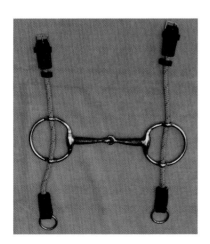

The snaffle bit acts by pinching the corners of the mouth where the upper and lower lips unite and has a lesser effect on the lower jaw. The principal benefit of the snaffle is that constant contact can be maintained with the horse's mouth. A simple snaffle is a mild bit, but like all bitting devices, its severity can be increased with the addition of twists, breaks, material, size, diameter and weight. Whether with a solid (unjointed), straight or curved mouthpiece, the bit pulls back against the front molars. A jointed mouthpiece increases the action and adds pressure to the roof of the mouth. The smaller the diameter of the mouthpiece, the greater the severity. Further addition of gag cheeks and/or draw reins, or both, changes the action of the snaffle and, therefore, its severity.

There are many snaffle variations ranging in severity from rubber through rubber-coated, Dr. Bristol, twisted, jointed, double-jointed, wire, chain link to double twisted wire. In addition, each can be fitted with

Cheltingham Egg Butt Snaffle Gag

different rings ("cheeks"). A loose ring provides some movement and is most prevalent. Egg butt snaffles are stationary and less sensitive except in a gag, where they are more severe.

Any of the above bits that are made to slide up and down the cheek straps are called gag bits. A gag changes the action of the snaffle by pulling up on the upper front molars. This slide-pulley action gives the rider more leverage, but also raises the horse's head and puts added pressure on the poll.

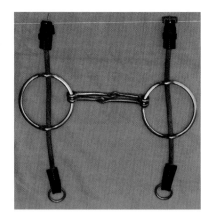
Large Ring Barry Gag

Gag cheeks are made with two holes to allow cheek straps to go completely through the rings rather than attach to them. There are many types of rings available, the most common being the large Argentinean style that more easily accommodates draw reins.

The Curb

Unlike the snaffle, the curb rests on the bars of the horse's mouth, between the incisors and molars, and a chain in the groove under the chin. It applies pressure to both those areas and the poll. Its severity is related to the length of the cheeks, and, as with all bits, to its size, weight and construction, as well as the length of the "curb chain." The curb is a device that causes the horse to flex its neck.

Like snaffles, curbs come in a wide variety. They can be flat, ported, rollers, spaded, fixed or movable, and, of course, their shanks are of various lengths. A port can allow room for the tongue or apply pressure to the roof of the mouth. Spades apply pressure to both roof and tongue, which can be very severe if used incorrectly.

The Double Bridle

A double or full bridle is created by adding a small ringed snaffle (bridoon) to a curb bit. The double bridle first gained acceptance in the mid-19th Century.

A double bridle is not two bridles, but it is the most sophisticated bitting devise because it combines the direct action of a snaffle with the leverage of a curb. The snaffle, often called a bridoon, works on the corners of the mouth while the curb acts on the bars of the mouth and the tongue. Because of its complexity, it is useful for not only polo, but for every horse discipline. Because this bitting combines the action of both snaffle and curb, it is a very exacting device. In use, the bridoon should be engaged first for mild checking and turning. The curb should be engaged only when abrupt stopping is required.

Weymouth Double Bridle

By adding draw reins, the bridoon becomes more severe. It increases the contact to the curb so that the full benefit of the double bridle is achieved. One popular variation is the gag snaffle and curb combination known as a Miller Gag. It works well when more control is desired with horses that are used to going in a gag. It bears repeating that the double bridle is a very exacting device and should only be used by experienced hands.

Mullenmouth Pelham/
Vulcanized Bar

The Pelham

The Pelham bit is a popular device that attempts to duplicate the action of the double bridle in one bit. One reason for its popularity is the belief that it is less severe than the snaffle/curb combination and less difficult to use, because the mouthpiece automatically engages before the curb comes into play. The Pelham's clever design can be rendered useless if the curb is engaged before the snaffle. Like all bits, a Pelham can be made and used in a severe manner. Adjusting the curb chain tighter increases the curb's effect. Popular Pelham bits found on the polo field are the Hartwell, Mullen, and Kimberwick.

Pelham/Ported Copper Bar

Both Pelham and snaffle bits should be adjusted snugly against the corners of the mouth. Some suggest that there should be one wrinkle induced by bit placement. In the double bridle the snaffle is adjusted similarly and the curb a half-inch (one hole) longer. The curb chain is adjusted according to the desired severity.

Exercise Bridle

Most polo barns keep an exercise bridle fitted with a mild bit and an easily adjustable headstall with one rein. The purpose is threefold. First, since the pony is only going to loped or led in a set, a mild bit is all that is needed to control the horse. Secondly, a mild bit may "freshen" a pony by working or resting differently on the bars of the mouth. Thirdly, a mild bit will probably work on almost any horse in the barn making it easy to switch between ponies. Western style headstalls without throatlatches work well for ease of switching. But perhaps the biggest incentive to having a separate bridle for exercising is the time saving of not having to clean several sets of tack each day.

Some players prefer a simple snaffle, not a gag-snaffle, while others use a curb. Some like a bosal because there is nothing in the mouth. Players choose headstalls that have many adjustment options and can easily accommodate different bit configurations. Unlike game tack, leather durability is not a life or death matter so lesser quality, i,e, cheaper, tack is usually used. Modern innovation has brought us washable tack that is well suited for this purpose.

Bit Guards

Bit guards are those colorful, round rubber disks that are seen at the corners of a horse's mouth. They serve to protect the horse's mouth from being cut or abraded during a polo match and are not for aesthetics. Their use is strongly advised, not only for humane reasons, but because a horse with sores around the bit area may become difficult to control.

Bit guards are used on almost any type bit, with the exception of those with two mouthpieces (double bridle), but they are most effective on loose-jaw bits (gags, snaffles, etc.) that have a greater potential to pinch the horse's mouth.

Many players encounter difficulties installing this simple device, especially on bits with long shanks or large diameter snaffle rings. The easiest solution is to first place the guard over the longest shank, then loop a length of bailing twine through the loose end of the guard and over a tack hook or available post. By pulling the bit, the hole will elongate, allowing it to easily slip over the other side of the cheek piece. To further facilitate installation, some people heat the rubber in boiling water or use a lubricant. Heating the rubber guard in a bucket of hot water and using a lubricant can help on those really large bits.

Cavesons, Breastplates, and Other Tack

Cavesons, or nosebands, are essential because they are the best way to attach a standing martingale or tie-down. Several styles of nosebands are used in polo, depending on the pony and the type of bit. Most common is the plain leather caveson. Drop, figure eight, and rope nosebands can be useful additions. Take care when using a drop noseband not to affix the bottom strap so low on the mouth that it interferes with the horse's ability to breathe.

A standing martingale is used for polo and, like all polo tack, takes tremendous abuse: it is one of the most often broken pieces of equipment. Therefore it should be made of extra-heavy leather and have substantial hardware on an adjustable tongue. A martingale reduces the ability of the horse to raise his head very high, thereby defeating the bit's effectiveness. Polo martingales come with single or double adjustments. Rubber stoppers should be used to keep the yoke from slipping up and down the chest strap. The chest strap should be loose from the stopper to the girth, not binding. Fitted properly, a standing martingale should be adjusted so that it can be drawn up to meet the pony's throat-latch when the horse is in his natural standing position.

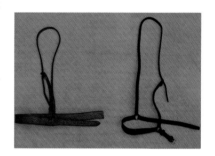

Caveson and Drop Nose

Likewise, breastplates (collars) should be heavy-duty racetrack types and adjustable at both sides, where they attach to the girth and on the strap that goes over the withers. Center adjustment types are also popular, because they are easier and faster to fit from one horse to another. Usually the breastplates are one inch to one-and-a-quarter inches wide. Some are lined with bag leather. The collar itself should be extra-wide so as not choke off the horse's windpipe.

Boots and Bandages

Commonly known as leg wraps, bandages are an extremely important piece of polo equipment. They not only protect the horse's legs from blows from mallets, balls and other horses' legs, but also help support the tendons.

Whether wool, felt or tubular knit cotton and wool combinations, they should be about nine feet long to wrap around enough times to give adequate protection and have wide Velcro closures to keep them on securely.

Some players prefer the tubular construction because of the dual layers of protection. However, these leg wraps require tighter winding due to their tendency to slip. Still others prefer synthetic wraps, because these are more elastic and stay up better. Manufactured with a stretchable nylon core and covered on both sides with acrylic nap, they are less bulky and, when washed, less likely to shrink. However, they will lose their elasticity over time.

The more traditional alternative is felt-lined leather boots. Although they do not offer as much support and can become heavy when soaked with water or sweat, it is almost impossible to over-tighten them, thus causing injury to the horse. A new variation of the old leather boot that is becoming increasingly popular is sports medicine boots. Made from foam neoprene or plasticote

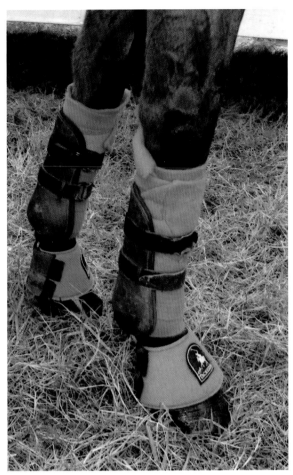

Italian tendon boots over traditional wraps with Tackeria corronet Boots.

polyurethane and covered with a napped acrylic fabric, they offer superior support and increased protection around the fetlock joint.

According to recently conducted tests (Birmingham University, UK) wool and cotton bandages absorb only about seven percent of the impact of a blow, while leather boots are twice as effective. The new sports boots absorb about three times as much force and weigh only a few grams more than leg wraps. In addition, they are less prone to unravel or come loose. Some like the Professional Choice because they protect the fetlock joint as well.

Recently, Italian Tendon Boots applied over traditional polo wraps have gained widespread acceptance. The wraps give good support, and the hard outer shell of the tendon boot, lined with a force-distributing material, provides protection from a blow, mallet, or hoof. Together, this combination is less cumbersome than the neoprene sports boots and allows the horse greater freedom of movement.

For added insurance against injury, many players further protect the coronet band with bell or coronet boots made out of rubber, neoprene or leather. Pull-on rubber is the lightest and least expensive but tears easily. Plastic is slightly more durable. More expensive leather-covered felt is long-lasting and, therefore, prevalent, but acrylic nap-covered neoprene with Velcro closures is beginning to gain in favor. Bell boots offer good coronet band protection for horses that "scalp"-toe of front foot scrapes rear; "forge" (toe of rear foot hits the heel of the front foot); or "brush" (the insides of either front or rear hit each other).

Rugs, Blankets, Sheets, Muzzles

Horse clothing can be divided into three main categories: rugs, blankets, and sheets. The main difference is in thickness and coating. Horses can destroy any blanket, so be aware that each type has a relatively short useful life.

The first rule of horse clothing is that it has to fit the horse properly. Blankets come in inch sizes. Measure the horse laterally from the center of the chest to the middle of the buttocks. The second rule is to make sure that the horse is neither too warm or too cold.

Rugs and blankets usually have hind leg straps to insure that they won't shift during movement. The best designed clothes have straps that buckle in the front of the hind legs so that the fasteners remain free of manure. Those with permanently attached fasteners keep the straps from getting lost in cleaning are preferred, because they are more difficult to repair if broken.

Rugs

Rugs are heavier-weight blankets that are usually coated to resist wet weather and protect the horse from wind gusts. The most popular rugs in use today are made from New Zealand heavy canvas and polymer-coated. Rugs are designed for both indoor and outdoor use but are predominantly used outside, hence their other name, "turnout blankets." They are either waterproof or water-repellant. Be careful on warm days: coated rugs don't breathe, and a horse can overheat.

Blankets

Blankets can be the same weight as some rugs but are not coated. They are used mostly on stabled horses and come in various weights and fabrics. A blanketed horse is easier to groom, and his coat will more readily retain its natural oils because a blanket makes the hairs lie flat. Therefore, be consistent. If a pony is usually blanketed, make especially sure that he is covered on chilly nights, because he will be more susceptible to chills than a horse that is unusually uncovered.

Sheets

Sheets are lightweight blankets that usually cover the horse's neck as well as the body. They help horses retain natural body heat and protect them from slight breezes. Like blankets, they are made in a range of fabrics depending on the local climate. Sheets can also be used as blanket liners to increase warmth, because they are constructed from fabrics that breathe. Synthetic fiber sheets help minimize chafing.

Like tack, all horse clothing should be cleaned regularly and kept in a good state of repair. Fleece linings that look great when new, mat quickly and retain dirt and hair, eventually becoming a source of irritation.

Muzzles

Regardless of the level of polo played, players try to feed and train their ponies to perform at their optimum athletic ability. Horses that are fat, or have massive muscles or those with big stomachs are severely limiting their natural athletic ability and health.

A muzzle is the tool of choice for weight management. Horses want to constantly graze, whether in a stall or a paddock. Whether grass or not. A muzzle can limit intake of fiber while allowing free water intake. Thus a pony can be turned out for added exercise and relief from the boredom of being in a stall all day

Various types of grazing muzzles–ugly but effective.

without overeating or eating bedding while stall-bound. When turning out a horse on fresh grass the horse is not used to, a grazing muzzle can be a useful tool in avoiding colic or founder (See page 138).

Another useful device is the exercise muzzle. Pictured at left, it has extra large and adjustable nostril openings. It will keep a horse from nipping at another while being ponied but not inhibit air intake.

Polo tack should be cleaned with pure glycerin saddle soap (liquid or bar) after each use to remove dried sweat and dirt. Sweat and mildew are the number one destroyers of tack. One of the many common misconceptions about cleaning tack is that water ruins leather. Wear and tear eventually ruins all leather and stitching. Use plenty of water and a small amount of soap to free up grime. Bits should be rinsed off in clear water to remove any caked saliva so that the pony will always have a "fresh" bit.

To prevent mildew, tack should be air-dried in *indirect* sunlight after cleaning. Bridles should be hung from the top of the headstall, and the reins should be loosely looped and allowed to hang down from the bit in approximately the same position as when in use. Leather has a tendency to assume the shape of its most accustomed position, therefore it is best to try to approximate the same shape for storage as when in use.

While all of this sounds easy, it is all too common for tack to get just a lick and a promise or no cleaning at all during a hectic playing schedule. By the end of a tournament or season, tack usually needs more thorough cleaning and oiling.

The first step in thorough cleaning is to take the tack apart by unbuckling all the pieces, removing keepers, bits, browbands, etc. Briefly soak all leather parts in a bucket of lukewarm water mixed with a couple of tablespoons of liquid glycerin soap. Use just enough soap so that the water feels slightly filmy. Swish all leather parts around in the bucket and then use a lightly soaped scrubbrush and wash-type pad to gently scrub all leathers. Use the abrasive side of the pad for really stubborn spots. A soft toothbrush is useful for those hard-to-reach places around buckles, hook studs and stitching. After cleaning a piece, swish it around again in the bucket to remove any loose dirt and then towel-dry any excess moisture and leave in an airy dry place, but not in direct sunlight, for about a half hour or so to complete drying.

Remove stirrup leathers from the saddle and clean the leathers as above. Obviously, it is impractical to dunk a saddle in a bucket, so use a soft sponge to go over the entire saddle, paying special attention to the underside where the saddle contacts the horse. Even if a saddle pad is used, sweat will come through and the dried sweat (salt) will dry and crack the soft leather around the panels. It is important to at least wipe the underside of a saddle after each use. Girths should get scrupulous attention, because they are the weakest link. When cleaning girths, each buckle and strap should be checked for durability.

After the tack has dried sufficiently, handle each piece and check the stitching and buckle turns to make sure that they are not in need of repair. Those that feel supple and soft are ready for use. Any pieces that are stiff need oil. Herein lie two more misconceptions: one, that oil ruins leather and stitching, and two, that heating the oils will cause them to penetrate better. Tanning leather permanently closes and seals the hide's pores so that they can't respond to heat like living skin. Hot oil can actually damage leather fibers much as a hot iron can damage cloth. The bottom line is, if the leather is dry and brittle, oil it. If it isn't, don't. Leather that comes in direct contact with the horse, the underside of saddles, girth, breastplates, etc. will probably require the most oiling.

Use a light oil like hydrophane or even pure olive oil. Commercial vegetable cooking oils (Wesson, Puritan, etc.) will turn rancid. Oil and soap combinations such as Lexol are not rich enough to penetrate dry leather and often leave a sticky film. Neat's-foot oil, which is very strong and penetrating, irritates some horses' skin and breaks down stitching more rapidly than other oils.

Use a dry, clean piece of terry cloth, sheepskin, natural sponge or fingers to apply a thin light coat of oil. Flexing the leather as the oil is applied will help penetration. Use a generous amount of oil under the panels and flaps of the saddles, but do not oil the outside or seat. The outside of the flaps and seat do not come in contact with the horse and don't get as dirty as the underside. Besides, you don't want to get your clothing oil stained. If the leather still feels stiff after the oil has been absorbed and the surface no longer glistens, apply another coat. Especially dry tack may take several coats before it is rehabilitated.

Mildew, which can form on tack stored in damp, humid conditions, is the bane of all leather and stitching. The moment it is spotted it should be removed with a solution of one part ammonia to seven parts water. After cleaning the mildew off with the solution, place the tack in direct sunlight. It is actually the sunlight that kills the mildew and keeps it from coming back. Once mildew has set in, it is very hard to kill and may require several treatments to completely eradicate any traces.

If the tack is to be stored for a while, clean all tack as above and then coat all leather with a heavy dressing such as Ko-Cho-Lin to create a barrier against moisture. If it is impractical to store the tack in a dry, warm (about seventy degrees) place, wrap it in brown paper to absorb any moisture residue and then seal it in a plastic bag. In general, tack in use will keep better than any storage regimen.

Personal Equipment

"Owing to the number of fatal accidents
all officers must wear hats."
A British commander in India, 1890

Helmet (Rule 4a)

Ill. #33: Traditional (Locke Style) Helmet with Face Mask

Don't be fooled by those old polo prints depicting players wearing school caps or, worse yet, are bareheaded. From polo's earliest times, records show that there was considerable concern over headgear and safety. In India, some English players were upset over the native players wearing turbans, because it was felt that they held an undue advantage and could play with "unnatural abandon." In 1877 the first recorded polo fatality occurred when Bob Darley, an uncle of *Modern Polo*'s author E. D. Miller, landed on his unhelmeted head when his pony tripped over another's legs. This led to a profusion of various "safety caps" and inspired a debate as to the relative merits of silk versus wool in protection. Oversized visors were added to forage caps to shield the eyes from the sun, and military men adopted the pith helmet, which became quite the rage for a while that lasted almost seventy-five years. Eventually, the two styles were combined into the Locke type, constructed of a cork shell wrapped with a cloth cover that is still popular today.

It is fortunate that the single most important piece of personal equipment is unquestionably also the one that benefited most from modern technology. After three years of research and development, the Oxley Safety Helmet with a rigid outer shell and a styrofoam liner was introduced in 1963. Over the ensuing years there have been several new attempts as materials and technology have improved. In 1979 Wayne State University created the first standard testing regimen and performance requirements for polo helmets. Most of the currently available polo helmets have undergone strenuous tests by the USPA® and, although the results are conclusive, low-scoring Severity Index helmets (below 1100) have not become the rule. According to the (NOCSAE) (National Organization Committee for Safety Athletic Equipment) the standards for testing polo helmets are the most stringent of any sports helmet. Since the test's inception, there have been several additional tests and re-tests. The most recent (1998) results appear below, with Bond Street 98 and Polo Gear 2000 garnering the best scores. Unfortunately, helmets manufactured in South America are not subjected to any testing standard.

Chin straps come in a variety of styles. The traditional continuous loop has been augmented to include plastic or metal buckles, chin cups and ear protectors.As long as the strap holds the helmet in place, no particular style has demonstrated an advantage over another.

Chart No. 3a/Wayne State University Standards

HELMET	FRONT	SIDE	REAR	TOP
Patey*	**1638**	**589**	**949**	**1181**
Grattan*	1401	647	1614	1244
Argentine	**3270**	**1903**	**3059**	**2509**
Polo USA Gear*	3263	818	1585	1380
Polo USA Gear	**1806**	**1145**	**2708**	**2420**
Polo Gear 98*	1161	801	1202	939
Bond Street	959	858	964	648
Bond Street 98	740/1028	594/584	806/1078	598/975
Spectra	**1181**	**804**	**1278**	**965**
Falcone 2*	1291	938	1885	1188
Falcone l*	**1131**	**691**	**1064**	**1114**
PoloGear2000	1212	457/707	842/1064	640/1003
Spectra 2*	**1259**	**770**	**1197**	**1160**

*When the same helmets were re-tested, the Severity Index results were dramatically worse. This suggests that those helmets that tested well (1100 or below initially) should be discarded after a severe blow to the helmet. Helmets no longer manufactured are the Lodsworth, Townsend, Cowdray and the Bell Pacer.

Face Masks

Face masks made of various materials and designs began to appear in the mid-1960s. Space-age materials and high-tech designs, while proven safety aids, never gained widespread usage. Many players complained of limited visibility and range of motion. To others, the newer helmets were ugly and heavy. It didn't help that most of the high-goal players preferred the traditional cloth-and-cork-style helmets.

Grattan Helmet/Mask

Polo Gear Helmet

Patey Helmet/Mask

A USPA® safety committee study found that facial injuries comprised nineteen percent of all injuries suffered by polo players, making them the second most common type of bodily injury. Ninety-four percent of all facial injuries were lacerations, contusions and abrasions. Six percent were fractures. Sixty-five percent of facial injuries occurred to the players who did not wear facemasks.

According to a study done by the New England Eye Institute at Tufts University, stainless steel face masks may offer protection against a polo ball traveling at the speed of eighty-four miles per hour when the face masks is no more than two-and-one-half inches from the helmet brim. USPA^Æ is presently unaware of any injuries actually caused by the stainless steel face masks, although such injuries may be possible. An anecdotal study by the USPA Safety Committee suggests that facial injury is reduced eighty-three percent when a facemask is worn in outdoor low-goal polo.

More recently, after still more serious injuries, helmets with low Severity Indexes have gained in popularity. In 1995 Horacío Hegey (10h. ARG) was struck in the eye by a hard line-drive ball. The resulting loss of his eye has driven many players, including his cousin Edúardo (10h. ARG), to wear shatterproof goggles.

Boots

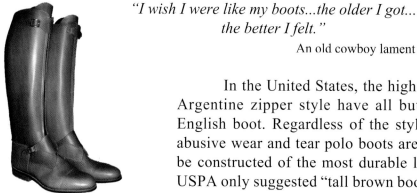

"I wish I were like my boots...the older I got... the better I felt."

An old cowboy lament

This pair of polo boots is custom-made of exotic full grain side-leather cowhide by E. Vogel, Inc. of New York City. They feature Argentine style zippers with ankle guards and plain toe-tips with double leather soles.

Italian oiled four strap Velcro® polo boots with reinforced inside and Vibram® light tread sole by R Custom of Westport, CT.

In the United States, the high-top Western boot and the Argentine zipper style have all but replaced the traditional English boot. Regardless of the style, due to the tremendous abusive wear and tear polo boots are subjected to, they should be constructed of the most durable leathers. Prior to 1993 the USPA only suggested "tall brown boots," but that language was subsequently dropped from the rules.

The most notable features that polo players look for are low-heel counters (side) to permit maximum ankle mobility and an underslung heel. In the U.S. the popular choice is the Western (Cowboy) style with a one-and-three-quarter or two-inch heel. The underslung Western heel minimizes the danger of getting a foot trapped in the iron in the event of a fall, and pointed toes make it easier to regain a lost stirrup. Many are made with a shank (arch) that is reinforced with iron for long durability. The characteristically high arch forces the foot deeper into the stirrup iron. Many who swear by cowboy boots say they are less tiring. These higher-arched shanks often require shorter stirrup lengths than the flatter English and Argentine boots.

The Argentine style features a front zipper and has a less underslung but shorter heel that also allows the player to ride "shot home" without fear of being unable to release. The zipper offers the two additional advantages of trimmer fit and ease of taking on and off, which have made the "Argie boot" the international popularity leader.

Many players prefer thin-leather (domestic or French calf) construction because they say that they get a better "feel" of the horse. Others prefer the durability of lined cow leather or even the tougher "buffalo" hides. A lined boot will hold its shape better, but linings tend to wear out before the outside skins. The tops should be nineteen inches high (or just under the knee break) to protect against impact. If they feel a little high initially, don't worry; the boot shafts will drop with use as the ankle wrinkles.

A boot should fit snugly across the ball of the foot and be fairly loose everywhere else—not so loose that it moves and rubs or so tight that it is a chore to pull on. In spite of what the salesperson may say, a well-fitting boot does not require a break-in period. Initially there might be some slight pinching at the heel, but a boot should be **easy** to put on and take off. Remember when purchasing a pair of boots that the breech or trouser leg has to fit inside the boot, probably with a rather heavy sock to aid in wicking.

Stetson's® new three strap polo boot. This new model features a computer designed molded last and square toe for maximum comfort. The Vibram® sole is contoured for the proper toe/heel alignment. The field boot style lacing and padded ankles plus loops to retain knee guard straps are other added features.

Knee Guards

Polo photographs of the 1920s and '30s show that players did not use knee protection of any kind. If used at all, knee-guards were applied to protect a previous injury. About thirty-five years ago players, mindful of preventative rather than remedial action, broke with tradition and began wearing knee guards to protect their knees in a ride-off and from being hit with balls and mallets. Initially bulky, their design has been refined, and there are now several popular models. Today it is rare to see players without knee protection. Still, there are some, like Joe Barry (9h. USA), who shunned any protection in favor of more sensitive contact with the pony.

Either foam rubber or felt covered with ribbed or smooth leather is the most common. Some types are reinforced at the critical kneecap (patella) and small bone on the outside of knee (fibula) areas.

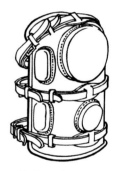

Ill. # 34: Full-size Hipwood style knee guards offer the most protection at the critical points, patella and fibula, and will stay securely in place.

The Julian Hipwood (9h. UK) designed type, introduced in 1980, have gained wide spread popularity over the smaller Argentine, Pakistani and English models. Hipwood knee guards are reinforced and come in two sizes: short with only two straps, and long with three straps. The extra length offers added shin protection.

Another new entry is made of foam neoprene covered with a napped acrylic fabric and fitted with Velcro closures. These knee guards are more comfortable than hard leather and permit closer contact with the horse, but the closures wear out over time.

Whips and Spurs *(Rule 4c)*

"It's (too) easy to kick the wind out of a horse with spurs and they won't make a horse go faster."
Ray Harrington (9h. USA)

In polo, where instant obedience is necessary, whips and spurs are used to encourage an immediate response rather than to beat a horse into submission. Since most trainers use a whip when making a pony, just carrying a whip can alter a pony's attitude. Often a light tap is all that is needed to signal the horse.

Spurs are useful for initiating quick starts, especially on lethargic ponies, and in moving a horse into a ride-off, but they are more often used to "draw up" a pony to make him stop on his hocks. The whip is used to lengthen the stride to encourage speed, while spurs are used to shorten stride and "collect" the horse.

Because the whip and reins are carried in the same hand, a long whip is desirable so that it can be used without a simultaneous tug on the reins that could mitigate a signal. A polo whip needs to be about thirty-nine inches long and flexible enough to strike the horse with minimal wrist movement. For this reason, polo whips usually have a fiberglass, rawhide, or steel shaft. The shaft is then wrapped with thread, nylon cord, linen or leather or rawhide. The heel of the handle is usually fitted with a larger protruding "button" to prevent the whip from sliding through the hand and a wrist sling to avoid an inadvertent loss.

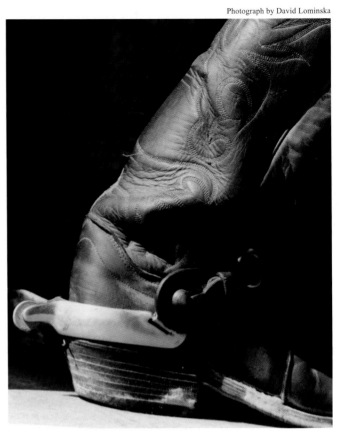

Photograph by David Lominska

Heavyweight Western style polo spurs rest on the low heel counter of a Western style polo boot. They feature smooth small diameter round rowels. Many players tape the rowels so that they won't turn and pinch the horse's hide.

Unless used by a competent rider who is in the habit of wearing them, spurs should be avoided in polo except when absolutely necessary. When turning the leg out in the act of swinging, it is very easy to inadvertently jab the horse. In addition, spurs can send mixed signals to the pony, especially if you are trying to rate the horse while it is being spurred. Other than hitting the horse in the head with a mallet, it is one of the more notorious reasons why ponies get in the habit of shying away from the ball.

If you do plan to wear spurs, make sure they don't have sharp rowels as they are forbidden by USPA Rule 4(1) c. Some players prefer the heavier Western type with small diameter round unpointed rowels, while others use the traditional English Prince of Wales or Cavalry types. The latter two come in various weights and shank lengths.

Gloves

Gloves have become very popular, because they make it easier to grip the reins, especially in the rain, and prevent blisters. Most that are in polo use today have been adapted from other sports and come in a variety of colors to match your team colors.

Leather-palmed racquetball gloves are made in light deer skin and slightly heavier goat skin. Baseball batting gloves are similar but slightly heavier. Roping gloves are heavier than both former types and have a reinforced thumb and forefinger, offering greater durability. One popular model uses sticky leather for the palm that is especially good in the rain.

Today's manufacturers offer so many different options that gloves have become a matter of personal preference. Some players don't wear any, while some only wear one on their rein hand, saying that they get a better "feel" of mallet without a glove. Whichever type you choose, remember that leather will absorb sweat. When it dries, the gloves become brittle. Regular cleaning and light oil will make them supple again, but even with good care, they have a short useful life.

Mallets

There is more to a mallet than meets the eye, and players give far too little thought to mallet selection. Understanding how the three components—cane, head, and grip—are constructed is key to choosing the right one and being able to replicate it consistently.

Although mallets have had a tremendous metamorphosis since the days of *chaugán*, they have not changed very much in the last fifty years. Although there are several mallet makers using "New Age" materials such as graphite (Argosy of England, Centaur, Gladiator and Vectra of the USA), these non-cane mallets are rare, although they can be standardized to specific personal tastes and duplicated more easily. Impervious to climate, easier on the arm due to their lighter weight and greater resiliency, composition mallets are rapidly gaining converts, such as Julian Hipwood (9h. UK).

Canes

Most of the commercial sticks in use today are made from bamboo (rattan, malacca, moonah, etc.) cane that grows underwater in the Far East and Malaysia. Rattan, currently the most popular, has a typically light "bamboo" color. It is chosen for strength, closeness of joints, and flexibility. Malacca is darker, stiffer, and lighter in weight. Honey-colored moonah is a compromise between the two. The canes are hand-straightened and "cured" in an oven under medium heat (about one hundred degrees) for several hours. For this reason, both heat and moisture are enemies of a finished mallet.

Bamboo cane has a thin bark on the outside that seals out the moisture from the inner fibers. The cane grows in spurts, which creates numerous joints. The number, placement and degree of taper of the joints account for the cane's inherent "feel." Mother Nature has made it almost impossible to find two canes exactly alike. Variable head weight can further increase the mallet's 'feel' and whippiness.

Today's more prominent custom mallet makers to the stars are more likely to use Manau cane, a thorny member of the Palm family that is predominantly found in Asia. It grows above ground and can grow 600 ft. long during a lifespan of fifteen years. Starting from the part closest to the root where the cane is strongest, 9 ft. lengths are cut and then boiled in a mixture of diesel and coconut oils until they becomes golden yellow. The finishing process consists of a wet sand wash. The custom mallet maker will then heat the shaft over an open flame to "cure " the cane and cut the finished stick from the part of the cane most suited to specific requests of the player, ie: amount of of whippiness and where on the cane to set the head.

Heads

Mallet heads are chosen to compliment the cane. A heavy head on a light cane would produce a very whippy stick and one that is prone to break close to the head and, therefore, undesirable. There are four basic woods used to make malletheads: bamboo, tipa blanca, maple, and mulberry. Tipa blanca comes from a tree that is native to Northern Argentina, Paraguay and Brazil and is hard and brittle. Because of its brittleness, it can break very easily and does not take a large cane diameter well, since it leaves the wall too thin. In some countries locally grown wood, such as sycamore and oak, is substituted quite successfully.

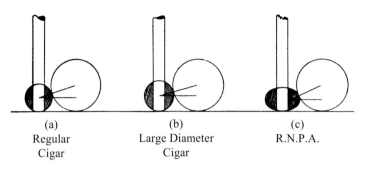

(a)	(b)	(c)
Regular	Large Diameter	R.N.P.A.
Cigar	Cigar	

Ill. # 35: Variations of Cigar-Shaped Head indicating the different points of impact.

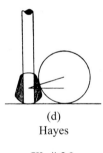

(d)
Hayes

Ill. # 36:

More available in the US and UK, maple is similar to tipa, but even harder. Because of its heavy mass, many players prefer it for distance. Mulberry is used because it is characteristically like maple, but less brittle. Bamboo is the most popular by far, because it offers the best compromise. It is reasonably durable, and its resiliency makes it easier on the arm. Bamboo is fibrous and, although less brittle, given to peel or shred. The so-called "female head" has a root hole core that is filled to add strength and mass.

In addition to different woods, mallet-heads come in several shapes, sizes and weights. The size and density of the wood dictates the weight. The most common shapes used today are cylindrical (see ill. #35 above) , with the same diameter throughout; cigar, which has both ends tapered and usually a trimmed heel; Skene (named after the famed ten-goaler who designed it), which is cigar-shaped with a flat rather than rounded bottom; and the RNPA (Royal Naval Polo Association), which features a squashed oval with a broad base. The RNPA style permits the head to contact the ball further below the equator than the Skene and is preferred for knock-ins and penalty shots.

While a heavier mallet may drive the ball a greater distance, it is also less handy and takes greater effort to swing quickly. The cigar head is a clever compromise, because it is wider at the center where, presumably, the ball will be hit. However, if the ball is not met exactly in the center (sweet spot) of the head, the tapered end will adversely affect aim. The flatter the head, the easier it is to get under the ball, thereby gaining loft. This can be especially useful when playing on long cut grass. On the other hand, you can get too much loft and sacrifice distance when playing on short grass.

The end of the cane, where it attaches to the mallet-head, is usually wrapped with cord to protect the bark and absorb shock. Sometimes rubber rings are added for further protection, but they can interfere with the ball if the wrist is behind the mallet when the ball is struck. Some heads are treated with vellum, linseed oil or paint to protect them against moisture damage.

Grips

By gluing a block of wood to the round cane, grips can be manufactured in almost any shape and size. Round, flat, vee, notched or not, they are all covered with rubber, cotton terry cloth or leather depending on the climate where used. Rubber grips range from smooth to varying degrees of roughness.

Mallet handles are basically variations on the standard rugby grip. Experimental grips like the elbow-bend, rimless, and finger-notched grip have proven to be passing fads, but some players do customize standard grips to suit their personal tastes in thickness and size.

Length

Mallets are made in various lengths in inch increments to suit a player's height and arm length as well as pony size. Some players prefer to use one length regardless of the size of the pony being ridden. They argue that it is easier to adjust aim mentally than physically and add that different-length mallets have a different "feel." Other players find it easier to use different-length mallets on different size horses. Yet others may use one length and/or type when playing different positions. Nevertheless, the longer the mallet, the greater the corresponding arc will be, resulting in greater distance. However, a shorter mallet, while sacrificing distance, should increase accuracy and handiness. Most professional players advise using the longest mallet that feels comfortable.

Selection

It is not unusual for high-goal polo players to spend hours selecting mallets. Often they are unhappy with their last selection. A favorite stick may be used for years, requiring endless repairs because the owner swears that there is not another one like it to be found. Mallets are made from natural substances. Even if they look the same, feel the same, and weigh the same they will rarely play the same.

Other than making your own, there are two ways of obtaining mallets: custom-made or from a retail inventory. Either method requires an arduous amount of trial and error. It is best to enlist the aid of a more experienced player who knows the first-time buyer's physical and equestrian abilities. Beginners should note that starting out with a mallet that is unsuited to their physical attributes might do irreparable damage to their muscles, tendons and ligaments.

After determining the length of stick needed, systematically go through all the mallets that are available. Immediately discard those that are obviously not right. Cull from the rest until a few are found that feel comfortable to wield and are well balanced. Then check for desired whippiness. Canes that have a narrower diameter and fewer joints will be whippier. Grasp the mallet-head in the left hand while still holding the grip and flex the shaft. Check for bendability and notice where along the shaft the maximum flexation occurs. Many players who like slightly whippy sticks prefer the maximum flex in the bottom third of the shaft. This usually occurs when the growth rings are close together near the grip and widen out closer to the head. This done, test the feel and whippiness by abruptly halting a partial swing.

Lastly, still holding the grip, twist the head. If the shaft of the mallet twists as the head is turned the mallet is a "ringer" and useless. Having found a good one, the whole process needs to be repeated again and again to choose two or three. Once a group is selected, each mallet should be weighed. Marking the weight at the exact center point of balance on the shaft for future reference will prove most fruitful.

If you know what you want and are close to a custom mallet maker, he will probably be able to replicate your old prized mallet more easily and in greater quantity. Equally important, he can also customize the handle to precisely fit your hand by using various grip materials and slings. Another nice touch is that the heads can be custom-painted with colors and initials, which makes them easier to locate in a hurry.

Mallet Care

Just like horses, mallets don't appreciate changes. If it were possible, mallets should be kept in a temperature- and humidity-controlled environment. Both heat and moisture can be absorbed by the cane, which will affect its whippiness. Mallets should be stored in a dry place out of the sun.

When stored, mallets should hang *freely from their slings*, which allows gravity and the greater head weight to pull the cane straight down. Under no circumstances should a mallet be left in the glaring sunshine.

Mallets that have weathered poorly may need to be re-straightened. It is best to use two hands and your knee to make several small bends to realign the shaft rather than banging it against your boot or stirrup, which can damage the bark and leave the cane open to greater moisture retention.

Ground moisture can destroy heads very quickly, since they absorb water. Heads treated with protective coatings that vary from linseed oil, vellum, varnish and paint are of some help. Striking a ball with a moist head, even a "protected" one, will shred the fibrous material with just a few shots. Save an old mallet for those rainy days and dewy mornings.

Transportation

If you own some polo ponies and want to play at a location other than where the horses are stabled, a method of conveyance is a must. For the polo player, commercial horse transporters that are often used for horse shows are impractical, as well as cost-prohibitive. In the United States today, the preferred method is a truck and "gooseneck" trailer rather than a solid-bodied van. This combination, commonly called a "rig," is the polo player's lifeline so it gets almost as much care as the ponies. In the United Kingdom, New Zealand and Europe solid bodied single chassis horse vans or "boxes," as they are called, are more prevalent.

The Truck

The number of horses to be carried will dictate the size and "pulling power" of truck needed. By far the most common vehicle in use today is a one-ton pick-up truck with dual rear wheels (Dually) and a towing ball in the middle of the truck bed, designed to pull a fifth-wheel-type trailer. These trucks come with heavy-duty suspensions and either gas or diesel engines capable of towing ten thousand pounds. Although today's pick-up trucks come with as many options as the family sedan, the two most important for the horse hauler to consider are gas vs. diesel and auto transmission vs. standard.

Diesel fuel is less expensive than gas, and if you are going to be hauling great distances, the saving can be meaningful. There is a slight sacrifice in pulling power even with turbochargers. Automatic transmissions tend to burn more gas, but enable even the feeblest drivers to give the horses a smooth ride. Standard transmissions offer greater control of power and braking and are preferred in hilly environs. With a competent driver at the wheel, they are more economical and capable of providing a similarly smooth ride. Unlike playing polo, when it comes to truck motors, it is better to be over-horsed.

128

An overdrive reduces engine wear and fuel consumption and is, therefore, useful on long, flat turnpike driving. If the transmission keeps shifting unnecessarily ("hunting") to find the proper gear, overdrive should not be used. Too much shifting can cause excessive heat buildup that can destroy bearings and seals. An add-on electric brake controller is a necessity. The device senses changes in the tow vehicle's inertia and sends impulses to the trailer brakes to apply appropriate pressure. Be careful when purchasing a vehicle with anti-skid braking capabilities. Special brake controllers are a need and hooking into a hydraulic system is more convoluted. On bigger rigs, air over hydraulic brakes is advisable. Other useful options include heavy-duty battery and alternator, transmission oil cooler, heavy-duty suspension, and extra large fan.

The Trailer

Having decided on a typical polo "rig," a one-ton Dually hauling a six-horse combination/stock trailer, the next decision to make is steel or aluminum.

Although aluminum is far and away today's most popular choice, there are many diehard steel fans who cite many more virtues than just the fact that steel is one third the cost of a similar aluminum trailer. Because aluminum dents more easily than steel, the cost factor may be mitigated by the higher cost of repairs to the frame or shell. Aluminum welding is more difficult, therefore costly, and not as readily available, especially on the road.

On the other hand, aluminum requires almost no maintenance on account of weather. Steel rusts and requires costly sanding and repainting every two to four years depending on climate.

The lighter weight is less of a benefit than aluminum fans think. A 4,800-pound steel trailer will weigh about 4,000 pounds if made in aluminum. The same two trailers loaded with six thousand pounds of horseflesh will weigh 10,800 versus 10,000 pounds respectively. It is still a saving, but now that 800 pounds represents only eight percent weight savings!

Steel fans say aluminum's lighter weight and tensile strength cause it to vibrate more and that aluminum does wear quicker at stress points. In addition to increased wear, the added vibration is not beneficial to horse's legs. Yet aluminum flexes better than steel, which may render the question moot.

One option that seems not to present a conundrum is axles. Rubber torsion axles are preferred over conventional axles with leaf springs. They definitely give the horses a smoother ride and are easier to pull (better gas mileage), but springs are easier to replace. A six-horse trailer should have axles rated at at least seven thousand pounds, but preferably eight thousand. In addition to torsion axles, rubber floor mats are customary because of better footing and ability to lessen the concussive effect on the pony's legs.

Regardless of the final choices, trailer design and configuration are important. Seven or eight feet wide and seven feet high is the standard. The horses will stand at slightly more of an angle in a narrower trailer but narrower trailers are easier to see around when driving.

Although ponies have been put in trailers every which way including loose, today's more scientific approach dictates that they should be placed on a slight angle, facing rear with heads curbside. (It has been demonstrated that if you place a horse untied in a trailer by himself he will naturally prefer to stand that way.) In addition to headroom safety, the added height allows for better heat dissipation, which is always desirable, as are many roof vents.

Partitions limit the number of ponies that you can squeeze into a trailer and can cause innumerable problems in a wreck. However, they greatly reduce inter-horse injuries especially on hilly, curving roadways.

Wide rear doors are the consensus because they facilitate passage, but a ramp is another question mark. Proponents agree that a horse is less likely to injure himself loading on a ramp than jumping on and off. Rampless devotees point out that unless the trailer is on perfectly flat ground the ramp will wobble, scaring the animal and eventually causing him to refuse to load.

The tack compartment should also have a wide door to facilitate entry while carrying armfuls of tack. Saddle racks are a welcome option and there are never enough bridle hooks. A hinged bar to keep your stowed gear from falling out of the over-the-goose neck compartment is a good idea as are a pair of fold-away steps on the inside wall so you can climb up to get items. A water tank (fillable from the outside) with an electric pump is a worthwhile option.

Trailering Tips

Horses should not be on a trailer for more than ten hours, and eight (four hundred miles) is preferable. It is a good idea to stop for at least fifteen minutes every four hours to let the horses relax and drink, if they will. Smooth driving techniques protect the horses and tow vehicle. Take corners slowly and avoid sudden stops and starts.

Many experts recommend feeding only hay for forty-eight hours prior to travel and a bran mash for the last meal before departure. It is not a good idea to tranquilize horses for shipment. Some chemicals can heighten the fear factor and can mask other vital symptoms. Some even contribute to choking and "dry throat." Even a pony that is a "good shipper" will have an elevated state of nervousness and a somewhat dry mouth. For this reason it is wise not to feed hay or grain during the trip.

Tie ponies in a way that leaves enough play in the lead rope to allow a horse to use his neck to balance, but not so long that he can get a leg over the rope. It is easier on a horse's anatomy to face rear. Likewise, there is less chance of a pony being hit in the eye from debris and splashes of passing cars if he faces curbside. It is also less dangerous to check or water the horses if the driver is not standing on the passing traffic side.

Overheating is a major shipping concern. Ideally ponies shouldn't break a sweat during a haul. Nor should they have a cold draft blowing down their backs, especially if it is raining. Weather conditions can vary immensely between mornings and evenings and changing altitudes. Modern trailers are made with roof vents, windows, and sliding plexiglass. Roof vents can be angled to allow air to blow in or to exhaust heat. Use these devices to regulate the climate inside the trailer, and check it frequently.

CDL

On April 1, 1992, compliance with the Commercial Vehicle Safety Act of 1986 became mandatory in the USA. The effect of this regulation on the polo player is that, unless he is transporting his own horses for a non-business purpose, the driver must have a special Commercial Driver's License (CDL) to drive a truck and trailer or van that has a *combined* weight of 26,000 pounds or more.

An individual who is transporting horses that are not his own for furtherance of commercial enterprise in any type or weight conveyance also must have a CDL. The U.S. Federal Highway Administration (FHWA) has an extremely broad definition of "furtherance of a commercial business purpose," and includes playing professionals, show riders, breeders, trainers, etc.

The Accident

In the event of the unthinkable, an accident with a loaded trailer, assessing the damage and injuries and communicating them to rescue officials so that suitable help is dispatched quickly can make the difference in whether a horse lives or dies.

See if any horses have been trapped in the trailer. If any are loose, locate and tie them out of harm's way. If the trailer has flipped, make sure it is stabilized before entering the box to work a horse loose. Even a slight movement by a thousand-pound horse is enough to make a precariously perched trailer roll again, and a spooked horse in a rocking box can cause further injury. Consider destroying any severely injured ponies, especially if they are trapped in the box with other uninjured horses. A horse with a badly broken leg can still cause problems and make extracting the other horses more dangerous.

To avoid personal injury attach a strong nylon halter with an extra long lead shank (ten feet or more) that can be manipulated from outside the trailer. Try to approach a trapped or fallen horse from the rear and attempt to reach over the body to grab the legs. If possible, one person should hold the horse's head to soothe him while another person works the legs. In some instances a blanket or jacket placed over the horse's eyes will help to settle a nervous animal; although sometimes just the opposite is true. Here again, it is important to know your horses. If the site is noisy, earplugs (rolled up stockings work well) can also be effective. In most accidents, even very serious ones, trapped horses will usually lie quietly until they are freed. Before opening the trailer door(s), make sure that the doors are not keeping the box from collapsing. Then tie them open so that they stay out of the way. If necessary, cut through the roof or walls.

Use soft cotton lead ropes tied with half hitches to pull the front legs up to the girth and the hind legs forward and up to the belly. A rope tied to the tail below the vertebrae can be useful in pulling the horse backward. With legs secured, a horse can be rolled onto his back, and backboards (common rescue equipment) can be used to slide the horse out.

If the horse must be lifted, construct a rope harness to support the horse under the chest. Never try to pull or lift a horse by his pasterns (ankles).

Avoid the use of drugs. Not only can they mask symptoms and make the vet's job tougher when he arrives, but some drugs also act as stimulants to a horse in a stressful situation.

Part Five:
The Support Team

Grooms are the unsung heroes of polo. By virtue of the fact that they spend more time with the horses than anyone else, they can make or break a polo player. A good groom is as hard to find as a world-class high-goal professional or a top-notch pony. It is no coincidence that they will usually be found together.

Perhaps the reason why there isn't much talk about grooms amongst polo players is because, if they have a good one, they don't want anyone to know about their good fortune for fear of losing the groom to a competitor. Likewise, if they are not fortunate they still want to keep it to themselves, because they don't want to turn the spotlight from their own ability and "string" (horses).

Besides being resigned to working long, hard hours, the best grooms love horses and are completely dedicated to their equine stablemates.

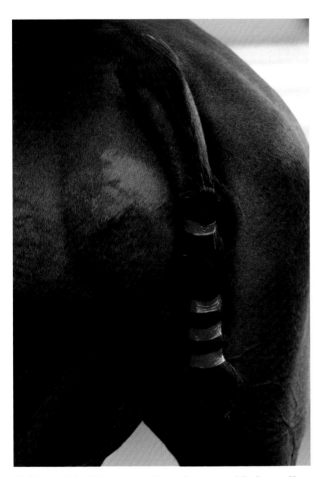

Tails are "tied" to prevent interference with the mallet. Sometimes tape is added for insurance. Note that this tail has been clipped at the dock to make a tight fit. A more aesthetic look can be achieved by "pulling" the hairs out by hand.

Many have developed, and are known for, special skills, such as managing leg injuries, "schooling" ponies to sharpen their proficiency, and breaking and training green horses. Grooms can be divided into two distinct groups: those that aspire to become players, and those whose fulfillment comes solely from a well turned-out string.

The more knowledgeable the horse owner, the easier it is to find a suitable groom and communicate to him exactly how the work should be done (see "The Daily Routine," page 29). Although most grooms work from a system, the better ones will know when to abandon their system for a pony that needs individual attention. Aside from the normal groom's duties of feeding, mucking, grooming, clipping, and tacking up, a polo groom should be proficient at bandaging legs, pulling and tying tails.

Around the turn of the century, polo players in India had the luxury of having one groom (*syce*) per horse. In the USA in the1920s it was not unusual to employ one groom for every two ponies. Today we expect a groom to take care of six to eight ponies. Obviously, this is a lot of work. The job, which is a seven-day-per-week undertaking, tends to be more than full-time and requires not only dedication but also extensive knowledge, experience and skill. In the final analysis, grooms are more than grooms.

They are full-time trainers, exercisers, veterinarians and caretakers of horses that compete in the most demanding equine sport.

Aside from the groom's normal caregiving chores, a good groom will be proficient at clipping, roaching manes, and "pulling" or trimming tails. Some may even "float" teeth or do minor farrier work. At a competition, a good polo groom should be aware of how the match is going and have the next pony at the ready. If the player needs to change a mallet, spurs or whip with the new horse, the groom should have these items ready when the player changes mounts. Also, the groom should have a spare mallet ready should the player need to change sticks during the chukker. When a pony comes off the playing field, the groom should be able to instantly recognize the horse's vital signs and do everything to insure the quickest recovery possible in case the pony may be asked to play another chukker.

Since the player often sees his string only when he comes to the field, he relies heavily on the advice of his groom as to the condition and temperament of the horses to be played. For this reason the groom usually has total control of what horses are played and when, and the player is wise to heed his groom's advice.

Farriers

"For want of a nail the shoe is lost,
for want of a shoe the horse is lost,
for want of a horse the rider is lost."
George Herbert (1593-1633)

Nobody can make or break a polo player quicker than a farrier. Ninety percent of all lameness in horses is due to problems from the knee down. Improper or too infrequent shoeing has been clinically proven to cause serious lameness, sometimes permanently. One carelessly placed nail can instantly render a pony unplayable. The horse's hoof structure is very sensitive to stress and pressure. Therefore, choosing a farrier is one of the most important horsecare decisions any horse owner has to make. It is especially critical for the polo player, due to the tremendous amount of stress a polo pony's legs are forced to endure.

Unlike the usual heavy-duty design of most polo equipment, polo ponies are shod with relatively thin, lightweight shoes similar to racetrack training shoes, to enhance their ability to run as fast as possible. Consequently, they have to be reshod more often than most horses, approximately every four weeks. So-called polo plates are used on the front feet. They are made out of a standard steel bar, double-rimmed on one side, with one rim slightly higher than the other. The shoe is then curved with the higher rim on the inside to conform to the USPA Rule 6's ban on sharp outer rims. The double rimmed-design allows the foot to pivot during lateral turns while still providing

Polo Shoes

protection and increasing traction. Hind feet are shod with a lightweight regular-type shoe, like Diamond's Classic or St. Croix's Lite Heeled Shoe, that have slightly elevated heels (caulks) on both ends to prevent slipping.

Caulks are designed to give added traction and come in various different sizes as well as different sharpness. The horse's conformation and use will determine what type of caulk is best. Some players prefer to elevate the inside caulk slightly more than the outside. (High, sharpened outside caulks are also prohibited by the USPA and HPA.) While increasing traction, caulks, especially high ones, can place undue stress on a pony's legs. Generally speaking, they should be used only by experienced players who can take care not to turn a horse while its feet are firmly planted and supporting total body weight. For fear of injuring the pony, even experienced players use high caulks only when absolutely necessary on very wet greensward.

Again uncharacteristically, thin, lightweight nails like #5 City Heads, #5 Slim Blade, or #5 Combo Specials are used to attach the shoes to the hoof wall. In addition to not adding much weight to the foot, they are designed to break easily so that the shoe will come off under extreme stress. Toe clips are used only occasionally and then, one center clip, usually only on the hinds. Hunter-type double clips are to be avoided totally. While clips may help to keep the shoe on, they don't help the pony's legs or feet in any way.

With all the stress placed on a polo pony's feet and legs, precise trimming of the hoof is critical. The hoof wall should be straight from the coronet band to the ground. The bottom of the hoof should be absolutely flat and level to insure even contact with the ground. Polo farrier Bill Brennan, who accompanied the 1979 USA team to the Argentine Cup of the Americas Tournament advises, "Keep the toes trimmed short to avoid clumsiness and pressure on the tendon." Care must be taken that the heels of the hoof are not trimmed too short. Some players believe that short or underslung heels enable the horse to run faster, but there is no definitive proof to substantiate this belief. On the other hand, there is proof that short heels place a tremendous amount of increased pressure on the tendons. Corns are usually due to improper heel fit or one set of shoes being left on too long.

Trimming the hoof is the farrier's true art and requires understanding of the horse's anatomy. Mother Nature should dictate how a horse is shod. If a horse has feet that naturally turn out or in, it is better not to try and correct the idiosyncrasy by orthopedic shoeing, because this will place unusual stress further up the leg. A healthy foot should require minor trimming and no adjustment. Improper hoof angle, especially a long toe, can cause a horse to 'pull' a suspensory ligament and overextend the fetlock joint. Horses' feet do not grow down as commonly believed, but rather, they grow forward, increasing the tension on the deep flexor tendon. The toe and heel do not grow at the same rate. In addition, they are under different degrees of stress. If a horse's hoof angle is altered, special care must be taken until the pony adjusts to the new angle. The sole of the foot should be concave to prevent pressure buildup and bruising. If a horse has a particularly thick, heavy foot, it is sometimes desirable to scoop out the sole of the foot to promote spreading in the hoof. A scooped sole aids in traction and shock absorption. In general, it is not wise to work a freshly shod pony excessively or ride in deep or sandy footing. Some horses have tender feet and require a day or two to get used to new shoes.

Is the Farrier Doing a Good Job?

Because of the high concentration of horses around a polo club, several farriers experienced in shoeing polo ponies are usually available. If you are located far from a local club, ask your veterinarian for a referral. Although many may disagree, in a pinch, a blacksmith with racetrack experience is the next best choice to a polo specialist. Unlike England (Farriers Registration Act of 1975), the USA has no laws governing farriers, so it is wise to ask for recommendations from fellow horsemen. According to the *American Farriers Journal* (1999), the cost of trimming and reshoeing all four feet runs from $25 to $100 in the United States, with the national average being $60. At present, it costs about $55 for a pony to be reshod by a specialist. Emergency service may cost more.

A good farrier is punctual and able to work calmly with even the highest-strung pony. He will be happy to explain his work and answer any questions. He should take pride in his work and be able to confer with the veterinarian about any problems. During the polo-playing season farriers' schedules are usually fully packed, so they will appreciate having the horses caught and ready for shoeing when they arrive. A clean, flat, spacious area in which to work is a must for a farrier to do a quality job.

Polo players look for the hoof to be properly aligned with the column of bones in the foot, correct shoe length, even medial/lateral balance, and proper nail placement. Front feet carry sixty percent of the load and are rounder than the more egg-shaped hinds. Some horsemen arbitrarily believe all polo hooves should be trimmed to perfect a fifty-, fifty-five-, or sixty-degree pastern angle (from pastern to ground). Others think that the angle should follow the line of the shoulder. The current consensus among knowledgeable vets and farriers alike is that the lower foot bones should be aligned. The small bones of the foot between the fetlock and hoof dovetail into one another. If they do not fit together perfectly straight, undue pressure is placed on the unions, which weakens the resiliency of the joint. Straight alignment (when viewed from the side) permits forward and backward rotation of the bones and maximizes support.

The hoof walls should be trimmed so that there is no flare at the bottom. Ideally, the shoe should be bigger than the hoof. Shoes should be long enough to slightly extend past the end of the heel to support the leg and assist heel expansion of the hoof. The toe of the shoe should be very slightly "rockered" to decrease tension on the flexor tendon. The age-old "quarter test" is as good as any tool to determine proper shoe width. Sufficient shoe, approximately one-sixteenth of an inch, should extend out past the hoof wall to permit a quarter-size coin to roll on its edge from the quarter back to the end of the shoe on both sides. This allows the hoof to expand.

The shoe should be set on the hoof so that the center of the frog points directly at the center of the front of the shoe. Nails should be placed plumb to the ground, neither up- nor downhill. To facilitate hoof expansion, nails should not be placed farther back than the widest part of the hoof. The nails should extend from the hoof about three-quarters of an inch up the wall. The nail ends are then cut off and bent over ("clinched") tightly into tiny troughs. You should be able to rub your hand over the hoof wall and not feel the clinches.

Before the farrier leaves, trot each horse out to make sure that he is tracking properly and there is no overstepping ("forging"). Look for any "paddling" or "winging" of the feet.

How to Pull a Shoe

Often a shoe will come loose or pry slightly apart from the foot. If the nails are bent, it is dangerous to try to bang the shoe back on because you can't foretell where the nail will come out, or worse, if it will at all. The safest remedy is to pull the shoe.

Farriers use a dull chisel-like instrument called a clinch cutter to loosen the clinches by unbending the nail ends. (Rasping clinches off should only be used in an emergency because, unless done very carefully, it may excessively damage the hoof wall.) The cutter is placed flat against the hoof wall, and the hammer driven up toward the coronary band, either breaking off or unbending the nail ends. After the clinches have been straightened, use lever action to pull the shoe off with a large flat-headed pliers-type device called a shoe puller. Insert the edges of the puller between the shoe and heel of the hoof and lever angle toward the toe. Work from the heel forward. Alternate sides, a little at a time and taking care not to shear through any nail. Support the hoof with your free hand to minimize leg strain and don't try to lever the shoe off with one quick jerk.

Orthopedic Shoeing

Although many farriers recommend the judicial use of pads in special situations, clinical tests of pads of various materials placed between the shoe and the sole indicate that they do not significantly reduce concussion. Leather pads make the foot sweat, and grit can become lodged between the sole and the pad. Synthetic pads can offer some relief to a pony with especially thin soles or one recovering from an injury. There are many new-age materials that offer new alternatives that are gaining acceptance when used properly.

Glued on shoes, a more modern innovation, have proven to be extremely effective in remedial shoeing or for horses that frequently throw shoes or, due to poor hoof wall, can't hold a shoe. Although glued-on shoes stay on very well on a semi-active horse, they do not last as long on polo ponies and are more costly. If they must be used for polo, gluing on a regular polo plate is preferred over specific shoes that are made by Glu-Strider and Ibex, because the plastic shoes are prone to slip on certain grasses.

Veterinarians

Although the elevated amount of stress to which a polo pony is subjected has been mentioned several times herein, it cannot be overstated. No other equine athlete has such a long competitive life or is put under more stress for longer periods. It is no wonder, then, that a veterinarian specializing in polo ponies forms a unique bond with the player. Most of the horses he deals with are only "polo sound," and keeping them in playing condition requires delicate sensitivity as well as knowledge.

Choosing the Right Vet for You

Naturally, it is important that you feel confident and comfortable with the vet's knowledge and experience. They should be used to looking at polo ponies and understand the value judgments inherent in such a strenuous sport. But equally important, the horse owner/caregiver must be able to communicate easily with his vet, who should answer all of the owner's questions willingly and thoroughly. If the caregiver doesn't know how to perform a necessary task, the vet should take the time to show and train the caregiver.

It is desirable to get to know the veterinarian before becoming a client. Is he an alarmist? Is he old-fashioned or up to date with the latest techniques? How is his clinic and equipment? Does he like to get second opinions? And, last but not least, how far away is he and how responsive is he apt to be to emergency situations? Willingness to come when you need him is one of the most important factors. Once you know the vet's capabilities and he understands your needs, it will be easier to define a care regimen.

Of course, the more knowledgeable the owner, the easier it is to communicate with the veterinarian. Believe it or not, this factor usually affects the vet's punctuality. The vet is invariably busy when you call. If you can pinpoint the problem and provide some basic life-sign information, the vet is more likely to know if he has all the necessary medicines and equipment with him and correctly predict how soon he will arrive.

Some Common Ailments

Part of being an accomplished polo player is keeping one's string in good playing condition and minimizing stress. Polo is tough on horses and, like many professional athletes, ponies are often played with minor injuries. Every horseman should be able to evaluate his horse's vital signs—pulse (32–44 beats/minute), rectal temperature (99–100.5° F), respiratory rate (8–15 beats/minute) and gum color or capillary refill time (1–3 seconds). Each horse must be examined carefully after every chukker and continually monitored when not playing. Any maladies should be attended to immediately, often fieldside, because even minor injuries can become major emergencies if allowed to go unattended until a vet can be found.

The following is not to be intended as medical advice, but rather an overview of some of the more common ailments polo players are likely to encounter at some point during their career. Remember: **DO NOT ADMINISTER ANY MEDICATIONS THAT MAY MASK SYMPTOMS OR CONFUSE DIAGNOSIS!**

Colic

Colic is easily one of the most common and most dangerous equine diseases. Because of the horse's uniquely designed digestive tract, he is highly susceptible to digestive problems. Colic is incorrectly oversimplified by calling it a horse "bellyache."

The horse's digestive mechanism is designed for large quantities of food to pass from the mouth to the stool very quickly. When there is an interruption of the flow, those same bacteria and protozoa that produce enzymes to aid digestion ferment and cause a painful buildup of gases, which is usually accompanied by a high fever. Liquids and gases build up and the bowel becomes distended and pushes against the diaphragm, compressing the chest and making it difficult to breathe. Colic is painful, because the nerves in a horse's gut are extremely sensitive. While a horse can tolerate cuts and punctures rather well, it is the intestinal stretching that the horse cannot stand. Although painful, it is not colic that kills horses but rather colic's side effect—endotoxic shock. The reason why colic is so dangerous is because the condition can escalate from a barely perceptible backup of gas to fatal shock in just a few hours.

There are two categories of colic: strangulating and non-strangulating. Fortunately, most colic cases are non-strangulating (simple colic)—minor backups of gas, impactions or spasms that rarely require surgery. Strangulating colic (twisted gut), when the bowel and blood vessels are twisted closed cutting off the blood supply, is much more life-threatening and usually require surgery.

Although colic can be generally controlled by diet, there are many factors that can cause a horse to colic. Remember that colic is largely a man-made disease and rarely found in wild horses. Feeding a horse extra fiber will maintain looser stool and minimize colic. A good parasite control program also reduces the chance of colic.

Horses that are turned out in sandy terrain, eat off a dirt floor, or have a habit of trying to vacuum up the last morsel in a close cropped or overgrazed pasture are susceptible to sand colic, because they ingest the sand along with their feed. Slowly the sand builds up in the intestinal tract, causing irritation and, eventually, impaction. The symptoms and treatment are usually the same as for regular colic, but if there is a large sand buildup that cannot be dislodged with medication, surgery may be required.

Heat (Estrus)

When mares are ready to ovulate they are said to be "in heat." Some mares have more obvious signs of being in heat than others. Usually mares will rub their tail against their stall wall. Their urine will be cloudy and their ears may point forward and tails may be raised. During estrus mares may "squirt" often in small streams and also "wink," open and close their vulva. During this period mares may exhibit abnormal behavior such as a change in personality which could be either cranky or affectionate—but noticeable in any case. Some mares may be difficult to play during this period. This is especially true when the mare is actually ovulating which is usually 24 to 48 hours before the end of her heat period. Depending on temperament, a mare in this condition may be more interested in other male horses on the field than concentrating on a rider's commands.

Diarrhea

Diarrhea in an adult horse is a serious condition and should be addressed immediately. Diarrhea causes an imbalance in a horse's water and electrolyte supply. This imbalance can quickly affect the large intestine and is the most common cause of colic. Aside from the obvious signs of diarrhea, lack of appetite and a dull coat may be signs of bowel irritation that, if not corrected, may lead to colic.

Heaves

Horses get heaves much the same as humans get asthma. Inhalation of dust, mold spores, and other allergens that are always plentiful around a barn can cause horses to heave. The main symptom is a soundless cough. Annoying more than a serious health impediment, heaves can be managed with a variety of measures, from wetting down the hay to corticosteroids. Sometimes switching feedstuffs or stall location will stem an allergic reaction.

Founder/Laminitis

Founder or, more correctly, laminitis is inflammation of the laminae and can have serious consequences. The laminae is the elastic tissue that support and aid flexation of the hoof, as well as act as the horse's shock absorbers. Founder is a symptom, not a disease. Once it has appeared, it takes on a life of its own and can escalate rapidly. Anything that disrupts the flow of blood to the feet can cause laminitis—colic, diarrhea, too much grain, some medications, new pastures, drinking cold water when overheated, hormonal imbalance, long-distance hauling, and even plain old stress are some of the more common causes that can make a horse founder. Almost anything that upsets the horse's intestinal bacteria can induce laminitis. It takes twelve to twenty-four hours before the onset of lameness and, if not resolved within forty-eight hours, the laminitis becomes chronic. Therefore it must be treated as quickly as possible.

Sudden lameness for no apparent reason can be an indication of founder, especially when following any of the events noted above. Laminitis is more likely to affect the front feet. If a pony is tenderfooted and you can feel a strong pulse and heat in his hoof, there is good reason to believe that he has foundered. The underlying cause of the laminitis must be cured first before a vet can treat the horse to stimulate blood flow. It is often suggested to walk the horse while waiting for the vet. The hoofs pounding the ground help to increase blood flow. After forty-eight hours, exercise is not beneficial. Other horsemen recommend soaking the feet in various solutions, both hot (to increase flow) and cold (to decrease pain and reduce blood requirement).

Horses that become sound within forty-eight hours enjoy a good prognosis, but it will take several weeks to determine the horse's future usefulness. If the laminitis is chronic, there are remedies like shoeing with pads and/or egg, heart or web bar shoes, and sand bedding can be helpful.

Thrush

The cause of this highly common condition in horses is a ubiquitous fungus. Thrush attacks the frog of the hoof and, because the frog is composed of dead tissue, poses no major heath hazard. Only in rare cases does it cause lameness. But oh, the smell! The stench can often be smelled without lifting the horse's leg and may be accompanied by a thick black discharge.

Thrush thrives in stabled horses forced to stand in dark, damp and dirty stalls for long periods of time. Excessive hoof dryness and lack of exercise can also cause thrush. Horses that are shod with pads are predisposed to thrush, as are horses that do not receive regular hoof care. Be sure to pick out hooves regularly and often.

There are several effective commercial remedies for thrush available without prescription. There are many popular remedies like bleach, but care must be taken to dilute properly. The same goes for many of the commercial products that contain caustic agents. Regardless of which product you choose, the key to proper treatment is to make sure that the remedy reaches every part of the infected area, including the crevices and is begun when the first signs of thrush are noticed. You will probably need to scrape and trim the frog and then spread the deeper crevices before applying the treatment. It's a dirty and smelly job, but unless the agent is thoroughly applied, thrush can be difficult to rid.

Ankle (Fetlock) Problems

All horses encounter ankle problems at one time or another, which polo players realize more often than others because of the tremendous stress to which their ponies are subjected. Horsemen say that a horse has "ankles" for a variety of problems: windpuffs, distention, osselets, sesamoid, suspensory ligament enlargements, and plain old "stocking up." How are these different ailments recognized and treated?

A horse can remain in work with many common ankle injuries if he is managed properly. A polo player should be familiar with his string's appearance in order to recognize any changes. The first question the vet will ask is how long you have noticed the condition. After determining the pony's appearance, touch will tell if the enlargement is hard or soft.

Often poultices, icing, mineral gels, white lotions, DMSO, and other astringents produce beneficial results to new injuries. Heat is usually a better solution for managing old or long-term injuries. Mild alcohol 'sweats' (Biegeloil, Absorbine, etc.) produce heat that increases circulation and reduces swelling. Wrapping a dressing increases its effectiveness. A nonporous wrap like plastic increases effectiveness more than cloth or roll cotton. Brown paper such as butchers use to wrap meat, is a popular compromise. Bandaging may also help in reducing edema and keeping the filling down.

Windpuffs are caused by a fluid buildup brought on by strain to the tendons (deep flexor and superficial). Because the tendon's sheath extends down to the fetlock, the puffiness associated with windpuffs is usually located toward the back of the fetlock. Once a windpuff develops, it may never go away. It is all right to keep a horse in work as long as the windpuffs stay soft and the horse isn't lame.

Distention

If the enlargement is on the front and outside of the ankle, it is usually caused by a buildup of lubricating (synovial) fluid in the capsule surrounding a joint. More common on the front legs, it can be brought on by almost any kind of severe strain, chip or fracture. If the swelling is only on the front of the leg it is more likely to be the result of a blow and is called a "false bursa." If the swelling doesn't subside in twenty-four to forty-eight hours with rest and mild treatment, call the vet. The problem could be serious.

Osselets

Osselets occur on the front of the fetlock joint and are usually a response to high-speed stress. Osselets involve bone growth and, unlike windpuffs and distentions, are hard. The tissue at the front of the joint becomes thickened and solid. Although the osselets may never go away, unless they are where two bones meet, a horse can continue to work. In some instances a horse with osselets will have a reduced range of motion. If a chip is involved, it may require surgery.

Sesamoids

Sesamoids are bones at the base of the fetlock. Sesamoid damage is caused by wear and tear to the fetlock joints. Horses that work at speed can develop bone density loss and ligament damage. Hard enlargements on the back of the ankle can indicate sesamoid damage. It is a condition that can only worsen over time, but if the horse is sound and not in pain, he can be used in light work. The key is relative change, which can only be assessed by X-ray.

Suspensories

Although some fluid builds up in the damaged area, "suspensories" are caused by a thickening of the soft tissue in between the suspensory ligaments. Located further forward than windpuffs and sesamoids, the enlargements are solid and flatter. They often coincide with a sesamoid problem because the ligaments are attached to the sesamoid bone and support the fetlock. Early awareness and rest are critical to dealing with suspensory problem, but surgically splitting the sheath will probably be required for a polo pony.

Rather than actually splitting the tendon, small longitudinal incisions are made through the sheath surrounding the suspensories tendon to let the entire area heal simultaneously. While this may take longer to heal (six months to a year) than conventional therapy, it has been proven to provide better and longer lasting results.

Stocking-up

Unsightly swelling, usually on the hind feet, from just above the fetlock down to the coronet band is called stocking-up. This condition is caused by a buildup of fluid (lymph) that the horse's veins are unable to return to the bloodstream.

Stocking-up is usually noticed on the morning after a strenuous workout. In order for the horse to return the extra secreted fluid, he must remain moving so as to be able to fight gravity and pump the fluid up the legs. If the horse is stabled after a strenuous outing and isn't inclined to move around in his stall a lot, the chances are that he will stock up. This is especially true in older horses, whose lymphatic system may be compromised.

The good news is that stocking-up rarely interferes with or bothers a horse. It isn't painful and will usually go away after a short walk or turnout. Bandaging the legs with a mild brace and icing the leg for a short (ten to fifteen minutes) periods after exercise will greatly reduce the chance of a horse stocking up.

Splints

A splint is a tear of the thick, fibrous ligaments that run down both sides of the shin and attach the two thin splint bones to the weight-bearing cannon bone. Because of their close association with ligaments and tendons, and because they are unprotected by tissue, they are particularly susceptible to external trauma during polo and can be as painful as a fracture. Splints most commonly develop on the inside of the front leg, about midway between the knee and fetlock. Splints that form higher up toward the knee are more worrisome. When the area is no longer hot, swollen or painful, the splint is said to be "set."

Splints usually occur the day after a match and can be easily diagnosed by small bumps on the shin that are painful to the pony when touched.

Once set, a splint does not disappear, because calluses develop at the site, but over time it can disappear. Splints that are closer to the knee can affect stability and put undue pressure on the suspensory ligament.

Bowed Tendon

Also called tendonitis or tendon sprain, a bowed tendon is a sudden tear of the superficial digital flexor or deep digital flexor, or both. These are the tendons that flex the fetlock joint, knee and hock. Bows are usually the result of stress and overwork, an accident such as a stumble or fall, or an external blow from a mallet or ball. Horses that are not in playing condition when asked to perform, or ponies played without proper and timely shoeing, are also susceptible to bowing.

The tear of a tendon can be likened to a fraying rope. The tear causes blood to leak into the tendon, painfully separating the fibers, causing inflammation; it is readily recognizable to the naked eye as a bulge along the tendon path.

A bowed tendon is one of the most feared injuries to a polo player because, although curable, horses that have bowed rarely return to their prior performance levels and remain susceptible to re injuring the same area because the repaired tendon is never as strong.

The good news is that, except for severe cases, rest–sometimes up to one year–will usually remedy the problem, since horses have the ability to repair the fibers. However, the injury must be properly treated to control the hemorrhaging and inflammation.

Superficial Injuries

Superficial cuts, scrapes, abrasions and tears can be serious because how much and, more importantly, how quickly the blood is lost can be disastrous to horses, especially if the blood loss happens during a polo match. Blood pressure is elevated during exercise, and excitement from the trauma will only raise it further.

These minor injuries can be easily overlooked, because there usually isn't much pain associated with them initially. Pain comes from inflammation, which takes a while to develop. The deeper, wider and dirtier the wound, as well as its proximity to weight-bearing entities in the leg, the faster the onset of pain.

So, no matter how minor these injuries might appear, they should be treated immediately. It only takes a few hours for bacteria to take hold and start an infection. Usually, irrigation with saline solution and an antiseptic dressing under a bandage will short-circuit any serious problems.

Heat Exhaustion

Although heat and humidity are impediments to good performance, more often than not polo is played in hot weather. All horses experience a rise in body temperature during exercise. Some elevation (one or two degrees) in body temperature is desireable, warming up. The harder the horse works, the greater the *rate* of elevation.

Horses with leaner body mass dissipate heat faster than larger, highly muscled ones. Watch for typical heat stress in your ponies. Lethargy, profuse sweating, higher respiratory and pulse rate (the best place to check pulse rate is under the cheek bone near the throatlatch), all can be signs of heat stress. At the end of a chukker, a pony's respiratory rate can be elevated to one hundred twenty to one hundred forty beats and the pulse rate to eighty to one hundred beats per minute. The normal respiratory rate is ten to twenty beats per minute, but may remain slightly (sixty to eighty) elevated to aid the horse in cooling. After only a few minutes, a well conditioned pony's pulse rate should drop to forty to fifty beats per minute.

If weather conditions are inordinately unfavorable and/or your ponies are more susceptible to heat problems, it is a good idea to carry a rectal thermometer when you go to matches. At rest, the horse's normal temperature is around one hundred degreees. It is expected that a horse's temperature will rise one or two degrees during exercise. On extremely hot and humid days, when evaporation is poor, the temperature can rise three or four degrees. Anything over one hundred and six degrees calls for immediate and aggressive cooling efforts.

Cooling (Tying-up)

During the heyday of polo up until only a few years ago the accepted method of cooling a hot horse was to walk him slowly in small circles, "hot walking.". Cold water was frowned upon and drinking was an absolute no-no. Fortunately, there have been studies on various cooling methods and the results have been eye-opening.

"Hot walking," has been shown to have neither a beneficial or negative effect on cooling and if done incorrectly, can add exercise and delay the cooling process. The best way to cool a hot horse is with water and plenty of it. The water should be at normal cold water tap temperatures (35-40ºF) and not too cold. The pony should be thoroughly doused from head to tail. If a hose is not available, use a bucket or sponge, but do not drape wet towels over the horse's body because it will impede evaporation. The water will heat up to the horse's body temperature almost immediately. As soon as the pony is fully doused, quickly scrape of the excess water and repeat the process. If possible, find a place to put your horse in the shade.

After a few minutes it is permissible to allow the horse to drink *small* amounts (no more than eight gulps) of water if he will. Traditionally, letting a hot horse drink was taboo for fear of colic and founder. Here again, the water should not be ice cold.

Waiting for the Vet to Come

Not calling in a veterinarian for even minor injuries is a mistake. Many horsemen don't want to "bother" the vet for minor injuries, but many seemingly minor injuries can become very serious very quickly. If you really want to help the vet, be prepared to give an accurate assessment of the problem.

In addition to visual signs of the problem and the cause of its onset, if known, the horse owner should be able to offer the horse's vital signs. Also, specific time sequences should be noted for bowel movements, water and feed consumption, etc., and should be noted on a log for the vet to see upon arrival.

The Horseman's Medical Chest

Every traveling polo player should carry a medical kit and be able to perform basic care giving and handle superficial injuries. A typical kit might contain the following:

Rectal equine thermometer	Scissors, tweezers and hemostat
Gauze and sterile patches	Rolled cotton and tape
Alcohol and astringent	Feurocine and gall salve
Saline solution and eye cup	Ice bags and boots
Twitch	

The following drugs are mentioned only for the poloist's enlightenment. Although they can be readily found in every barn's medicine chest, it is not suggested that they be administered by the layman.

Ace (acepromazine) is a tranquilizer that can ease constriction of blood vessels and is often used for horses that founder. Although it will calm a nervous animal, it should not be given prior to a vet assessing the injury, because it can mask diagnosis and can have disastrous side effects.

Azium (dexamethasone powder) is a drug used as an analgesic and to suppress histamines that develop as a result of injury, infection or, most commonly, allergic reactions.

Banamine (flunixin meglumine) is used to control inflammation primarily associated with colic and muscle injuries.

Bute (phenylbutazone) is an anti-inflammatory and analgesic (pain killer) and can be beneficial in treating colic. It is easy to use because, besides tablets, it is available in gel or paste form.

Maintenance Remedies

Bandaging

> *"Bandaging a horse's leg can be learned in*
> *minutes. And mastered over a lifetime."*
> Anonymous

Photograph by David Lominska

A Templeton groom wraps legs before a match. Note that he is wrapping the bandage clockwise, inside-out, and pulling it tight across the front of the cannon bone.

from the front or back, always pull taut toward the back so that pressure is never applied at the tendon, but rather across the cannon bone. Try to make each turn uniform so that the bandage isn't fatter in one area than another. Wrap clockwise (outside to inside) on the off-side and counter-clockwise on the near-side.

The most common bandaging error is wrapping too loose or too tight. Try to maintain constant tension by pulling taut on each pass. Do not make several turns and then pull the loose end tight. When finished, secure by a Velcro™ closure. Avoid string ties, as they can bind and cause injury.

Check the bandage when finished. The ideal job is wrinkle- and lump-free. The bandage should be tight enough to stay on, but loose enough to slip a finger between the top and bottom of the wrap around the entire leg. Continue to monitor the wrap. Any swelling above the wrap is an indication that the bandage is too tight.

The most common errors that beginners make are unrolling the wrap so the inside is against the leg, unrolling too much bandage at a time, beginning to high, unevenly overlapping the wrap, and using uneven tension. If you are uncertain of your abilities, a friend's forearm is a suitable practice dummy since it is about the same size as a horse's leg.

Poulticing

Applying a poultice to a horse's leg is an excellent and time-proven remedy for sore legs. Poultice is a gooey, clay-like material that often is medicated. Several products such as UpTite™ and Icetight® are sold for the purpose of reducing heat and swelling in the leg.

Make sure that there are no cuts, sores or raw abrasions on the leg before you start. Soak some pre-cut lengths, about ten or twelve inches long, of Kraft brown paper (if not available, shavings or grocery bags will suffice) in water. If the poultice is too dry, add a little water so that it is the consistency of peanut butter. The wetter your hands are, the less the poultice will tend to stick to them. Pre-wet the leg and apply the poultice liberally and evenly, starting with the back of the leg just below the knee. Make sure to cover the ligaments and tendons. It isn't necessary to cover the front (cannon bone) of the leg, because the poultice is ineffective in that area. Take care to insure that the poultice touches the skin by pushing and molding the clay through the hairs. Usually applying the poultice about one-quarter-inch thick is sufficient, but if you are dealing with an injury, a thicker application of about one-half inch will draw out more heat and inflammation. The poultice should not be so thick as to obscure the shape of the leg.

After the poultice has been applied, place a pre-soaked piece of brown paper over the dressing. The wet paper will help maintain the cool wet poultice longer. Be sure to cover the ankle as well. Now apply a quilted wrap, and then a stable bandage. Leave the poultice on for twelve to eighteen hours. Then unwrap and check for any hot spots. Unbandage and remove the poultice by hosing down the leg while gently rubbing the clay off with your hand.

Removing the poultice is a messy and tedious process requiring scraping with your hand and fingernails while continuing to run water down the leg. One old vet used to say that the removal process—running cold water over the leg for the twenty or so minutes it takes to remove the dressing—that is therapeutic rather than the poultice itself. The water is certainly soothing, but it's the poultice that will draw out the heat and soothe the aching tendon. The cold water won't hurt, however. Some players poultice their ponies regularly regardless of any injury, just to maintain the tendons and ligaments in the best condition.

Dewormers (Anthelmintics)

All horses are subject to parasite infestations, but not necessarily to the same degree. Four horses turned out on ten acres will have less chance of infestation than ten horses turned out on four acres of pasture. Likewise, horses turned out in the high altitude and generally colder climate of Wyoming will have fewer parasite problems than those residing in Florida. Although there are mitigating factors, all horses need to be placed on a regular de-worming program. It is best to consult a veterinarian in your local area to develop a program suitable for your personal needs.

Internal parasites, (large and small strongyles, ring worm, pinworms, bots, roundworms, tapeworms etc.) begin when the horse grazes in a pasture and ingests eggs or larvea from manure droppings. The larvae travel to the intestine where they mature and lay eggs that pass out of the horse's body through manure...creating a vicious cycle. The cycle can be significantly impeded by regular cleaning ("picking") the paddocks. The eggs and larvae are not always visible to the naked eye in the droppings.

But even with good paddock maintenance a de-worming program is necessary. Although there is a large choice of de-worming drugs, they don't all target the same parasites. Parasites are easiest to kill during the larvae stage and most of the current products are effective against most larvae. However, all products are not equally effective against adult small stronglyes. For this reason, veterinarians usually recommend that horse owners rotate their choice of class of de-worming drugs. Keep in mind that changing the brand of drug is not sufficient. For example: Eqvlan, Zimecterin, Rotation, are all the same class (Ivermectin) as are Strongid and Rotation (Pyrantel Pamoate).

To Pro or Not to Pro

"No player shall pay or receive payment for playing polo."
HPA (UK) rule enacted in 1933–abolished in 1934

With the advent of corporate sponsors spending as much as $100,000 on a single tournament and high-goal *patróns* willing to pay pros $20,000 to $30,000 per month to play in a single tournament, professionalism has become a popular, if controversial, reality. Although there have been polo players who have augmented their income as horse traders, club managers, equipment dealers, etc., the true professional, one who is paid just for playing, is a recent phenomenon. As in other sports that are competing for sponsorship and cash purse tournaments, world-class professionals or "hired assassins" have become rising commodities in the last decade. However, it is a job with very little security. Professional polo players never know if the next great dash downfield to goal will be their last.

Actually, players who received "appointments" and were often known as Masters of the Horse, to run their employer's farm and play on his polo team had been around for years. The distinction "hired assassins" came to fall upon those who were paid solely for playing the game.

Ever since the end of World War I, there have been players whose expenses have been paid or, at least, partially met, or whose horses were provided by a *patrón*. However, it wasn't until Harry Payne Whitney assembled the "Big Four" (brothers Lawrence and J. M. "Monty" Waterbury, Devereux Milburn, and himself) who went on to win the 1909,1911 and 1913 International Championships without losing one match along the way, that professionalism became *de rigueur*. At the time, Mr. Whitney was handicapped at 9 goals, thereby avoiding the common pitfall prevalent today, where high goal teams often have a low handicapped *patrón*.

Until the mid-1950s, when each team was introduced by position prior to the opening throw-in, amateurs were introduced as "John Doe," and those players whose income was directly attributed to their polo playing were introduced as "Mr. John Doe." In those days there were many high-rated amateur players, and the only way casual spectators could distinguish who was who was by the "Mr."

There is little question that the prevalence of professional high-goal pros has increased the level of polo throughout the world. Yet the same problems evident in other professional sports, for years absent in polo, have added a new dimension to the game and fueled a heated argument on whether or not to hire a pro.

On one side of the argument are those who feel that "hired assassins" place too much emphasis on winning and that much of the fun, camaraderie, sportsmanship and consideration of the horses is diminished. But there are just as many poloists who feel that raising the level of play is beneficial to all by giving players a chance to play with and against better-caliber players.

Professionalism is prevalent not only at the high-goal level. Even at the low- and medium-goal level, players find that there are many benefits in hiring a pro. Aside from making up half of a team and thereby being assured of playing more certainly and regularly, there is the consistency of playing with the same teammate and of readily available private instruction. There is a big difference between the high-goal and low-goal pro.

Patróns

There is no doubt that without *patróns* to sponsor high goal polo most of us would never get to see first class polo and all those professionals players might be deprived a living.

There have always been *patróns* in polo. During polo's nascent period the sponsor were the Royal Court (hence the Sport of Kings). In polo's Golden Era (1920s and 30s) the *patrons* were more likely to be wealthy scions of industry. However, there is one major difference between today's sponsors and those of yesteryear. Belmont, Bostwick, Corey, Gerry, Guest, Harriman, Igelhart, Phipps, Rumsey, Strawbridge, von Stade and Whitney were all rated at eight goals or higher! With a very few notable exceptions, today's sponsors tend to be rated at two goals or less.

Players enjoy the game the most when they feel that they have contributed to the teams success. For sure, being able to supply horses and financial backing is a major part of how well a team will perform. However, the most satisfaction comes from contributing on the field on a par with the other team members. Also, polo teams tend to be more successful when they are "balanced"—the team's aggregate handicap is evenly divided among all four players.

Almost all polo in North America is sponsored by low goal *patrons* if, for no other reason, there are less than a handful of higher rated players with the ability or inclination to do so. Most of these *patróns* sponsor teams at the low and medium goal levels. By doing so they are able to stabilize their rosters to insure that they will be able to participate in the tournaments they wish to play.

Open class polo in this Modern Era is limited to twenty-six goals. That translates into three high rated players and a low goal playing *patrón*. The predictable result is that the *patrón* does little on the field and rarely touches the ball. Their place on the winner's stand is sufficient gratification...but woefully unrewarding if the outcome is a loss.

High goal polo in Argentina is almost entirely corporate sponsored. That is the reason why truly Open class polo only exists in Argentina and begs the question: Does present American sponsorship protocol inhibit the growth of amateur talent?

High Goal

Unless the whole team is sponsored the sponsor, or *patrón*, is usually the weakest player on the team, rated at 2 goals or less. This means mounting any team over 32 goals is impossible and, even at the 24- to 30-goal level, very costly.

Since there are very few 7- to 10-goal professionals, there are often scheduling conflicts. This problem is exacerbated by the fact that most contractual arrangements are verbal, and even further by sponsors waiting until the last moment to finalize their arrangements in case of any handicap changes or injuries.

The "hired guns" come in two styles, mounted and unmounted. Herein lie more problems. The first is money. Given relative ability, the mounted pro is more expensive than his horseless counterpart. The second difficulty arises if the *patrón*'s string is not sufficient enough to allow the pro to play *his* best. In that case he probably won't take the job, because he wouldn't want to risk a poor outing causing his handicap to be lowered and thereby lessening the amount he could charge future *patróns*. Even if he does, the *patrón* won't get what he bargained for.

The professional has to consider his next engagement as well. If he is mounting himself, is he playing his best ponies or saving them for the next tournament? If he uses the top of his string, is he asking the horses for all they can give? Perhaps the only offset is the *patrón*'s option of replacing the pro with a better and possibly less expensive player.

Unless the pro is hired for a fairly long period, at least a season, he will probably do little more than show up and play. Since there is tremendous pressure on the professional to win in order to retain his handicap, he will be prone to accept jobs on teams that have a chance of winning and that play in large polo venues where his skills and horses will be noticed by other prospective employers.

Low Goal

Low-goal pros who in most cases aspire to the high-goal level have a somewhat different perspective. Since they are more numerous than their high-goal counterparts, they are not likely to be called on to play for various *patróns* in far-flung corners of the globe. They are more interested in full-time employment and the opportunity to play frequently as well as, in some cases, in making green ponies. In addition to supplying his direct remuneration, the *patrón* may be asked to support the pros string and to augment it from his stock. In return, the *patrón* may gain the services of a professional trainer and the first pick of any horse that he makes.

The annually employed lower goal pro will usually act as the *patrón*'s polo manager who is responsible for logistics and overseeing other employees. In addition to being in charge of general horsecare, he will coordinate veterinarians, farriers and feed supplies.

The "Foreign Player" Rule

As of January 1993, the USPA has implemented a rule that no foreign player rated at 5 goals or less can play in sponsored 20-goal or higher tournaments. A similar rule adopted by the Hurlingham Polo Association limits teams to no more than two foreign players.

In addition to creating more employment for the local pros, these rules inhibit the use of "ringers," relatively unknown foreign low- and medium-goal players who can play well above their rating. The jury is still out on the effectiveness of this rule.

Part Six:
Polo Quotes and Poetry

On a stone plaque by an ancient polo field in Gilget, North Pakistan:

> *"Let other people play at other things,*
> *The King of Games is still the Game of Kings."*
>
> J. K. Stephen (1859–1892)

"No sport, save possibly steeplechasing and football, is so good a school in this respect than polo. This element of personal risk is not a drawback but a decided advantage. No matter how brave a man may be he is none the less a creature of habit. If his most lethal experience prior to battle has consisted of dodging automobiles on city streets the insinuating whisper of bullets about his sacred person will have a more disquieting influence on him than would be the case had this same person received a few cuts and broken bones on the polo field."

Captain (General) George S. Patton, 1906

"We have been having a simply dee-lightful time....We have been having great fun here with polo.... I tell you a corpulent middle-aged literary man finds a stiff polo match rather good exercise."

President Theodore Roosevelt, 1888

"At the end of a few weeks' play, the beginning poloist can keep him and his pony out of danger; can make spasmodic stabs at the ball; and has perhaps learnt to get angry when shouted at. He gets, however, much strenuous exercise, his liver is shaken up, and he acquires an excellent thirst; all of which fortifies him in his opinion that there is no game like polo."

Lieutenant General Wilmont G. H. G. Vickers, 1923

"Pluck, endurance, submission to discipline, good temper, calmness, judgment, quickness of observation, self-control are all qualities as essential in a good polo player as in a good soldier; and last, but by no means least, there is no finer school in which to acquire the art of riding."

J. Moray Brown, 1891

Of all of our relations with the dumb creation, there is none in which man has so entirely the best of it as the one-sided partnership that exists between the horse and his rider.

Anon.

For daring turn and skillful stroke
The ever quickening stride,
The ring of the stirrup, the clash of the stick,
And the rush of the furious ride;
The cheer when the ball through the goal is driven
By steady hand and eye,
Have a wild delight in themselves alone
That can never grow old or die.

H. C. Bently, 1880

"Polo is a social game and some of its most serious
hazards are encountered at parties and entertainments
which are such an inevitable feature of all tournaments."

HRH The Duke of Edinburgh, 1984

Man is a ball tossed into the field of existence,
driven hither or tither by the polo-stick of destiny,
wielded by the hand of Providence.

Ancient Persian dictum

TO POLO
Our young men still may spur the heel,
And sport 'cap', 'coat' and 'leathers',
Compared with covering wrought of steel
Almost light as feathers:
Heads once were made to carry weight,
And not to carry knowledge;
But all that's past and out of date—
Heads now bring brains from College.

The lance exchanged for polo stick,
The sword for cutting whip,
We catch sounds of willow click
And sight of good horsemanship.
It's still a mimic of war of course,
With each one quick as a cony.

Not mounted on an armoured horse
But on a polo pony,
Not striking at a block of steel
But at a ball of wood,
And twisting with it like an eel
As brave as 'Robin Hood'.

And if there chance an accident—
A 'charger' slip or fall—
It's ten to one no detriment
To pony, man and all.
Long live the fighting polo game,
Buckmaster with it too—
The old Cantab whose famous name
Stands first in Sports Who's Who.

G. A. Fathergill (1868–1945)

The Ball no Question make of Ayes and Noes,
But Right or Left as strikes the Player goes;
And He that toss'd Thee down into the Field,
He know about it all—He knows—He knows.

Rubiat of Omar Khayyam
Translated by Edward Fitzgerald, 1859

"I have participated in nearly all sports that men have invented to harden their
bodies and temper their spirits. Now I ride no more; my strength and skill and even the
fortune which enabled me to live so regally are spent. But if I had to do it all over again,
I would follow exactly the same way. It was life of pure delight."

Foxhall Parke Keene (10h. USA) 1938

No game was ever worth a rap
For a Rational man to play,
Into which no accident, no mishap
Could possibly find its way.

Adam Lindsay Gordon
Galloping Rhymes (1870)

"Never confuse love and polo. The same passions might apply for a time,
but horses are forever. No surprise then, is it, that the only prince
to give up a kingdom for a woman played golf, not polo."

Adam Snow (9h. USA) 1985

"If there are no horses in Heaven I have no desire to enter."

Aristotle (384–322 B.C.)

A buyer needs a hundred eyes, the seller not one.

Old Proverb

A WINNING GOAL
By Will H. Ogilvie
What though 'twas luck as much as skill that gathered up the pass,
Before us lies an open goal and eighty yards of grass.
Now, all ye gods of Hurlingham, come hearken to my call,
Give pace unto the twinkling feet that fly before them all.

Their Back is thwarted on the turn; their Three's out-thrown and wide;
Their One and Two can scarce get through however hard they ride;
So stretch your neck, my swift Babette, and lay you down at speed,
There's not a flyer on the field can rob you of the lead!

The dancing ball runs straight and true, the ground is fast as fire;
To us the single stroke to crown our heart's desire.
With purple on their ponies' flanks they close on either side,
But you will keep in front, Babette, whose only spur is pride!

One drive to make the trophy ours! One glorious goal to get!
The slow ball hangs and curves away. Swing in! Swing in, Babette!
Now! How the tingle of the stroke through arm and shoulder spins!
A hefty hit...a deadly line...*a goal! The goal that wins!*

POLO PONIES
Beneath the rainbow silks they sail
Like birds that wheel and cross
Then, all their speed of no avail,
Come round to bit and martingale
With heads that reach and toss.
The ceaseless stick beside them swings,
The torn turf marks their track,
To heaving flanks the dark sweat clings
And from their fretted bridle rings
The foam comes feathering back.
But well they know there is no game
That men their masters play
Can fan like this their hearts to flame
And make them one with every aim
That fills the crowded day.
And if the sweat's on sobbing flanks,
And necks are lathered white,
Have they not won from Beauty's ranks
Caress and kiss and whispered thanks
For this their hard-fought fight?
Will H. Ogilvie (1869–1963)

"Superficial observers consider it mere play.
Men of more exalted views see in it a means of learning promptitude and decision.
It tests the value of a man and strengthens the bonds of friendship."

Fazi-i-Allami (Abu-l Fazl), c. 1590

"There's something about the outside of a horse that's good for the inside of man."

Sir Winston Churchill (1874 –1965)

When asked, *"What goes first when a polo player begins to fall*
apart–his legs as in boxing or his eyes as in baseball?"
Lois E. Stoddard, Chairman of the USPA® from 1922 to 1936, replied, "his money."

"Chukka by chukka the game is played,
So goal by goal point by point is made,
I hope I am never too old and staid
To play the game of Polo."

H. St. C. S., 1922

One white foot, buy a horse,
Two white feet, try a horse,
Three white feet, look well about him,
Four white feet, do with without him.

Old Rhyme

In the choice of a horse and a wife, a man must please himself, ignoring the opinion of others.

A perfect horseman knows neither fear nor anger.

George John Whyte-Melville (1742-1811)

Heavy hands make hard-mouthed horses.

John Adams, 2nd US President (1735-1826)

There is no secret so close as that between a rider and his horse.

Robert S. Surtees (1803-1864)

The horse must obey with the proud obedience of a soldier.

Lord Archibald P. Wavell (1883-1950)

Part Seven:
Bibliography

BOOKS

"A Lover of the Game", *Letters on Polo in India,* Thacker Spink Co., Calcutta, 1918.

Ames, Joseph B., *Chaps and Chuckkers*, A. L. Burt & Co., 1928.

Ainslie/Ledbetter, *The Body Language of Horses,* William Morrow & Co. New York, 1980.

Aldrich, Nelson W., *Tommy Hitchcock: An American Hero,* Fleet Street Corp., Gaithersburg, MD, 1984.

Archetti, Eduardo P., *Masculinities: Football, Polo and the Tango in Argentina,* BERG/Oxford Press, NY, 1999.

Ashton, Chris, *Geebung*, Hamilton Pub. Co., Sydney, Aus., 1993.

La Asociation Argentina de Polo, *Cien Anos de Historia, 1893-1993.*

Badger, Lt. Col. T. R., *A Record of My Horses*, Raithby, Lawrence & Co., Ltd., Leicester, UK, 1937.

Barton, Frank T., *Horses & Practical Horse Keeping*, Jarrold & Sons, London, 1912.

Bailey, Thomas A., *The American Pageant,* D. C. Heath & Co., Boston, MA, 1937.

Baumer, Wm. H., (Ed.), *Sport As Taught and Played at West Point*, The Military Publishing Service, Harrisburg, PA, 1939.

Beal, Carlton, *Into Polo*, Dummond Advertising, Midland, TX, 1993.

Bent, Newell, *American Polo*, The Macmillian Co., New York, 1929.

Beverage, Bert, *A Little Bit of Remembering*, Private Publication.

Board, John, *A Year with Horses*, Hodder and Stoughton, London, 1953.

A. S. Barnes, *Polo,* Countryman Press, VT, 1955.

Board of Governors, The, *Onwentsia,* Onwentsia Club, Lake Forrest, Ill., 1984.

Boniface, Col. J. J., *Riding*, A. S. Barnes, New York, 1940.

Brooke, Lt. Col. Geoffrey, *The Way Of A Man With A Horse*, J. B. Lippincott, Philadelphia, PA, 1929.
    Horse-Sense And Horsemanship Of Today, Charles Scribner's Sons, New York, 1924.
    The Way of a Man with a Horse, J. B. Lippincott, Philadelphia, 1929.
    British Sport and Sportsmen (Ed.), *Polo and Coaching,* Sport & Sportsmen, Ltd., London, 1930.

Brown, Paul, *Hits and Misses*, The Derrydale Press, 1935.
    The Horse: His Gaits, Points, and Confirmations, Charles Scribner's Sons, New York, 1943.
    Polo, Charles Scribner's Sons, New York, 1949.

Burri, René and J. L. Lanuza, *Gauchos*, Takarajima Books, New York, 1994.

Compos Carlés, M. J., *Campieonato, Argentino, Abierto de Polo*, La Assn. Argentina de Polo, 1993.

Carberry, Don, *Pedestrian's Guide Polo*, Carberry Assoc., PA, 1965.

Chambray, Pierre & Macaire, Lionel, *Polo*, C. Lavauzelle, Paris, 1979.

Churchill, Winston S., *My Early Life: A Roving Commission*, Odhams Press, Ltd., London, 1947.

Clayton, Hilary M., *Conditioning of Sport Horses*, Sport Horse Publications, Saskatoon, Saskatchewan, Canada, 1991.

Clayton, Michael, *Prince Charles: Horseman*, Stanley Paul & Co., London, 1987.

Courtney, Nicholas, *Sporting Royals*, Hutchinson/Stanley Paul & Co., London, 1983.

Cullum, Grove, Selection and Training of the Polo Pony, Charles Scribner's Sons, New York, 1934.

Crocket, Albert Steven, *When James Gordon Bennett Was Calif of Baghdad*, Funk & Wagnall Co., New York, 1926.

Dale, Rev. T. F. (Stoneclink), *The Games of Polo,* A. Constable & Co., Westminster, UK, 1897.
    Riding and Polo Ponies, Lawrence & Bullen, London, 1902.
    Polo, Past and Present, Charles Scribner's Sons, NY, 1905.
    Polo at Home and Abroad, The London & Counties Press, 1915.

Danckwerts, Brian, *A Century of Polo in Rhodesia/Zimbabwe,* Private Publication, 1995.

Daniels, John H., *Nothing Could Be Finer,* John Culler & Sons, Camden, SC, 1996.

Dawnay, Maj. Hugh, *Polo Vision*, J. A. Allen & Co., London, 1991.

Dawson, Capt. Lionel, *Sport in War*, Collins, London, 1936.

Dailey, Fred, *Polo Is a Four Letter Word,* Topgallant Pub., Honolulu, HA, 1986.

deLisle, Gen. Sir Beauvior, *Tournament Polo*, Eyre & Spottiswoode, London, 1938.
           Polo In India, Thacker & Co., Bombay, 1913.

Deim, Carl, *Aisiatsche Reiterspiel,* Olms Presse, Hildesheim, GR, 1982.

Devereaux, Jr., Walter B., *Position & Teamplay in Polo*, Brooks Bros., New York, 1924.

Disston, Harry, *Beginning Polo*, A. S. Barnes, Cranbury, New Jersey, 1973.
           Horse and Rider, A .S. Barnes & Co., New York, 1944.
           Know All about Horses, Wilshire Book Co., Hollywood, CA, 1977.

Dorling, Taprell ("Taffrail"), *The Hurlingham Club 1869–1953*, The Hurlingham Club, 1954.

Drybrough, T. B., *Polo*, Longmans, Green & Co., London, 1906.

Durand, Sir Edward, *Ponies' Progress*, Charles Scribner's Sons, New York, 1935.

Earl of Suffolk & Berkshire, The (Ed.), *The Encyclopedia of Sport,* Lawrence & Bullen, Covent Garden, UK, 1897.

Edward, Elwyn E., *The Kingdom of the Horse*, Crescent Books, New York, 1991.

Edwards, Elwyn Hartley, *The Encyclopedia of the Horse*, Dorling Kindersley, New York, 1994.

Ferguson, Maj. Ronald, *The Galloping Major*, Macmillan, London, 1994.

Fitch, C. G., *Queer Horses and Queer People*, H. Gurst & Blackett, Ltd., London, 1947.

Follmer, Shinitzky, *The Endless Chucker*, Polo Publishers, Gaithersburg, MD, 1978.

Forbes, Allan, *Sport in Norfolk County*, Houghton Mifflin Co., Boston, MA, 1938.

Forbes, William Cameron, *As to Polo*, G. H. Ellis, Boston, 1919.

Ford, Sewell, *Just Horses*, Mitchell Kennerley, New York, 1910 .

Fritz, C. & D. Rylance, *Ever Westward: To The Far West,* The University of North Dakota Press, Grand Forks, ND, 1982.

Fritz, John H, *Champion Horses and Riders of North America*, J. B. Lippincott Co., Philadelphia, PA, 1975.

Galvayne, Sydney & Fred, *The XXth Century Book of the Horse*, Belliére, Tindall & Cox, London, 1907.

Gilbey, Sir Walter, *Ponies Past & Present*, Vinton & Co, London, 1900.

Goldschmidt, Lt. Col S. G., *The Fellowship of the Horse,* Charles Scribner's Sons, NY, Country Life, London, 1930.

Grace, Peter, *Polo,* Macmillan Publishing Co., New York, 1991.

Halford, V. (Ed.), *The Polo World 1994, 1995,* Heinz Dorler/Polo World, Ltd., London, 1994.

Halpin, Warren T., *Hoofbeats,* J. B. Lippincott & Co., Philadelphia, PA, 1938.

Hamer, David, *Care of the Stabled Horse,* B. T. Batsford, Ltd., London, 1993.

Hatch, A., & F. Keene, *Full Tilt: The Sporting Memoirs of Foxhall Keene*, Derrydale Press, New York, 1938.

Hawcroft, Tim, B.V., *The Complete Book of Horsecare,* Weldon Publishing Co., Willoughby, Australia, 1983.

Heguy, A. P. & D. M. Paez, *Polo de Alto Handicap Argentino*, Fundatión de Polo Enrenamiento Integral, BA, ARG.

Higginson, A. Henry, *Try Back: A Huntsman's Reminiscences,* Huntington Press, New York, 1931.

Hill, John, *The Polo Pony Stud Book*, The Polo Pony Society, London, 1894.

Hobson, Richard, *Polo and Polo Ponies*, J. A. Allen, London, 1976.
   Riding: The Game of Polo., J. A. Allen, London, 1993.

Jackson, Noel, *Effective Horsemanship*, Michael Russell (Pub), Ltd., Salisbury, 1967.

Kays, D. J., *The Horse*, A. S. Barnes & Co, New York, 1953.

Kendall, Paul G., *Polo Ponies, Their Training & Schooling,* Derrydale Press, New York, 1933.

Kimberly, Earl of, *Polo*, Lonsdale Library, J. B. Lippincottt Co., Philadelphia, PA, 1936.

Knox, N. R., *To B. A. and Back...Again*, Private Publication, Buffalo, NY, 1966.

Knox, S. H., *To B. A. and Back,* Private Publication, 1932.
   Polo Tales & Other Tales, Vol. 2, Private Publication, Buffalo, New York, 1973.

Laffaye, Horacio A., *El Polo International Argentino*, Private Publication, Argentina, 1989.
   Diccionario de Polo, Private Publication, Weston, Conn.T, 1995.

Langdon, William G., *Polo: A Way of Life*, Langdon Enterprises, Inc., Colbert, WA, 1964.
   Team Play—Polo Manual, Langdon Enterprises, Colbert, WA, 1985.

Little, K. M. Fouler, *Polo in New Zealand,* Whitcombe & Tombs, Ltd., Wellington, NZ, 1956.

Loving, Nancy S., DVM, *Veterinary Manual for the Performance Horse*, Equine Research Inc., Grand Prarie, TX, 1993.

Lloyd, J. & M. Roberts, *The PIMMS Book of Polo*, Trafalgar Sq. Publishing Co., 1978.

Lyon, J., *A Polo Ball.*

Lyon, Maj. W. E., *In My Opinion*, Constable & Co., London, 1929.
　　　　The Pegasus Book, Constable & Co., London, 1931.

Mackay-Smith, Alexander, *Speed and the Thoroughbred*, The Derrydale Press, Lanham, MD, 2000.

McBane, Susan, *The Horse and the Bit,* Howell Book House, New York, 1988.

McMichael, E. H., *Polo on the China Pony*, The Mercantile Printing Co., Shangai, 1931.

Macnie, Capt. J., *Work & Play in the Argentine*, T. Werner Laurie, Ltd., London, 1925.

Marco, *An Introduction to Polo*, Charles Scribner's Sons, New York, 1931, RNPA Edition, 1960.

Marshall, R. Q., *The Polo Umpire's Primer*, Carleton Beal, Midland, TX, 1989.

Meisels, P., *Polo*, Collins Publishers, San Francisco, CA, 1992.

Melvill, Col. Philip Teignmout, *Ponies and Women*, Jarrolds, London, 1932.

Mihanovich, Iván, *Polo—En Sintesis*, Iván Mihanovich, Buenos Aires, Arg., 1993.

Milburn, Frank, *Polo, The Emporer Of Games,* Alfred A. Knopf, New York, 1994.

Miller, Capt. E. D., *Modern Polo*, Hurstand Blackett, London, 4th Edition, 1922.
　　　　Fifty Years of Sport, E. P. Dutton & Co., New York, 1927.

"Moki" as told to Fred Dailey, *Polo Is a Four Letter Word*, Topgallant Publishing Co., Honolulu, HI, 1986.

Ogilvie, Will H., *Galloping Shoes*, Constable & Co., London, 1922.

Paterson, A. B. (Banjo), *Off down the track*, Angus & Robertson Publishers, Australia, 1986.

Patten, William (Ed.), *The Book of Sport*, J. F. Taylor & Co., New York, 1901.

Pearce, Capt. James J., *Everybody's Polo*, Robert Hale, Ltd. London, 1949.

Peek, H. & F. Aflalo, (Ed.), *The Encyclopedia of Sport*, Lawrence & Bullen, Ltd., London, 1898.

P. O. V., *"PRACTICAL POLO"*, C. H. Smiley, Mission Press, Jubbulpore, See: C. P. Vickers.

Ramsay, Maj. Gen. F. W., *Polo Pony*, Gale & Polden, Aldershot, 1932.

Richardson, Charles, *Cassell's New Book of the Horse*, The Waverly Book Co., London, 1912.

Ricketts, Brig. Gen. R. L., *First Class Polo: Tactics & Match Play*, Gale & Polden, Ltd., UK, 1928.

Roberts, Monty, *The Man Who Listens to Horses*, Random House, New York, 1966.

Roy, Frederic, *Polo,* Stadium Polo, West Palm Beach, Florida, 1992).
        Your Polo Game, Stadium Polo Inc, West Palm Beach, Florida, 1993.

Russel-Stoneham & Chatterdon-Newman, *Polo at Cowdray*, Information Bureau, London, 1992.

Saunders, Ray, *Ownership Stabling and Feeding*, Sterling Publishing Co., NY, 1982.

Sawaya, Jorge, *Primera Guia Argentina de Polo*, La Associacion de Polo, BA, 1993.

Self, Margaret Cabell, *The Horseman's Encyclopedia*, A. S. Barnes, New York, 1963.

Smith, Harry Worcester, *Life and Sport in Aiken,* The Derrydale Press, New York, 1935.

Smith, Sharon B., *The Performance Mare,* Maxwell Macmillin International, New York, 1993.

Spencer, Herbert, *Chakkar: Polo Around The World*, H. Spencer, England, 1971.
        A Century of Polo, World Polo Association, Cirencester, England, 1994.

Steinkraus, William, & M. A. Stoneridge, *The Horse in Sport*, Stewart Tabori & Chang, New York, 1987.

St. Quintin, Col., Thomas A., *Chances of Sports of Sorts in Five Continents*, William Blackwood & Sons, London, 1912.

Story, Loftus H., *The Training of Man and Mount for Polo*, The County Polo Association, UK, 1948.

Summerhays, R. S., *From Saddle and Fireside*, Country Life, London, 1936.
        Horse and Ponies, Frederick Warne Ltd., London, 1978.

Taylor, Louis, *Bits: Their History, Use and Misuse*, Harper & Row, Inc., New York, 1966.

The Editing Committee, *The National Pony Stud Book*, Vol. XX, The National Pony Society, UK, 1930.

The Pakistan Polo Association, *PAKISTAN POLO ASSOCION HANDBOOK 1954*, Messers Ferozsons, Peshawar, 1954.

The Rasp, 1914, Ed. Lt. Geo. S. Patton, Lt. J. G. Quekemeyer, U. S. Army, Ft. Riley, KS.

Thorne, Diana, *Polo*, The Moray Press, Edinburg & London, 1936.

Vernon, Arthus, *The History and Romance of the Horse*, Waverly House, Boston, MA, 1939.

Vickers, Lt. Gen. G. H., Practical Polo, (J. A. Allen, London, 1950's).

Vischer, Peter, *Horse and Horsemen*, D. VanNostrand & Co., Princeton, NJ, 1967.

Vosburgh, W. S., *Thoroughbred Types 1900–1925*, Private Publication, New York, 1926.

Watson, J.N.P., *The World of Polo Past and Present*, Salem House Publishers, MA, 1986.
A Concise Guide to Polo, Trafalgar Square Publishing Co., North Pomfret, VT, 1989.
Hanut: Prince of Polo Players, The Sportsman's Press, London, 1995.

Webber, Toni, *Mouths and Bits*, Threshold Books, London, 1990.

Weir, Brown, Dale, *Riding—Polo,* Badminton Library, Longmans Green & Co., London, 1891.
Riding—Polo, Badminton Library, Longmans Green & Co., London, 1895.

White, Capt. Wesley J., *Guide for Polo Umpires*, USPA, New York, 1963.

Whitney, C. V., *High Peaks*, The University Press of Kentucky Press, Lexington, KY, 1977.

Wrench, Frank A., (Ed.), *Horses in Sport*, William Morrow & Co., New York, 1937.

Young, Major H. P., *Hints on Sport*, A. J. Combridge & Co., Bombay, 1907.

Younghusband, George J., *Tournament Polo,* Pioneer Press, Alahabad, 1897.

PERIODICALS, MAGAZINES

Horse & Horseman, 1936-39, ed. Peter Vischer, Editor, Polo Magazine, Inc., New York, 1936–1939.

Horse Review, Ivanahoe Publishing, Ltd., Oxford, UK.

Polo, 1927-35, Edited by ed. Peter Vischer, Polo Magazine, Inc., New York, 1927–1935.

Polo, Vols. 1–4, 1969 to date, Polo Publications, Gaithersburg, Maryland.

Polo Quarterly International, Vols. 1–5, ed. Heinz Dorler, London, UK, Vols.1, 2, 3, 4, & 5.

Polo Times, 1998-2003, Oxfordshire, UK.

Polowest, ed. A. G. Webbe, Denver, CO, 1995.

Sidelines, Vols. 1–13, ed. Samantha Charles, West Palm Beach, FL, Vols. 1 thru 13.

The Horseman's Year, *ed.* Editor: Lt.-Col. W. E. Lyon, Lt. -Col., Collins, London, (1947), Jack Gannon, Jack, Collins, London, (1952), Lt.-Col. W. E. Lyon, W. E. Lt.-Col., Collins, London, (1954), Jack Gannon, Jack, Collins, London, (1957), Dorian Williams, Dorian, Collins, London, (1960), Harold Sebag-Montefiore, Harold, Collins, London, (1961), Jack Gannon, Jack, Collins, London, (1963), Dorian Williams, Dorian, Collins, London, (1969) (London: Collins).

The Polo Annual 1985, Nau-Mokal Publications, Cirencester, England, 1985.

The Polo Monthly, The Polo Monthly, Cirencester, Eng. UK, 1939.

USPA Newsletter, USPA, Lexington, Kentucky.

PAMPHLETS

D'Oench, Derry (Ed.), *"Polo Sweepstakes"*, Pittsfield Riding & Polo Assn. Inc., 1951.

Hale, S. S. , *"Polo by Hale"*, Pvt. Pub., 1992.
 "The Polo Handbook", Fleet Street Corp, Gaithersburg, MD, Corp., 1977.

King, Bucky, *"Big Horn Polo"*, Still Sailing Publications, Sheridan, WY, 1987.

Linfoot, Dr. William, *"Linfoot on Polo"*, Polo Publishers, Inc., Gaithersberg, MD, 1978.

Smith, M. M., *"Trailers: How to Tow & Maintain"*, Trailer Visions, South El Monte, CA, 1982.

Storey, Loftus H., *"The Training of Mount and Man for Polo"*, The County Polo Association, London, 1948.

Tuke, Diana R., *"Getting Your Horse Fit"*, J. A. Allen, London, 1977.

Zollinger, Bernard, "Polo Riding & Practising", Swiss Pioneers Polo Club, Switzerland.

ARTICLES

Foote, Robert Ordway, "Polo on the Pacific Coast", "The Men Who Organized The Sport and the Opportunities It Offers For Winter Play", Robert Ordway Foote, Outing, 1914.

Goodwin, Alfred Henry, "The Game of Polo," *Country Life In America*, July 1905.
 "The First Match for the Westchester Cup: The American Narrow Win," *The Ilustrated London News*, June 20, 1936.

Spalding's Athletic Library, *"POLO GUIDE...OFFICIAL RULES–1921"*, American Sports Publishing Co., New York, 1921.

Talbot-Ponsonby, Lt. Col. J. A., *"The Horseman's Bedside Book"*, B. T. Batsford, Ltd., London, 1964.

VIDEO

Blue Book Video Guide, U. S. P. A. Lexington, KY, 1993.

Polo, Transatlantic Films, Revel Guest Prod., Equestrian Video Library, Omaha, Nebraska, 1986.

Polo Power, Advanced Training, Sue Sally Hale, Graphic Productions, 1991.

The Masters of Polo, Grand Slam Productions, International Sports, Inc., West Sussex, ENG, 1993.

David Lominska–Photography

David was born in Sayerville, NY and began riding in his teens. While studying Animal Science at Cal-Poly in San Luis Obispo, CA, specializing in horse shoeing, David was introduced to polo and played on the College's first intercollegiate polo team. A summer job grooming polo ponies in Santa Barbara, CA was all it took for him to be hooked.

Instead of returning to college, he continued to groom and travel around the country for several prominent polo players eventually ending up in the USA's *Mecca* of polo, Wellington, FL where he lives and maintains his darkroom.

In the mid-'70s David began to merge his interest in photography with polo. His past polo playing experience and behind the scenes insights give him a unique ability to capture the beauty, grace, athleticism and yes, sometimes the agony of the "Sport of Kings." Soon his outstanding photographs made him sought after by players and publishers. It wasn't long after that that photography overtook his grooming and became his full time occupation. His photographs have graced the pages of *SPUR, Sidelines, The Chukker Collection* and numerous other polo publications

In the off season, David takes his kayak and beloved Pembroke Corgis through Colorado, Wyoming, Idaho and California where the water is fast and there is an opportunity to photograph wildlife and landscapes.

Alejandro Gambarini Lóizaga-Biomechanical Drawings

Mr. Lóizaga is a noted Argentine "Artista Plástico" whose anatomically correct work has illustrated many equestrian works, as well as professional medical publications. He first became associated with polo when he combined with Daniel Martínez Páez in the rehabilitation of Eduardo "Russo" Heguy when he broke his pelvis in England in 1998. After his miraculous recovery they collaborated with Alberto Pedro Heguy, famed winner of seventeen Argentine Open titles, to write the book, *Polo de alto handicap argentino*, in which Sr. Lóizaga's drawings first appeared.

The author wishes to thank Sr. Páez and Mr. Markus R. Tödtli of Bank Hofmann, AG, Zurich, Switzerland, sponsor of *Polo de alto handicap argentino* and Fundacíon de Polo y Entrenamiento Integral, its publisher, for their kind permission to use Sr. Lóizaga's drawings.

Author Biography

Bob Lubash was born in New York City but considers himself lucky to have spent most of his time in the surrounding "country," where his exposure to horses began at age five. He currently lives on a small horse farm in Southern Fairfield County, CT.

After a traditionally late start, a promising polo experience was sidelined by a motorcycle accident that severely mangled his left leg. Crazy as it might sound, eight years later he successfully decided to return to polo. It wasn't an easy row to hoe. The long trip back required re-learning to ride and to swing a mallet by compensating for his lack of physical conformity. As an avid collector of polo literature and memorabilia, he realized that there was no one repository of information where a polo enthusiast could look for help...hence this work.

He hopes that all his readers have as much fun playing the King of Sports as he has for the past forty years.

Photograph by David Lominska

The author (in red) on favorite mount, "LT," a fourteen year old
registered thoroughbred bay gelding.

USPA OUTDOOR RULES TEST 2003

1. Blue hits a long knock-in from the back line. The ball breaks and the larger piece lands well outside the 60 yard line. What is the call?
    a.___ Replay the knock-in.
    b.___ Play the larger piece until play stops.
    c.___ Throw-in from the point where the large piece lands.

2. White #1 is on the ROW. Red #4 crosses close in front to position himself for a near-side shot. White checks but retains possession of the ball. Red, realizing he may have caused White to check, does not make a play but permits White to make the next play. Red then rides White off and backs the ball.
    a.___ Foul Red.
    b.___ No Foul.

3. Blue rides with the LOB at a slight angle to his left. Red also rides with the LOB on his left but at a severe angle. Both will reach the ball at the same time. What is the call?
    a.___ ROW Blue only on his off-side.
    b.___ ROW Red only on his near-side.
    c.___ Both of the above.

4. Umpire A, in position following the play, sees Blue #4 drift back and forth in front of the ball carrier, Red #1. Umpire A blows the whistle, looks to Umpire B, points toward the goal Red is attacking and holds up 4 fingers. Umpire B, knowing that A had a good view of the play and seeing a zigzag foul himself, acknowledges with a hand signal. A then announces the foul and Penalty. Is this a correct procedure?
    a.___ Yes.
    b.___ No.

5. Blue prepares to back the ball from the goal mouth. As Blue starts his swing, Red rides over the ball and Blue is forced to check his swing. Blue had no offensive play to a teammate. Umpire A awards a Penalty No. 5 from the center. Umpire B suggests a spot hit as Blue only had a back shot and no offensive play. Which is the better call, spot or center?
    a.___ Spot.
    b.___ Center.

6.	White # 3 hits a neck shot at speed and now has the new LOB at a wide angle on his nearside. Blue # 2 following behind White # 3, turns up the line with a slight angle to the LOB on his offside. At speed, White # 3 rides to engage Blue # 2 before he reaches the ball, executing a ride-off, with both players meeting shoulder to shoulder. Upon impact, White # 3's horse falls breaking White # 3's collarbone. What should the Umpires call?

	a._____	Foul on Blue, since the White player got hurt.

	b._____	Foul on White # 3 because he came at the greater angle and being the aggressor caused the danger.

	c._____	Bowl in, no foul. Because the two players met shoulder to shoulder. Just the breaks of the game.

7.	Blue #3 hits a long ball. Red #4, well ahead, rides to the LOB, becomes parallel to it and backs the ball before Blue arrives to carry it on.

	a.____	Foul Red - Blue as last hitter has ROW.

	b.____	No Foul - if Red's play was without danger.

8.	Red #2 fouls as Blue #4 attempts to back the ball from goal. A Penalty No. 5 from the spot is awarded to Blue. Red #2 protests the call and the red flag comes out indicating a "technical" against Red. What is the correct procedure?

	a.____	Throw Red out of the game.

	b.____	Advance the ball placement to mid-field.

	c.____	Advance the Penalty No. 5 to Penalty No. 4.

9.	Blue #2 carries the ball and Red #3 rides with him attempting a near-side hook. Blue #1 meets the play with the LOB on his right. What is the call?

	a.____	Foul Red - meeting on the near-side.

	b.____	Foul Blue #1 - one meeting two.

10.	Blue knocks-in a short distance and canters to the ball to hit again. Red has positioned himself 60 yards out to meet the knock-in with LOB on his offside. As Blue hits the second time he is met by Red who steals the ball.

	a.____	Foul Red.

	b.____	Foul Blue.

	c.____	No Foul.

11.	Halfway through the third chukker the Blue Captain says he thinks the score is wrong. What is the proper procedure?

	a.____	Tell him you will work it out at half-time and keep the game going.

	b.____	Stop the game when the ball is out of play and work it out with the scorekeeper.

	c.____	Tell the Captain it is too late. He should have paid closer attention.

12.	Red rides from the left of the LOB to take the ball on his offside. Blue rides from the right of the LOB. The two players are at approximately equal angles to the LOB. Both plan to take the ball on the off-side and their extended paths will intersect at the ball. What is the call?

	a.____	Foul Blue.

	b.____	Foul Red.

	c.____	No Foul - 1st come, 1st served.

13. Blue #1 drops her mallet and rides to the sidelines to obtain a replacement. When play next stops, she asks permission to remove the mallet on the field. Should permission be granted?
   a.____ No - no time out for a dropped mallet.
   b.____ Yes - time out is not requested to retrieve the mallet, but to remove a potential hazard from the field.

14. As Blue #1 carries the ball down field followed closely by Blue #3, Red #4 rides from the right, attempts a hook, and passes behind Blue #1 and ahead of Blue #3.
   a.____ Foul Red - hooking at too great an angle.
   b.____ Foul Red - ROW infringement against Blue #3.
   c.____ No Foul.

15. Blue #3 hits an off-side back-shot away. Blue #2, following, turns, crosses the new LOB and prepares to carry the ball on. Red #3, also following, rides to the new LOB to meet the ball. Foul Blue #2 if he crosses the LOB at an unsafe distance ahead of Red #3. Foul Red if Blue's cross is safe and Red fails to keep the LOB on his right as he meets Blue. True or False?
   a.____ True.
   b.____ False.

16. In the closing seconds of a tied game, Red #3 carries the ball down the right-hand boards. Blue #4, defending, rides dangerously in front of Red just as Red #3 hits a beautiful shot to goal. Red #2, alongside the play, sees his teammate fouled, swings his mallet in a circular fashion and screams to attract the Umpire's attention. The Umpires agree that the crossing foul would usually be penalized with a 60-yard hit. They also feel the offensive "helicopter" should be penalized and reduce the severity to a Penalty No. 5 from the point of the infraction. Is this a proper call?
   a.____ No. The 60 gives Red chance to win and avoid overtime.
   b.____ Yes. Both fouled and the Umpire's decision is justified.
   c.____ No. The Umpires have to call one foul or the other.

17. Umpire A sees an infraction, calls the foul, and signals direction and Penalty to Umpire B. B was out of position and didn't see the play at all. Should the Umpires consult the Referee?
   a.____ Yes, unless they both saw the foul.
   b.____ No, there is no disagreement, just a single opinion.

18. Following the announcement of a foul and Penalty, Blue #3, the Captain, starts explaining to the Umpire how he saw the play. The Umpire reminds Blue #3 that the call has been made and the conversation is over. Blue continues. How does the Umpire handle the situation?
   a.____ Tell Blue that if he does not stop he will be penalized.
   b.____ Sound the whistle, award a "technical" and move the ball up.
   c.____ Call "Play" and try to move things along.

19. Red is awarded a Penalty No. 4 during a low-goal game on a rough field. As Red #3 is not a strong hitter, he asks Red #4 to follow him on the approach. Red #3 rides to the ball at an angle to dribble the ball to the right of goal. As Red #3 swings at the ball, his horse ducks out causing a clean miss and Red #3 rides past the ball. Red #4 follows to pick up the play. Blue #3 comes straight out from goal to play the now live ball. Red #4 and Blue #3 are going to collide at the still stationary ball. Who had the line and ROW?
   a.____ Blue. The line is from the goal mouth to the ball.
   b.____ Red. The line is the direction in which Red #3 was riding.
   c.____ Neither. The ball did not move so both Red and Blue must be very careful.

20. Blue holds up so Red #2 can clear a new line. Red clears slowly to give his teammate time to ride up and hook.

 a.___ Foul Red - making a play while clearing the ROW.

 b.___ No Foul.

21. Red # 2 concentrating on the ball, cocks his arm and begins his downward swing for a neck shot towards his goal as Blue # 3 rides at an angle with speed to ride-off Red on his nearside. As Red # 2 completes his swing, the mallet hits Blue # 3 in the face.

 a.____ Foul on Red because he is responsible for his mallet at all times.

 b.____ Foul on Blue for riding into the stroke. Blue entered the play late, and was not properly positioned (parallel to the Red player) before Red # 2 started his swing.

 c.____ Bowl in. Neither player was at fault. Just the breaks of the game.

22. Blue #2 hits the ball down field and follows with the LOB on his right. Red #3, well to the right of the projected LOB, rides to hook Blue. As Red hooks, his mount's head extends into Blue's lap. What is your call?

 a.___ Foul Red - dangerous riding.

 b.___ No Foul - once hooked, Blue loses all ROW.

23. Red #4 gallops with the LOB on the near-side. Blue #1 comes from behind to take the ball on the off-side. Blue #3 rides to meet the play and forces a foul on Red #4. What is your call?

 a.___ Foul Blue #3, once Red #4 and Blue #1 are engaged.

 b.___ Foul Red #4 if he can pull out but does not.

 c.___ Either of the above - a matter of timing.

24. Red #1 is on the ROW and carrying the ball at speed. Blue #4, defending, comes from Red's right at an angle to the line of the ball. As Blue flattens out to the line, his horses rear quarter drifts in front of Red's horse, forcing Red to check. Blue pulls back to the near-side, and concedes Red the next hit.

 a.___ Foul Blue - ROW violation.

 b.___ No Foul - Red kept possession, Blue conceded the next hit.

25. Blue taps a Penalty No. 4 forward and to the right and continues to dribble toward the goal mouth. As Blue nears the goal line, a Red defender is caught standing in Blue's path. What is the call?

 a.___ Foul Red - if Red had time, but did not attempt to clear the ROW.

 b.___ Foul Blue - if Red was not given a chance to clear the ROW.

 c.___ Both of the above.

26. A penalty # 3 is awarded to the Red team. Umpire A places the ball on the 40-yard line and rides to pick up a ball on the field. Red # 3 circles, hits the ball wide of the goalmouth before play is called by the umpires, and the ball hits a Blue player in the back who is positioned behind the end line. The Umpires should?

 a.____ Bowl the ball in at the 40-yard line.

 b.____ Allow a re-hit by the Red team.

 c.____ Award a free hit to the Blue team at the 40-yard line.

 d.____ Due to the danger, the Umpires have the discretion to award a more severe penalty; a center hit, a Penalty # 4, #3, or #2 to the Blue team.

27. Red hits a Penalty No. 4 and the ball breaks. What is your call?

 a.___ Goal - if the larger piece scores.

 b.___ Knock-in - if the larger piece misses.

 c.___ Re-hit regardless of where the pieces go.

28. Blue is dribbling the ball. As Blue taps and prepares to tap again, Red executes a ride-off on Blue's mallet side.
    a.___ Foul.
    b.___ No Foul.

29. Blue holds up to permit Red to clear a new line. Red clears properly, but Red's teammate uses the opportunity to ride up and hook Blue. Is this a legal play?
    a.___ Yes.
    b.___ No.

30. Both teams arrive at the center line and jostle for position as the Umpire prepares to bowl-in. What should the Umpire do?
    a.___ Bowl-in at once and get play started.
    b.___ Wait for players to position themselves.
    c.___ Blow the whistle and direct players to line up.

31. Blue is awarded a Penalty No. 3. How should the Officials position themselves:
    a.___ One Umpire behind the hitter, the other behind the left goal post, and the Goal Judge behind the right goal post.
    b.___ One Umpire behind each post, Goal Judge out of the way.
    c.___ One Umpire behind the hitter, the other on the line and the Goal Judge behind a post.

32. The teams line up, each on its own side of center, and move toward the Umpire as he prepares to bowl-in. The play should be stopped if they come within 5 yards before the ball is released.
    a.___ True.
    b.___ False.

33. Blue and Red, both with the LOB on their right, ride to meet or follow the ball. The player at the lesser angle to the LOB has the ROW and an opponent cannot play the ball unless he can do so at a safe distance ahead of the player.
    a.___ True.
    b.___ False.

34. After changing horses at the end of the field, Red #1 returns to the field on the wrong side of the lineup when the Umpire puts the ball in play. Red #2 hits a solid neck shot from the lineup to Red #1, who is 60 yards from the bowl-in. Red #1 hits the ball to goal and scores. What is the correct procedure?
    a.___ Award the goal to Red and bowl the ball in at mid field.
    b.___ Rebowl-in from the spot where the previous bowl-in took place.

35. Following a game, the Blue team gathers to review the video. They notice that a goal was incorrectly scored for their opponent in the 3rd chukker. The score, if kept correctly, would have given Blue a win rather than a loss. What now?
    a.___ Too late. The game is over and nothing can be done.
    b.___ Protest. The Tournament Committee may change the score.

36. Red #2 has ridden on the near-side of Blue #3 for several strides. Blue moves Red to the left and takes a hard off-side neck-shot to goal. Blue's follow through strikes Red's mount in the forelegs. What is the call?
    a.___ Foul Blue - striking into the legs of Red.
    b.___ No Foul - Blue was playing the ball.
    c.___ Foul Red - Once ridden off, Red should have pulled away.

37. Half way through the second chukker, Red #4 tells the Umpire that he is ill and unable to continue. How should this situation be handled?
    a.___   The Red Captain has 15 minutes to replace Red #4 or to remove a player from the opposing team.
    b.___   Red #4 may be replaced, or the team can play short-handed, but no extra time is provided.
    c.___   Red has 15 minutes to find a substitute or continue short-handed.

38. Blue #2 hits a strong off-side neck-shot. As he strikes, he crosses the new LOB extended back from the ball and turns to his left to follow up his hit. Red #3, following Blue #2, turns inside Blue and also rides toward the ball. Who has the ROW?
    a.___   Blue - the last hitter retains the ROW.
    b.___   Red - only if he plays the ball on his right side.
    c.___   Red - on either side as long as he is at the lesser angle.

39. Blue and Red are riding parallel on opposite sides of the ball. As they near the ball, Blue crosses the LOB, makes contact with Red, and takes the ball on his near-side. Foul on Blue for crossing the LOB?
    a.___   Yes.
    b.___   No.

40. Blue is approaching mid-field carrying the ball at speed. Red, riding behind Blue, realizes that he cannot catch up for a ride-off. As Blue prepares to hit a long ball, Red reaches cross Blue's horse and tips his mallet. What is your call?
    a.___   Foul Red. Penalty No. 5 from the spot of the infraction.
    b.___   Foul Red. Penalty No. 5 from the center of the field.
    c.___   Foul Red. Penalty No. 4.
    d.___   Foul Red. Penalty No. 3.

41. Blue #4 is hitting a Penalty No. 4. As he approaches the ball he sees Blue #2 changing mounts. Blue rides past the ball to approach again.
    a.___   Throw-in - Blue must hit on first pass.
    b.___   No problem - Blue can take all the time he wants.

42. Blue #4 prepares to hit an open near-side back-shot. Red #1 is riding parallel to Blue with the line on his off-side trying to poke the ball forward. Blue's mallet strikes Red's mount. What is your call?
    a.___   Foul Blue - hitting into Red's mount.
    b.___   No Foul - the striking of Red's mount was inadvertent.
    c.___   Foul Red - Red should have made way for Blue's stroke.

43. Blue #4 knocks-in and rides to follow up. Red #2 circles to Blue's left and slightly ahead. As Red will interfere with his ROW to the ball, Blue checks to avoid the collision. Red pulls out of the play and gives Blue safe passage to the ball. Foul or no foul?
    a.___   Foul.
    b.___   No Foul.

44. Red is awarded a Penalty No. 2 from a spot three yards from the goal mouth. The Blue players, assuming a score, ride to center field for the bowl-in. As Red approaches the ball, his horse ducks out and the ball is shanked to the right of goal. Foul Blue - the players were on the field and Red gets a re-hit.
    a.___   True.
    b.___   False.

45. Blue #4 and Red #1 gallop toward the ball. As Blue #4, with the ROW, begins his wind-up, Red #1 bumps him on the mallet side. Foul or no foul for riding into the stroke?
   a.___ Foul.
   b.___ No Foul.

46. Blue hits the ball down field. As Red closes to ride him off, Blue cocks his mallet and begins a downswing although well away from the ball.
   a.___ Foul Blue - hitting into Red's mount.
   b.___ Foul Red - riding into Blue's stroke.

47. Blue flips the ball to the side under Red's mount. Red, trapped on the new ROW spurs his mount to clear the way. As he rides clear, his mount kicks the ball spoiling the follow-up play for Blue. Foul or no foul?
   a.___ Foul Blue - intentionally putting the ball under Red.
   b.___ Foul Red - standing in Blue's ROW.
   c.___ Foul Red - only if his mount kicks the ball.
   d.___ No Foul.

48. The White team is awarded a Penalty # 2. White # 1 rides past the end line and 35 yards from the goal posts to change horses. While White #1 is changing horses, White # 3 miss hits the Penalty # 2 and the ball goes wide of the goal mouth. The Umpires should?
   a.___ Award a free hit to the Green team because White # 1 was improperly positioned.
   b.___ Award the White team a Penalty # 2 re-hit.
   c.___ Resume play with a knock-in by the Green team from the end line because White # 1 has the right to change mounts as long as he is safely positioned 30 yards from the goal posts and off the playing field.

49. Red starts with the LOB well to his right. Blue starts with the LOB on a slight angle to his left. Red rides directly to the   LOB then turns making his course parallel to the LOB. Blue continues his course and the two intersect at the ball. What is your call?
   a.___ Foul Blue - crossing ROW of Red.
   b.___ Foul Red - Blue started with a lesser angle.

50. A No. 2 Penalty is announced against Red. The Red Captain argues loudly that the call is incorrect. A violation of 35.g.2. is called. As the ball cannot be moved forward from a Penalty No. 2, the foul should be announced as a Penalty No. 5 (center hit) or a Penalty No. 4 (Umpire's discretion) following the conversion of the Penalty No. 2. True or False?
   a.___ True.
   b.___ False.

51. Blue carries the ball on the off-side. Red rides from the right to bump. Blue checks slightly, Red miss-times the play, and passes close in front of Blue. Foul or no foul?
   a.___ Foul Red - crossing.
   b.___ Foul Blue - Blue's check created the danger.

52. Blue #3 protests the Umpires' call loudly, abusively, and with a foul and offensive personal reference to the Umpire. An immediate ejection is justified. No preliminary warning or penalty is required.
   a.___ True.
   b.___ False.

53. Team Blue enters a 12 goal USPA event with a 12-goal team. After their first game, Blue #4's handicap is raised from 4T to 5. What are the consequences?
    a.___ The team must replace a player and remain at 12 goals.
    b.___ Continue in the event, but play off a 13-goal handicap.
    c.___ The player's handicap remains 4T for the remainder of the tournament.

54. Red #4 rides to turn a ball and taps the ball to his right creating a new line and ROW. As Red turns to follow the new line, Blue #1 riding fast down the old line takes the ball on the near-side passing at a right angle immediately in front of Red. Red reacts to the play by pulling his horse to a halt. What is your call?
    a.___ Foul Red - appealing for a foul.
    b.___ Foul Blue - crossing.
    c.___ No foul. The two acts offset one another.

55. Blue #2 is following the ball. Red #3 is riding hard to catch up and try for a near-side hook. Blue #1 is meeting the ball on his off-side planning a short back-shot pass to Blue #2. What is your call?
    a.___ Foul Blue #1 - one meeting two.
    b.___ Foul Red #3 - meeting Blue #1 on the near-side.
    c.___ Foul on either one - it is a matter of timing.

56. Penalty No. 3 is awarded to Blue. Blue #3 hits badly; the ball strikes a goal post, bounces back on the field and stops three feet from the post. What is the procedure?
    a.___ Ball is in play and LOB is from the post.
    b.___ Blue cannot hit or hit at the ball until Red has played the ball.
    c.___ Dead ball. Free hit to Red 12 feet from post.

57. Blue #3 changes horses following a goal. As a result, he is slow returning to the subsequent throw-in and his Captain asks that the throw-in be held up. Should this request be granted?
    a.___ No.
    b.___ Yes.

58. Red, hitting a Penalty No. 4, sees the ball move slightly as he approaches. Knowing the ball is now in a depression, he taps it out 5 yards, then hits toward goal. Should Red be penalized for endangering the opponents defending the goal?
    a.___ Yes.
    b.___ No.

59. Red carries the ball to goal with Blue riding him all the way. As Red crosses the 30 yard line and prepares to tap the ball through the goal, Blue reaches behind his back and cross-hooks. What Penalty is awarded?
    a.___ Penalty No. 2.
    b.___ Penalty No. 1.

60. Red #1 misses a goal and circles slowly as his teammate changes mounts. While Red #1 is circling, and his teammate is off the field, the ball is placed and Blue #3 is ready to knock-in. Should play continue and the ball be hit in with both players out of position?
    a.___ Yes.
    b.___ No.

61. Blue # 3 is awarded a Penalty # 5 from the spot. When Blue # 3 executes the Penalty # 5, he hits the ball about 15 yards towards his goal. As Blue # 3 approaches the ball to hit it again, the defending Red # 2, positions his mount to the left side of the LOB, clear of the ROW, within a horse length and on the nearside of Blue # 3, to make a defensive play. Blue # 3, elects to slow the play to a walk. As he taps the ball forward, the defending player moves into position for a ride-off. Blue # 3 checks and taps the ball to the left to avoid the defensive play by Red # 2. As Red # 2 advances to make a defensive play, Blue # 3 continues to dribble back to the right.

a.____ Foul on Red for making a defensive play on Blue.

b.____ No foul should be called because Blue # 3 has possession of the ball, Red did not enter the ROW and Blue has the ability to continue down the line of the ball.

c.____ The whistle should sound and the umpires should bowl the ball in for a walking-dribble violation.

62. Red #2 carries the ball on his off-side. Blue #3 waits to the right of the LOB for Red to reach him so he can hook. Red #1 rides to meet with the LOB on his off-side and will collide with Blue #3.

a.___ Foul Red #1 - one meeting two.

b.___ Foul Blue #3 - standing in the ROW.

63. Blue #4 is attempting a dribble turn. Red #2 turns inside and as Blue taps the ball, Red bumps shoulder to shoulder spoiling Blue's dribble.

a.___ Foul Red - riding into the stroke.

b.___ No Foul - Blue was dribbling.

64. Blue and Red ride to the ball on opposite sides of the LOB. As Blue comes to execute the ride-off, Red raises his mallet in preparation for a near-side back-shot. Foul or no foul?

a.___ Foul Blue - riding into the stroke.

b.___ No Foul - the stroke had not begun.

65. Red #3 knocks in and carries the ball toward the 60. Blue #2 rides ahead and slightly to the left squeezing Red toward the boards. Blue infringes Red's ROW, even though Red maintains possession of the ball. Should a foul be called against Blue?

a.___ Yes. Blue fouled even though Red maintained possession.

b.___ No. Red still has the ball, don't stop the play.

66. Blue hits the ball forward. The ball lands on a divot and bounces to the side. Red, previously out of the play, may now meet the ball fairly and assume the ROW. Blue can check and turn to remain safely out of Red's new path, but elects to ride through so as to be better positioned to defend Red's run down the field.

a.___ Foul Blue - not clearing the new ROW.

b.___ No Foul - bouncing off a divot is not a line change.

67. Team Red enters an 8-12 goal USPA tournament event with a 7-goal team. The Captain states that his team's handicaps are all in order and the team will assume the 8-goal minimum handicap. Can the Committee accept the entry?

a.___ Yes.

b.___ No.

68. In the 3rd chukker, Blue #3's horse slips and falls, injuring Blue #3's leg. Blue #3, a 4-goaler, is replaced within 15 minutes by a 3-goal player and the game continues. At the start of the 5th chukker, the 4-goaler comes out and announces that he is able to resume play. Is this acceptable?

a.___ No. Once Blue #3 is out, he stays out.

b.___ Yes. If recovered, Blue can return.

c.___ No. Blue is now substituting a 4-goal player for a 3 and you can't raise your team's handicap during game.

69. Blue #2 hits the ball well down field. Red #4 riding faster than Blue, passes Blue, placing himself safely parallel to the LOB and Red hits the back shot.
    a.___ Foul Red - crossing.
    b.___ No Foul. Blue must go to the near side.

70. Blue hits the ball up on the near-side. Red rides at a wide angle to the LOB from Blue's right. Red will get to the ball before Blue, but it will be close. What are the potential fouls?
    a.___ Foul Red - if he crosses the LOB and endangers Blue.
    b.___ Foul Blue - if he doesn't switch to his off-side.
    c.___ Both the above.

71. The ball is hit deep by Blue #2. As Red #4 rides to back it, Blue #1, coming from behind and to the left of Red #4, passes Red, safely enters the ROW, and carries the ball down field. Red #4 pulls his mount to a walk, looks over his shoulder to the Umpire, and holds up his mallet hand with the mallet hanging from his thumb. What is the call?
    a.___ Foul Blue for entering Red's ROW.
    b.___ No foul. Let the play continue.
    c.___ Foul Red - appealing. Spot hit to Blue.
    d.___ Foul Red - appealing. Severe penalty to Blue.

72. As the ball goes out of play over the sideline, Blue #2, riding a chestnut gelding, requests time out for broken tack. She shows the Umpire a broken rein and rides to the tie line. She returns quickly on a bay mare and joins the line up. The Umpire should:
    a.___ No foul. Resume play with bowl-in.
    b.___ Send the player off for the gelding and start play without her.
    c.___ Send the player off for the gelding and wait for her return.
    d.___ Award a "dead ball foul" against Blue.

73. Blue #2, following his own hit, sees Red #4 coming from the left to back the ball. Blue holds his mount to a hand canter, stands forward in the stirrups, and looks toward the Umpire while riding to the ball with mallet raised.
    a.___ Foul on Blue - appealing for a foul.
    b.___ Foul on Red - infringing the ROW.
    c.___ Offsetting Fouls.
    d.___ Any, or all, of the above.

74. Red is awarded a Penalty No. 3. As Red #3 positions the ball, he is joined by a teammate and they move the ball around for the right tee while discussing the play. The Umpire reminds Red #3 that he has only 5 seconds to finish teeing. Red is still teeing the ball after 5 seconds and requests more time. The Umpires should?
    a.___ Allow extra time because Penalties are important.
    b.___ Sound the whistle and bowl-in the ball.

75. Blue #3 raises his mallet, yells and looks to the Umpire for a foul. The whistle sounds and a Penalty No. 5 spot- hit is awarded against Blue for the infraction of Rule 35g. Blue continues to yell and the whistle sounds again. Which is the correct procedure?
    a.___ At the discretion of the Umpires, move the ball to a Penalty No. 5 from center field or a Penalty No. 4.
    b.___ Sit the player down for the remainder of the chukker with no substitute.
    c.___ Both a and b are correct.

76. A player injured, but not unconscious, and replaced in the first chukker recovers and wishes to return for the fifth chukker. Is this substitution permitted?
    a.___ Yes.
    b.___ No.

77. Blue #2 carries the ball on his off-side. Red #1 engages a ride-off on Blue #3 and prepares to take the ball on his nearside, meet Blue #2 at an angle to the LOB from ahead and to Blue #2's right. Red #1 and Blue #3 pass in front of Blue #2 at a close distance. What is your call?
    a.___ Foul Blue #2 - one meeting two.
    b.___ Foul on Red # 1 for creating a dangerous play.

78. Blue #3 is prepared to knock-in. Red #1 is standing at the 25 yard line, facing the hitter, when "Play" is called and Blue #3 hits the ball 15 yards toward Red #1. Red #1 makes a play on the ball. The whistle should sound and the ball moved forward to the 30 yard line because Red #1 was improperly positioned and influenced the play.
    a.___ True.
    b.___ False.

79. Red #3 and Blue #4 follow the ball on opposite sides of the LOB. Red rides Blue off and hits the ball straight forward on his near-side. As the two ride on, Blue pulls ahead of Red so his knee is even with the neck of Red's mount. Blue raises his mallet for a near-side back-shot. What is your call?
    a.___ Foul Blue if he hits into Red's mount.
    b.___ Foul Red if he does not immediately move to his off-side.
    c.___ Blue does not have a play, the two players are over lapped.
    d.___ Both a and c are correct.

80. Blue #3 turns the ball and starts up field. Red #2 also turns and is positioned well ahead waiting for Blue to hit up. Which of the following is true?
    a.___ Blue may hold the ball unless Red comes to defend him.
    b.___ If Red comes to defend and Blue does not hit, throw-in.
    c.___ If Red comes to defend and infringes Blue's ROW, foul Red.
    d.___ All the above.

81. The Umpires disagree on a call and the Referee signals for a conference. The Umpires should ride quickly to the Referee, each describe the call he made and answer any questions posed by the Referee. The Referee may uphold the opinion of either Umpire or void the call. Is this statement correct?
    a.___ Yes.
    b.___ No.

82. The ball breaks as Blue runs for the goal. What is your call?
    a.___ Stop play and throw-in when the ball breaks.
    b.___ Let Blue finish his run with the larger piece, then stop play.
    c.___ Play the larger piece until the ball goes out of play.

83. Blue is awarded a Penalty No. 4. As he approaches the ball, he taps the ball to the right to create a new LOB and perhaps draw a foul against a defending player attempting to meet the ball. The foul does not occur and the hitter is close to goal with little room to maneuver. Blue then hits a hard neck-shot to drive the ball through the pack of players clustered in the goal mouth.
    a.___ No Foul - Blue has the ROW and can do what he pleases.
    b.___ Foul Blue - Carelessly endangering other players or mounts.

84. Red #1 hits a short-shot down field. As Red rides to strike again, Blue #4 comes for an off-side bump. Red, seeing Blue approach, cocks his arm for a strong fore-shot. Blue bumps Red and hits the back-shot. Foul or no foul?
   a.____   Foul Red.
   b.____   Foul Blue.
   c.____   No Foul.

85. In the 5th period of a fast game, a cloudburst causes a suspension of play. Following the rain, a discussion starts as to whether or not to continue the game. Who makes the call?
   a.____   The Host Club Tournament Committee.
   b.____   The team Captains should talk it over and whatever they decide is it.
   c.____   The Umpires should make the call.

86. Red #4 taps the ball sharply to his right and turns quickly to follow. Blue #1, following, cannot check in time and knocks Red down. What is the call?
   a.____   Foul Blue - dangerous riding.
   b.____   Foul Red - not allowing time to clear.

87. White #4 rides on the LOB to hit an off side back shot. Purple #1 coming from White's left for a ride off, travels parallel to White #4 thirty yards from the ball. White #4 checks down to avoid the ride off. Purple #1 accelerates to the LOB and enters the ROW safely. As Purple #1 arrives at the ball, he slows his speed to carry the ball to goal. White #4, coming from behind, spurs his mount, accelerates, and runs into the rear quarters of Purple #1. What is the call?
   a.____   Foul on Purple for infringement of White's ROW. (White has the right to slow down on the ROW).
   b.____   Foul on White #4 for rough and abusive play.
   c.____   No foul, Purple entered the ROW and White got to the play late.

88. A new line catches Red across the ROW. Red moves properly to clear the ROW and in moving off his mount kicks the ball creating another line change and placing Red safely on a new ROW. What is the call?
   a.____   Foul Red - ROW infringement.
   b.____   Foul Red - at the moment his mount kicks the ball.
   c.____   No Foul - Red did nothing improper at any time

89. Blue hits for goal as Red #4 bumps and knocks Blue's mount off balance. The whistle sounds just before the ball passes through the goal. Does the goal count?
   a.____   No. The ball is dead at the sound of the whistle.
   b.____   Yes. If the foul against Red is confirmed.

90. Red #2 carries the ball down field with Blue #3 riding hard to hook. As Red #2 hits a strong neck-shot to goal, Red #3 takes Blue #3 out of the play with a dangerous bump. The ball is in the air when the whistle sounds and then passes through the goal. Does the goal count?
   a.____   No. The ball is dead at the sound of the whistle.
   b.____   Yes. The ball was in the air when the whistle sounded.
   c.____   No. Play was stopped by an offensive foul.

91.	The Red team enters a 10-goal team in an 8-12 goal tournament. Red # 2, a 5 goal player, has his mount stumble and fall, leaving him unable to continue. Since there are no 5 goal players available, Red requests a 2 goal player as a substitute. The Red team now has an aggregate team handicap of 7 goals. Is this a legal substitution?

    a.____ No, the Red team's aggregate handicap does not fall within the upper and lower limits of the tournament.

    b.____ Yes, once the game has started, the Red team may substitute an eligible lower rated player even though the Team's aggregate handicap falls below the 8 goal level.

    c.____ The substitute is not allowed and the Red team must continue with three players.

92.	Blue #3 crosses Red #2 and the whistle sounds. The foul is announced as a Penalty No. 4 against Blue. Blue #3 argues loudly that the call is incorrect. The umpire pulls a flag, a violation of 35.g.2. announced, and the ball moved to a Penalty No. 3. Blue #3 continues to argue the call. What now?

    a.___ Move the ball to a Penalty No. 2.

    b.___ Eject Blue for the rest of the chukker.

    c.___ Call "Play" and get the game going again.

    d.___ Both a and b are correct.

93.	Blue scores at the south goal and several players ride to change mounts. When all players line up and the ball is put in play, Blue is again attacking the south goal. Play continues and Blue scores again at the south goal. What now?

    a.___ Wrong goal - score for Red.

    b.___ No recourse - goal Blue and play goes on.

94.	A player is delayed in arriving for a game. He calls ahead and authorizes his groom (an eligible player with current handicap) to start in his place. The player arrives two minutes into the second chukker. The player may enter the game at the end of the chukker and complete the game.

    a.___ True.

    b.___ False.

95.	Red #1 loses a curb chain. When play stops, Red asks for time to make repairs. As the groom replaces the curb chain, Red sits down and rests. What should the Umpire do?

    a.___ Give Red #1 as much time as he wants, up to 5 minutes.

    b.___ See that the curb chain is repaired and call for a line up.

96.	Blue #2 carries the ball down field with the LOB on his right. At mid-field he is met by Red #4 and Blue #3 riding directly toward him. Blue #3 is attempting to ride-off Red #4 and clear the way for his teammate. What is the call?

    a.___ Foul Blue #2 - one meeting two.

    b.___ Foul Red #4 - meeting a player with the ball on the off-side.

    c.___ Foul Blue #3 - Riding Red across the ROW of Blue #2.

97.	Blue #4 hits a long shot to goal from the right side of the goal. Umpire A, leading the play, has no view of the goal. Umpire B, following behind the hitter, does not have an ideal perspective, but thinks the ball may have passed over the post, not between the posts. The Goal Judge signals a goal. What now?

    a.___ Goal Blue - the Goal Judge had the best view.

    b.___ No goal - unless the Umpires and Goal Judge all agree.

    c.___ Whatever Umpire B rules after talking to the Goal Judge.

    d.___ Umpire should get a consensus from the players.

98. A quick line change traps Blue on the ROW. Blue checks and pulls off to the right clearing the way for Red who has held up to avoid a collision. As Red moves on the new and now clear ROW, Blue executes a near-side hook and then plays the ball. Is this a legal play?
   a.___ Yes.
   b.___ No.

99. Blue #2 dribbles the ball down field at speed pursued by Red #3. As Blue leans forward to tap again, Red closes, rides Blue off shoulder to shoulder and backs the ball.
   a.___ Foul Red.
   b.___ No Foul.

100. Blue and Red ride to the ball on opposite sides of the LOB. As Blue moves to the right to execute a ride-off, Red also drifts to the right so contact is not made. As Blue prepares to hit on the near-side, Red raises the mallet and strikes across Blue's mount.
   a.___ Foul Blue - no contact was made.
   b.___ Foul Red - striking into the mount.
   c.___ Foul Blue - not taking the ball on the off-side.

Polo

The High-Tech Swing (parts I and II)

Hitting The Ball

© Copyright 1992
Polo Publications Inc.
656 Quince Orchard Road
Gaithersburg, MD 20878

MALLET HEAD — 16
R. HAND — 15
R. WRIST — 14
18 — FOREHEAD
R. ELBOW — 13
17 — CHIN
R. SHOULDER — 12
11 — L. SHOULDER
9 — L. WRIST
C.G.
10 — L. ELBOW
R. HIP — 5
4 — L. HIP
3 — L. KNEE
R. KNEE — 6
2 — L. ANKLE
1 — L. FOOT
R. ANKLE — 7
8 — R. FOOT
19 + 20 BALL
FIGURE 1

Frame by frame, the high-speed film is projected on an electronic screen and each reference point is touched with an electronic pen connected to a computer. With lines, the computer connects the points to create stick figures. Although all three men were mounted when the film was made, we subsequently removed the horses from the computer image in order to reduce confusion.

THE HIGH-TECH SWING

POLO Magazine sets out to unlock the mystery of 10-goal strokes using state-of-the-art technology. A mystery no more, we offer fresh promise to all who want to improve.

By Ami Shinitzky

Thankful be he who is blessed with God's gifts to athletes — remarkable coordination, quick reflexes and the ability to perform well without really knowing why. Still, when you can enhance God's gifts with scientific insights, the results can be even more astounding. For those of us whose athletic talents are less distinguished, however, the same scientific insights can play a much greater role. In fact, much of the credit for the improved performance in various athletic endeavors over the last decades is directly due to science — whether through better understanding of the biomechanics of sports or of exercise physiology. By contrast, over the same period, racehorses have not shown the same level of improvement because the sport has traditionally paid little attention to what modern

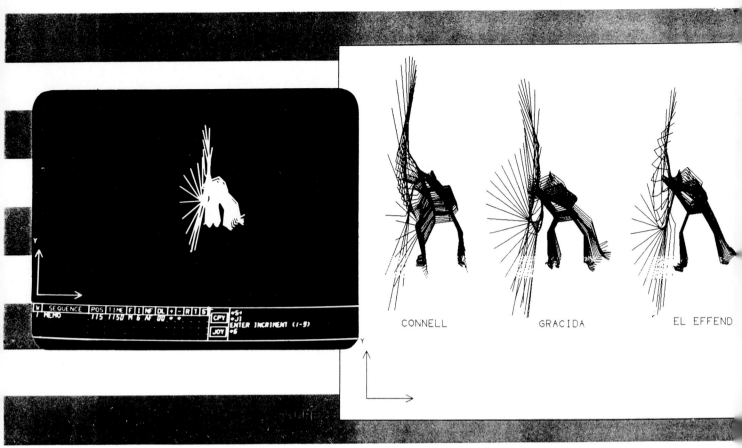

A frontal view of the three players through the stick-figure representation. Every fourth frame was used so that the elapsed time between each impression is about one twentieth of a second. Note how far the high-goalers lean out and observe especially the evenness of Gracida's stroke.

Also note their lack of mobility in the right knee and thigh and the line between their shoulder and hip. Connell, on the other hand, is far less steady.

science can contribute.

The better polo athlete, it's safe to say, has improved over time, if only because knowledge acquired through subjective experimentation has then been emulated by others and every player's performance has risen a notch. But ask five world-class players about the subtleties of their skills and you're likely to hear five different answers about something that all do equally well. Now consider the disadvantage at which new players find themselves when trying to master one of the most difficult sports man could invent — they have nothing but crude observations and meta-

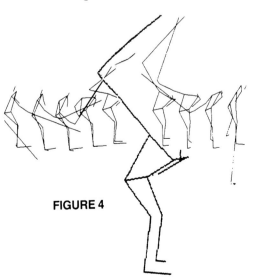

FIGURE 4

Memo Gracida in the arm-cocked position. Note the shoulder and arm creating a straight line. At about 45 degrees to the ground, the mallet is at a right angle to the arm, the elbow straight, shoulders turned from the hips and the body bent at the waist.

phors in their learning arsenal. A second-rate tennis pro can teach a beginner more tennis in a month than a first-rate polo coach could in six. The reason is simple. The tennis coach is backed by the well-researched and -documented body of knowledge in his sport. It is in an effort to bring the same advantage to polo that this project was undertaken. Right up front, though, let's acknowledge that polo is comprised of several unrelated skills: it's a stick-and-ball game like tennis, golf or croquet; it's a team endeavor like basketball or soccer; it's a horse sport like racing or jumping; and it's a high-speed contest like racing. Each of the required skills poses a separate challenge but, as with other things in life, a chain is only as good as its weakest link. If your weakest link is hitting, or if it could be strengthened, then read on. Read on, too, if you're at all curious about the polo stroke and the biomechanics of its many motions.

The task we set out to accomplish was a better understanding of the basic polo strokes: what makes for a good stroke and why a lesser one is deficient. Indeed, hitting a polo ball cannot be removed from the man-on-horse context nor isolated from actual game conditions, but first steps ought to be small ones and we decided to focus on the

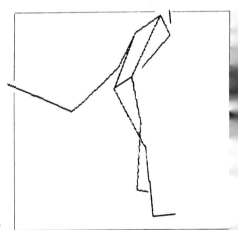

FIGURE 5

This is the point where the arm begins to decelerate. From this point until impact, less than a tenth of a second will elapse.

four basic strokes performed on a horse can tering toward a stationary ball. As we re searched the subject and the professional re sources available for such an undertaking, w discovered that the costs would exceed th magazine's means. To our delight, Royal Vi king Line agreed to underwrite the majo portion of the study and additional fund were provided by Alan Connell . . . we ar grateful to both. Unquestionably, this pilo study is the cornerstone for a new body o knowledge that will do more than anythin

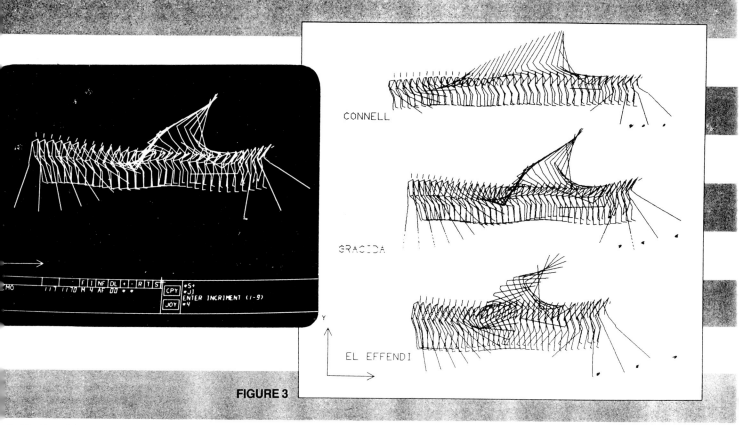

FIGURE 3

A side view of the same sequences, every fourth frame. Connell's horse traveled somewhat slower than the others, but his stroke also lacked the snap. Compare the three hitters' waist angle, the angle of their mallet at the stretched-arm position and the elbow position in the final phase of the stroke. Also note the ball. The first image was shot prior to impact and the other two afterward. In Connell's case the mallet head traveled faster than the ball even after impact.

hitherto to aid in teaching and improving the polo stroke.

The research group we selected was the world-renowned Coto Research Center (see sidebar on page 50), whose most recent accomplishment was the spectacular performance of the silver-medal U.S. women's volleyball team at the Los Angeles Olympics. The subjects chosen to represent the best in polo hitting were Memo Gracida (10) and Podger el-Effendi (8). The one for the low-goal stroke was Alan Connell. We didn't want to select a complete novice but rather a player who'd be more typical in ability of the largest segment of the playing population. At 1 goal and improving, Connell offered us that.

The first stage of the study took place at Palm Beach Polo & Country Club. Three high-speed movie cameras were positioned at three different locations and carefully calibrated so that data later fed into the computer would generate three-dimensional perspectives. The cameras recorded 100 frames per second; thus we could learn what happened at intervals of one one-hundredth of a second.

During the second step, the edited film was projected frame by frame on a large electronic screen. Twenty-one points on each frame were touched with an electronic pen, which the computer subsequently recorded as the relative position of each of these points, e.g. right shoulder, right elbow, right wrist, right hand, mallet head and so on (Fig. 1).

When this long and tedious effort had been completed, the computer began crunching and reams of different cross-tabulated charts were generated according to the variables stipulated. Also, by connecting the appropriate reference points with lines, the computer can generate stick figures that can be viewed from any angle — even above and below. The final step, of course, is a painstaking analysis of the results. Those presented here are for the off-side foreward stroke. Reports on the other strokes will follow in future issues.

First, some general observations. Our fastest ball traveled at about 84 miles per hour, and at a gallop, with more adrenalin flowing and the ball in motion, it will travel

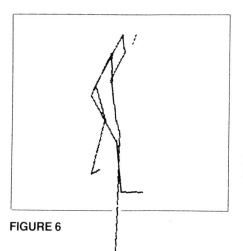

FIGURE 6

even faster. Still, the mallet, quite conclusively, is not a very efficient instrument. The relatively large size of the ball and its lack of resilience mean that the force which propels the ball will not translate into the same relative velocity as that of a golf or tennis ball — in those instances the ball will move faster than the objects that propel them, whereas in polo the ball travels considerably slower. That 84 mph ball was struck by a mallet traveling at 134 mph. There is, therefore, room for improvement in a polo mallet if greater efficiency is in the interest of the game.

Another consistent observation is the relative unimportance of the lower part of the body. In every other stick-and-ball or object-throwing sport, the lion's share of the power generated comes from the legs and torso. Not only does the ground act as a firm counter-force to the muscular effort, but the entire mass of the body contributes to the force generated while careful management of the legs' motion further maximizes the force of the impact or release. In polo, our biomechanical analysis revealed, the upper body does nearly all the work and, specifically, the most critical part is the right shoulder.

Lastly, the various charts clearly revealed how much the horse complicates the task of hitting the ball. In order to isolate some of the

An instant before impact. Note the straight arm. With the forward movement of the horse, the ball is almost under the player.

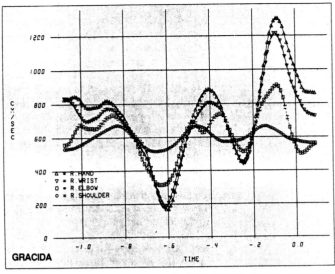

GRACIDA   **FIGURE 7**

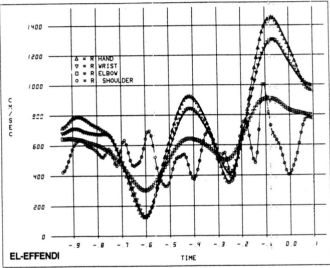

EL-EFFENDI   **FIGURE 8**

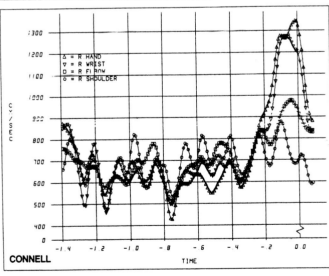

CONNELL   **FIGURE 9**

These charts show the resultant velocities of the four critical points of the body: right hand, elbow, wrist and shoulder. The peaks represent higher velocities and 0.0 on the X axis represents the point of impact. Note how smooth Gracida's motions are and how much more erratic (in the eyes of the computer, at least) Connell's are. El-Effendi's motions are also very rhythmic except for his right shoulder, which he uses especially as he brings his arm down.

The other thing to look for is the changing velocity of the arm along the four points in relation to the point of impact. In the cases of Gracida and el-Effendi there is a rapid deceleration *before* impact, while Connell's hand doesn't slow *until* impact. The curves show a slight deceleration in the elbow and wrist, but that occurs only because of the accelerating hand, causing a net effect of no acceleration at all.

variables and improve the basic hitting techniques, structured and purposeful work on a stationary horse is a must.

Let's look at our two good hitters first and see what goes into a good hit. At a canter, a horse moves at a speed of 10 to 12 miles per hour. From the instant a player begins to wind up until impact, the elapsed time is only about one second, a shorter period than the casual observer would expect. The time frame in which the arm is stretched above the head (Fig. 4) and the mallet motionless (except for the speed of the horse) is extended or shortened in order to allow for impact with the ball at the correct position. Obviously, striking too early or too late will result in a deficient hit. This motion of stretching one's arm overhead at about 45 degrees to the line of the shoulders with the mallet at a right angle to the arm is not just style — it is the very foundation for a good off-side stroke. Body leaning forward at the waist, the shoulder is cocked as far back as it will go; from that position the power of the swing begins. The elbow remains locked as the arm accelerates from the shoulder, and it doesn't bend until the instant following impact. Although the shoulders turn to the right during the windup, they are barely turned at the point of impact. Rather, to further reinforce the strong shoulder motion, the right shoulder rotates forward for additional body velocity and mass.

As the arm accelerates, you may think, it reaches its maximum speed at the point of impact. Wrong. In the case of the good hitters, the arm reaches maximum velocity when it's about in the position seen in Figure 5 and then, believe it or not, the arm begins to slow down. The head of the mallet, on the other hand, *because* of the deceleration of the arm, rapidly accelerates until the point of impact. The deceleration of the arm is slight and probably not even perceptible to a hitter (Gracida wasn't aware of it), but it's the second secret to good hitting.

In numbers, here is how Gracida's stroke looks: His wrist reached a maximum velocity of 29 mph and at the same point the mallet head traveled at 54 mph (a point on the circumference of a circle travels faster than a point closer to its center). At impact his wrist had slowed to 24 mph — a reduction of 17 percent in velocity — while the mallet head reached a velocity of 134 mph — a 148 percent increase from the instant his arm began to slow down.

I'd like to dwell on this phenomenon for a moment to underline its importance, more proof of which we'll see when we examine Connell's stroke, which doesn't exhibit this critical pattern.

An image or two first. You stand by the river with your fishing rod, you bring the rod back, rapidly throw it forward and then check your motion. Hook and sinker have thus been propelled to cover the desired distance. The mallet is not unlike a fishing rod. Or, when you are traveling in a car and you put your foot on the brake, the car slows down but your body wants to continue moving forward. The physical principle of inertia

COTO RESEARCH CENTER'S SUPERHUMAN EFFORTS

For the athlete, one special California facility works nothing less than techno-magic. When he has seemingly reached the pinnacle of "perfection," where does he turn? Fortunately, to the Coto Research Center (CRC), which has become an Oz of sorts for athletes who have exhausted all conventional means of improving their performances. Comprising almost 8,000 square feet of laboratories with highly sophisticated computer equipment, exercise and workout areas and support facilities, CRC is the dreamchild of two men — Dr. Gideon Ariel and Vic Braden — who have worked together since 1975.

The founders' primary goal is the optimization of efficient human movement in all phases of athletic and industrial performance as well as in daily living. CRC's various study results have been applied to sport and non-sport activities as well as product areas such as physical rehabilitation and industry.

Dr. Ariel, the originator of computerized biomechanical analysis, defines their work as "science serving industry, sports and human performance." Over the years he has worked with athletes such as Jimmy Connors, the Dallas Cowboys, world-champion discus thrower Mac Wilkins and now polo players.

Vic Braden is a well-known sports psychologist. He directs the high-speed film sessions used in the biomechanical analyses in addition to developing innovative and educational audiovisual teaching aids. His films and writings on tennis have also gained him international acclaim.

Ariel and Braden are joined by Dr. M. Ann Penny, CRC's Director of Research, who has served as president of Computerized Biomechanical Analysis since its formation in 1971. As coordinator of all incoming research projects, Penny supervises the crucial digitizing process.

Were it not for the Coto Research Center, the hand might still be quicker than the eye. . . . ○

ROYAL VIKING'S NEW PORT-OF-CALL: POLO

In the uncharted waters of polo's corporate sponsorships, one might say that the sport's sponsor ship has come in. It is embodied in a fleet of luxury liners known as Royal Viking Line. And in a gesture of goodwill, the San Francisco-based cruise line has largely underwritten the cost of our high-speed analysis of the polo swing.

Ever since the days when "posh" became an acronym for an elegant port-out-starboard-home cruise, the bows of Royal Viking's vessels have cut the waves toward 132 ports-of-call in exotic locations. Royal Viking's world-class service, exquisite accommodations and tempting cuisine have hit its competitors amidships. That same sort of adventuresome spirit marks its relatively recent involvement in polo through best-playing pony awards and tournament sponsorship.

Notes the cruise line's John Richards, Vice President of Marketing and Planning, "We are pleased and excited with the opportunity to become affiliated with the sport of polo, since many of its fans have enjoyed our fine cruise ships and hopefully will do so in the future." ○

arm begins to decelerate, the wrist closes more quickly, finishing on a straight line at the point of impact. This motion, however, emanates throughout from the shoulder.

Before we proceed to examine Connell's stroke, some comparisons between Gracida and el-Effendi are worth noting. The maximum velocity of el-Effendi's hand reached 32 mph while Gracida's was only 29 mph, yet Gracida's mallet head reached a velocity of 134 mph and el-Effendi's only 105 mph — a seeming paradox. The answer lies in that critical phase of arm deceleration. Gracida's rate of deceleration was more rapid, thus the head of his mallet snapped forward faster, reaching a higher velocity. In fact, his deceleration was rapid enough and his mallet perhaps more flexible to slow the head with the arm for about three-hundredths of a second before the rapid acceleration of the head commenced (from 54 mph to 134 mph in seven hundredths of a second).

Now comes the next surprise. In spite of the different mallet head velocities, Gracida's and el-Effendi's ball reached almost the same speed: 84 mph. We have no definitive explanation because some of the variables are by chance. (For example, although the trajectories of the balls were about the same, if one mallet grazed the ground more closely than the other, a good bit of the force could have been lost right there.) As far as biomechanical components, the weight of the mallet is, of course, part of the equation. Force is equal to mass times acceleration, and el-Effendi's mallet was heavier. Gracida's mallet weighed about 16.5 ounces while el-Effendi's was closer to 18. Also, el-Effendi makes greater use of his right shoulder (Fig. 8), thus adding to the body mass behind the mallet. When the velocity curves of the arm points are compared, Gracida's motion is exceedingly smooth, while el-Effendi's is smooth with the exception of the busy right shoulder, which at times works almost independently of the rest of his arm.

Watching Alan Connell hit the ball, his form looks pretty good. He hits the ball squarely, though not with the same "authority" as the other two. Upon examining the sequence of stick figures representing his stroke (Fig. 3), his subtle shortcomings become ap-

is what is in play here: a body in motion tends to stay in motion while a body at rest tends to stay at rest. Also, any acceleration (or deceleration) creates force in the opposite direction. Physics then determines that in order to maximize force and utilize the full benefit of the accelerating object's mass, there is a kind of snap at the point of impact so that the force is released at and not through it. Think of a karate chop. Even boxers, it's been found, pull their punches at the instant before impact so that their entire body mass participates in the blow, as opposed to only their arm — a kind of a massive snap.

If a polo mallet were made of an absolutely stiff material, the deceleration of the arm would begin much later, but given its great flexibility (even a stiff mallet is very flexible), the deceleration process must start earlier. Much like a fishing rod where the backward curve snaps forward in the casting process, the curve in a mallet cane becomes reversed in the hitting process. This reverse curve is as true of a golf club as it is a polo mallet.

A closer look at a few other details is highly revealing. For the good hitters, their knees serve as a firm base of support; there is especially little motion in the right knee area. At the outset, the upper body leans a bit behind the vertical but gradually bends forward to give more momentum to the stroke. Also, bending at the waist allows the hitter's arm to be stretched higher in the cocked phase prior to final acceleration. The wrist remains firmly flexed just until the point where the arm is parallel to the ground and then begins to rotate counterclockwise and close. As the

This is the point in Connell's stroke where the good hitters begin to decelerate. Note the bent elbow.

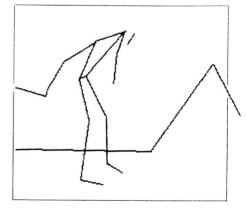

FIGURE 12

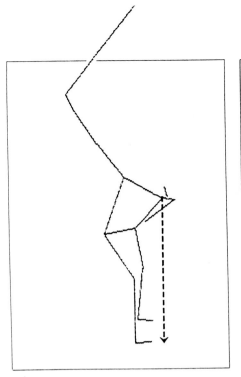

FIGURE 10

If you drop a plumb line from Gracida's right shoulder it will intersect his center of gravity. The ball at impact will not be far from this line, either. Gracida's head, as the broken line shows, is over his toes.

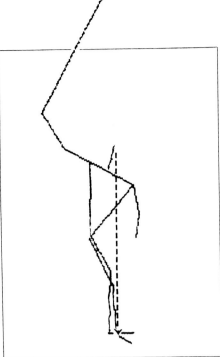

FIGURE 11

Connell's right shoulder isn't over his center of gravity. Thus he is deprived of the full benefit of balance and the power of his body. His head is over his toes.

parent. His horse travels a bit slower but he also starts his swing earlier. Connell lacks the crispness of the high-goal hitters; he doesn't make as effective use of his upper body, while his lower body and legs don't provide him with a sufficiently stable support.

Before we proceed to the velocity and displacement charts, let's take a closer look at the stick figures. Compare Gracida and Connell in Figures 10 and 11. During the critical stretched-arm phase, Connell's center of gravity is behind the vertical, causing him to be off balance. Of course, this means that his upper body cannot enhance the stroke — it actually hinders it. Draw a straight line from the top of the short line above the stick figure (it represents the forehead), and you'll see that Gracida's face is over his toes while Connell's is well behind with only the horse's back to support him. As mentioned earlier, the

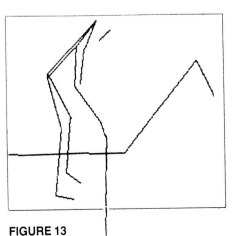

FIGURE 13

At the point of contact, Connell's elbow is bent, as is his wrist, while the ball is struck too far forward. These are common shortcomings of low-goal players.

failure to bend at the waist, even without getting out of the saddle, compromises a player's ability to stretch his shoulder and arm up to the maximum cocked position.

Examining the individual stick figures (Figs. 12 and 13) we can learn still more. Connell's elbow plays too much of a role. Even at the stretched position it is bent and bends still more as he accelerates his arm toward impact.

There are two enormously negative consequences to the bent elbow, and the greater the bend the worse they are. The first is that the bent elbow breaks the transmission of power from the all-important right shoulder, resulting in a stroke in which the right forearm takes over from the shoulder in order to generate enough velocity. That, of course, requires a greater muscular effort from smaller muscles with less support, in addition to the fact that the principles of physics are not actualized to their fullest advantage. The other negative consequence of the bent elbow is that it forces the wrist to compensate for the bend, creating a strain in the joint. When the flex of the wrist reaches its limit, the mallet may still not be in an optimal position for impact. In other words, if the elbow is bent too far and the wrist is flexed to the limit, the mallet head will point forward.

Examining the charts, we see that Connell also falls short on the second secret weapon of the good hitter (the first being the use of the

right shoulder). I refer, of course, to the deceleration of the arm and the resulting snap of the mallet. You remember that Gracida's arm or, more correctly, his hand, reached a maximum velocity of 29 mph. Well, Connell's reached a slightly higher speed yet his mallet head reached a top speed of only 74 mph compared to Gracida's 134 mph. His ball, it follows, also traveled slower — 47 mph versus 84 mph. Due to several inefficiencies, if you look carefully at Figure 3 you'll also see that after impact the mallet head was traveling faster than the ball.

Going back to the speed of the arm, what the data reveal is that at the point at which the good hitters begin to slow their arms down (Fig. 12) Connell's continued to accelerate until the point of impact and then slowed down. Without checking the arm's motion (remember the fishing rod), the mallet will not snap forward and, furthermore, due to the cane's flexibility, the head will tail the imaginary line extended from the hand, disrupt the timing and may drive the ball into the ground. (See Mel Bristow's "The Science of Hitting," POLO, May 1982.)

The deceleration of the arm is slight, and its timing and degree are functions of the flexibility of the cane and, to a lesser extent, the weight of the mallet head. This slowing down not only increases the velocity of the head but also results in better control as the arm stabilizes without the strain of acceleration. Trial and error will be required to master the skill, with a stationary horse being the correct tool. Needless to say, a periodic analysis such as we performed on our three subjects would be the ultimate way to optimize performance, but more on that in the future.

A few final observations. A longer mallet will drive the ball farther, as will a heavier mallet head. However, a heavier head will be harder on the wrist, especially when dribbling. A stiff mallet will always afford you better control, and the heavier the head, the stiffer the cane should be. The ball should not be hit in front of the horse as is often advised but rather as close to underneath the *hitter's* direct center of gravity as possible.

When striking the ball, hit it, don't hit through it. This may help the deceleration process. Another way of looking at it is to think of the relationship between a hammer and a nail — think of the ball as the nail. The follow-through is not really a part of the same motion but an extension of it. Stretching the arm up could be aided by consciously reaching for the sky and extending the arm to its maximum.

Here you are, wiser than you were half an hour ago and probably bewildered, thinking of how to teach the body what the mind now knows. That's our challenge, too. After we share with you the analyses of the other strokes, we'll work toward developing a complete manual. It will require, however, life's two most scarce resources: money and time. The project is nonetheless exciting and we hope that some of our enthusiasm is rubbing off on you, too. ○

THE HIGH-TECH SWING

Part II

The Near-Side Foreshot -- Less Snap, Ergo Less Power

By Ami Shinitzky

The more we know, the more questions we know to ask. The process is endless as we demand greater subtleties of knowledge and as improvements in performance are harder to obtain. In the first article of this series, "The High-Tech Swing," some brand-new biomechanical insights on the off-side forward stroke were introduced — insights that would most certainly improve one's hitting technique if properly understood and applied.

Here again are a few points of orientation about this new work on the polo swing. Sponsored by Royal Viking Lines and with additional assistance by Alan Connell, POLO Magazine and the Coto Research Center conducted an analysis of the polo hit in a way never before attempted. Three high-speed cameras (100 frames per second) were positioned at different angles to record the motion of a man hitting a stationary ball from a cantering horse. Each frame, therefore, represented an instant one hundredth of a second long while the three different perspectives allowed for computer reconstruction of a three-dimensional image.

Once the film was processed, critical points such as mallet head, hand, wrist and elbow were encoded on an electronic screen and fed into a computer that could plot velocity and displacement curves and could connect the various points with lines to create stick figures representing 1/100-second intervals — viewed from any perspective desired.

In the first study we traced 21 different points, many more than would be required in future studies. We know now that the lower part of the body, for example, plays a small role in the good hit. It must, of course, provide stability, but unlike other sports, the lower legs don't count for nearly as much. A tennis player or shot-putter will succeed or fail on the leg work. Not so in polo, where managing the *horse's* legs instead is all important.

The two most significant discoveries to emerge from the analysis of the off-side stroke were the role of the shoulder and the necessity of making the mallet snap forward in order to hit efficiently and long.

Although the entire body doesn't fully participate in the stroke, the right shoulder very much does. The effective stroke must start at the shoulder, and the only way to accomplish that is by stretching the arm well over the head with the mallet pointing forward at about 90 degrees to the forearm and 45 degrees to the ground (figure 4).

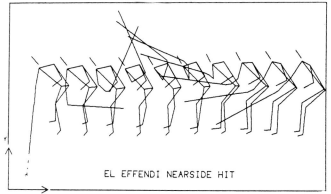

EL EFFENDI NEARSIDE HIT

Fig. 1

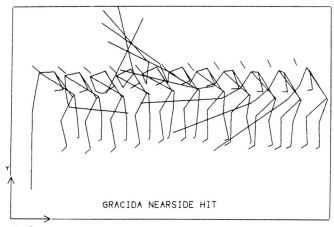

GRACIDA NEARSIDE HIT

Fig. 2

These stick figures are at intervals of about 1/10th of a second apart. The position of the mallet in the windup is similar to that of the off-side stroke, but note the bent elbow and turned body. In these sequences, which show the near-side shot from right to left, the last figure is just after impact.

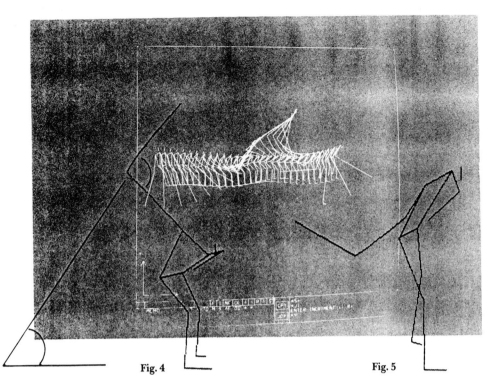

Fig. 4   Fig. 5

Figure 4 shows the point in the off-side windup where the arm and shoulder are stretched to their utmost. The mallet is at about 90 degrees to the forearm and 45 degrees to the ground. The power emanates from the shoulder. Figure 5 shows the point in the swing at which the arm begins to decelerate and the mallet begins to accelerate.

The elbow remains locked from this moment until the instant of impact (that's an imperative). The mallet head is the speeding end at the circumference of the circle and the entire power of the motion emanates from the shoulder. The moment the elbow is bent or the motion of the arm is not on an even plane, the muscle alignment is no longer maximized for the purpose of an effective stroke. The forearm and elbow participate in a compensatory way, the wrist is strained and the end result is a greatly compromised hit.

The other critical discovery (which had been suggested by some but was never before observed) is the deceleration of the arm before impact. Casual observation would have one believe that once a player commits himself and his arm begins its final downward motion, his arm will continue to accelerate until the mallet head drives the ball forward. Not so. In the proper swing, the arm indeed accelerates from its motionless position above the head, but just as the arm begins to point toward the ground it actually slows down (figure 5). What happens at this point we can loosely describe as the "fishing rod syndrome." When you cast a line, you bring the rod back, propel it forward and then stop it abruptly. It is this abrupt checking motion — or deceleration — at the bottom of the rod that causes the top of

the rod to snap forward in a reverse curve toward the water. This discharge of energy in the snap is the same force that will drive the ball much harder than a continually accelerating arm could by itself. In the case

of one of our subjects, 10-goaler Memo Gracida, his hand reached the maximum speed of 29 m.p.h. at which point the mallet head traveled at 54 m.p.h., (a point on the circumference of a circle travels faster than a point closer to its center). Then, about seven hundredths of a second before impact the checking process began and the hand slowed down to 24 m.p.h. But the mallet head snapped forward, reaching a velocity of 134 m.p.h. (figure 6) — a 148 percent increase while the arm slowed down by 17 percent!

There is, of course, a good bit more to it, as discussed at length in our anniversary issue (May, 1985).

As we look at the near-side forward stroke we find that the biomechanics are different than those of its counterpart on the off side. Let's look first at the obvious differences and then examine the more critical ones.

Setting aside the speed of a galloping horse, which can contribute to the ultimate velocity of a ball, the near-side stroke is predictably far less powerful. On the off side, Gracida's mallet head reached a top speed at impact of 134 m.p.h. and the ball reached 84 m.p.h.; on the near side, the mallet head's maximum velocity was only 67 m.p.h. and the ball's top speed was 66 and change. The other self-evident difference is that twisting of the torso to the left occurs at the expense of the more natural muscular flow possible when hitting on the off side.

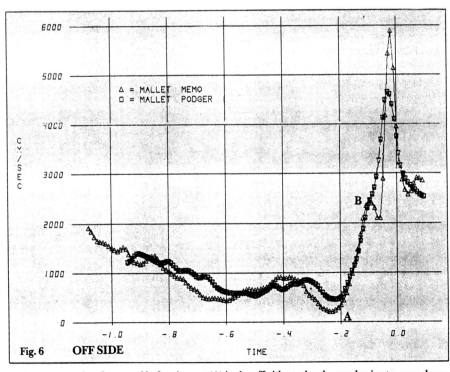

Fig. 6   OFF SIDE

At about two tenths of a second before impact (A) in the off-side stroke, the arm begins to come down. Point B is the when the arm begins to slow down and the mallet head snaps forward, as the change in the curve shows.

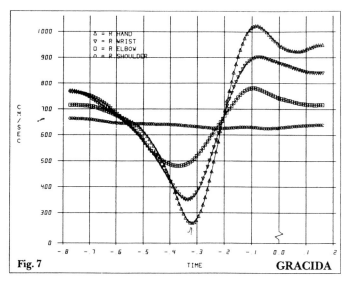

Fig. 7   TIME   **GRACIDA**

The highest point in each of these curves is the point of maximum velocity of the right hand, wrist, elbow and shoulder, respectively. Note that they occur 1/10th of a second or more before impact (0.0). They then begin to decelerate, reaching the lowest velocity at impact.

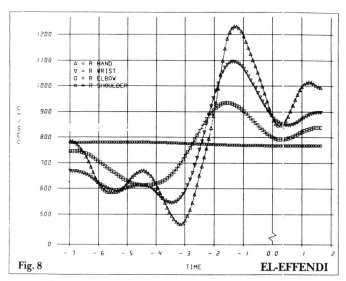

Fig. 8   TIME   **EL-EFFENDI**

Podger el-Effendi's hand reached a higher velocity and his rate of deceleration was greater too (steeper decline). That is why his mallet head reached a greater speed, 71 m.p.h. as opposed to 67 m.p.h.

The lesser but not absent contribution of the right shoulder in the near-side stroke, then, came as no surprise. The lack of significant deceleration of the arm in order to create the snap in the bottom part of the mallet (the "fishing rod syndrome"), however, was unexpected. Although the velocity curves of the elbow, wrist and hand (figures 7 and 8) do show some deceleration, it isn't sufficient or rapid enough for the mallet to powerfully snap forward — that is, rapidly accelerate — as it does in the off-side stroke. The mallet's rate of acceleration, as you can see in figure 9, remains almost constant from the beginning of the downward motion until impact. (Compare with figure 6.) This was true for both Gracida and 8-goaler Podger el-Effendi.

In numbers, here is a further comparison: On the off side, the mallet's velocity increased by 148 percent between the time that the arm began to slow down until impact, but in the same interval in the near-side stroke mallet speed increased by only 20 percent. Indeed, had the near-side snap been equal to that of the off-side, the mallet head would have reached 86 m.p.h. rather than 67 m.p.h. The reasons for this major difference are at least two: Firstly, given the stiffness of the cane (which can vary drastically and further complicate the equation), the mallet must travel fast enough to sufficiently bend in the process so that it can snap back. Secondly, the direction of movement of the arm and wrist in the near-side stroke offers less control for well-managed deceleration, with the wrist already straining more than on the off side.

Studying both the displacement curves

and the stick figure, additional differences become apparent. In the off-side swing the shoulders rotate almost 90 degrees but return to their normal position at impact. The windup motion adds further power to the stroke. In the near-side motion, though, the shoulders rotate counterclockwise early in the stroke and remain turned until almost the instant of impact. The right shoulder will move downward in the final phase of the stroke to add more power

to the swing.

In the near-side windup, much like that of the off side, the mallet is upraised, pointing forward and in about 45 degrees to the ground (figure 10). The same effort to stretch the shoulder to the maximum takes place here — a tight coiling motion out of which the final downward swing begins. In both strokes, this is an absolutely necessary phase that sets the tone for the rest of the stroke and one that low-goal players tend

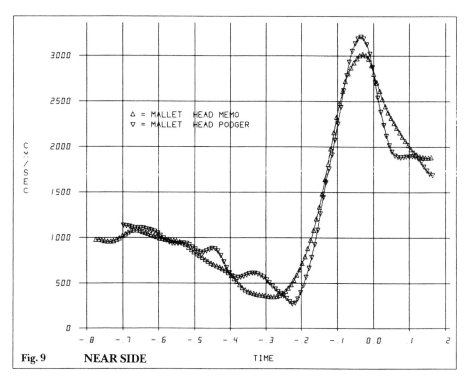

Fig. 9   **NEAR SIDE**   TIME

As the curves show, the acceleration of the mallet head is even. Although the arm decelerated, no real snap took place. That's not to say that none took place. Gracida's hand did slow down 7 percent while the mallet continued to accelerate, albeit with only a small kick.

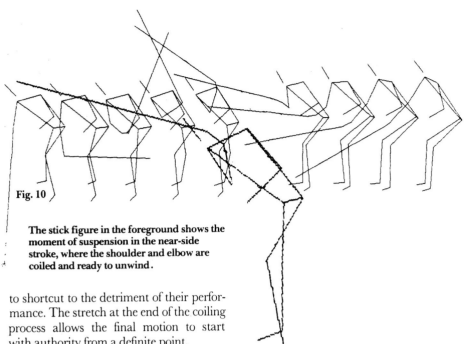

Fig. 10

The stick figure in the foreground shows the moment of suspension in the near-side stroke, where the shoulder and elbow are coiled and ready to unwind.

to shortcut to the detriment of their performance. The stretch at the end of the coiling process allows the final motion to start with authority from a definite point.

Unlike the off-side stroke, in which the elbow is locked until impact, the opposite is true on the near side. The elbow is bent at the start and the arm doesn't reach full extension until just before impact. Since the outside of the arm leads, the forearm muscles from the elbow down don't interfere, as they do in the off-side release, and the final motion is fundamentally the result of the built-up momentum. Another difference worth noting is a shifting in the center of gravity on the near side. Bringing the right shoulder across the horse's back to the left and then the additional bend at the waist has a clear effect on the balance of both horse and rider. A less secure rider might restrict his motion so as not to challenge his balance, while the horse with the center of gravity shifting to the left might instinctively follow it to keep his own balance. Needless to say, good horsemanship is essential to keep the horse on the correct course.

The awkward position of the near-side swing and the lesser force it can generate make the position of the ball even more important at the point of impact. If greater distance is the objective, then the ball must be right under the point of the right shoulder at impact in order to maximize the efficiency of the hit.

Putting the entire sequence in order, the near-side motion is not unlike the more powerful off-side forward stroke, except that the body position required doesn't allow for the same biomechanical potential to be actualized. As you approach the ball and turn your torso to the left, your waist is already bent forward to facilitate a full crossing over of the right shoulder to the near side. The thighs and knees are called upon to provide stability while the left

hand holding the reins must insure a steady course or even compensate to the right to counteract the pull of the shifting center of gravity to the left. The eyes are kept on the ball and, in the windup, the shoulder and elbow coil up so much that the shoulder touches the chin and the elbow is fully bent.

Again, as in all strokes, that moment of tight extension stretch over head is also a moment of suspension that can be lengthened to improve the timing of impact.

Once the arm begins to come down it accelerates until the mallet shaft is almost parallel with the ground (figure 11) at which time it begins to slow down to let the mallet head snap forward and to afford control (figure 12). Don't be misled by earlier statements about the lack of snap, or reverse curve, in the near-side swing. It's not much of a snap, but it's enough to allow the curve in the mallet to straighten out and even move slightly forward toward the ball. If this straightening out doesn't take place, the head of the mallet will not be at the ball when you think it is and ideal timing is off again. The action of the wrist tends to be more pronounced in the near-side strokes. This was even more evident with el-Effendi, who relies heavily on his strength. Gracida, on the other hand, is able to more subtly manage the motion with the resultant smoothness and efficiency.

The final concept to keep in mind is that the follow-through is not part of the stroke but rather an extension of it. Hit the ball, don't hit through it; let the mallet impact the ball and discharge all its energy there rather than letting the mallet merely carry the ball forward as it travels into the follow-through phase.

So much for theory. But remember, only practice makes perfect. A thorough understanding of these principles is necessary for improvement, and once you have them committed to your mind, carry them to the polo field. And may your body catch up. . . . ○

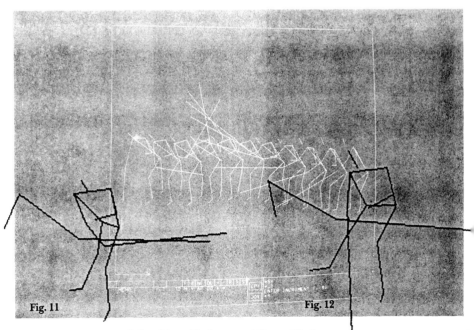

Fig. 11   Fig. 12

As the mallet nears a parallel position with the ground (figure 11), the arm begins to decelerate. The elbow is almost locked and the wrist rotates rapidly. Figure 12 shows the position of the near-side shot an instant before impact.

HITTING THE BALL

A SCIENTIFIC EXPLANATION *By Mel Bristow*

There is good news! After decades of guessing about what makes for a good hit, and years after other sports have reaped immense benefits from answering such questions, important discoveries have been made for polo. Mel Bristow, a polo player and scientist, answered the call, and POLO is proud to present the first installment of his work. It might take a couple of readings to assimilate all the ramifications of this article, but it will be well worth your effort. A proper understanding of concepts such as critical cane angle and reverse curve will unquestionably improve every player's stroke.

Look carefully at the strobe photo on the cover of the June 1981 issue of POLO, and you can see that while it is a technically impressive and beautiful photograph, the stroke is bad. With apologies to the hitter (hitting in the dark with strobes popping all around is not easy), let's examine the photo because it clearly shows the low-goal player's classic stroke.

In the cover shot, the ball is not only behind, but traveling more slowly than, the mallet. The distance from the ball image in Strobe Flash II (from left to right) to the ball image in Strobe Flash III is approximately 2.7 inches. The distance between the mallet head images in Flashes II and III is approximately 3.7 inches, or about 37%, farther. Thus, in the cover shot, the mallet head drove the ball into the ground, then passed over it before the ball bounced back up. For comparison, imagine what happens when a batter gets his bat ahead of a baseball! The result is a foul, an infield pop-up or a bounce in the dirt in front of home plate. The photo shows the polo equivalent of a ground hop to the pitcher. Since most of us make that shot once in a while, let's diagram it and see what happened (Figure 1).

TOPPING

The mallet's contact at A exerts a force through the center B in the direction AH. The force along line AH is divided into two components: a large vertical (down into the ground) component and a smaller horizontal (forward, down the field) component. So when the ball is hit 64° above the equator, 67% of the total

mallet force will drive the ball into the ground. Observation and strobe photo analysis show that:

1) the mallet passes over the ball
2) the wrist is jolted
3) the ball pops up
4) the ball is deformed by the mallet
5) the ground is dented

In a well-executed shot the energy of a rapidly moving mallet is meant to impart a force to the ball to drive it down the field. If instead that energy jolts the wrist, dents the ground and creases the ball, there is little energy left for "down the field." Topping, then, on a grass surface transfers energy from the ball to the ground with a 60 to 80% energy loss, with more on a softer surface and less on a harder one.

Suppose you put enough muscle into a stroke to hit 120 yards, but top the ball as shown in Figure 1. First deduct 67% of the distance lost to the vertical force. That leaves enough energy for 40 yards, but since 70% of that will be lost on wrist jolt and grass absorption, the ball will travel 11 or 12 yards. Big deal!

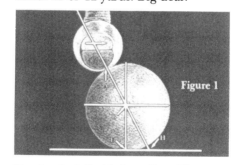

Topping the ball with the mallet striking at 64° above the equator

Even when the ball is hit halfway between its north pole and its equator, in other words at 45°, it is still topped

(Figure 2). Although 50% of the force is horizontal, one-hundred-and-twenty yards of muscle will produce only 18 yards. Hardly an improvement.

In Figure 2, Mallet Image I and Ball Image I were caught in the same strobe

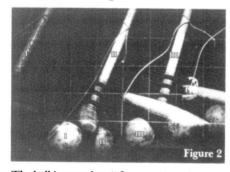

The ball is topped at 45°, approximately halfway between equator and north pole. The motion of the mallet and the ball are frozen at successive instances with the use of a strobe. The mallet moves faster than the ball.

flash. Ditto for each of the other numbered pairs. Between Strobe Flash I and II the mallet head struck the ball at approximately 45° north latitude. In Flash II, the mallet is starting to move over and pass the ball. This movement is completed by Flash III. Note the lower position of the ball in Flash II; it has been driven into the grass to which it also transfers most of its energy.

The string is the trigger for the electronic shutter release and the strobe flashes 100 times per second. The four-inch chalk-line grid on the black plywood allows angles and velocities to be measured with reasonable accuracy directly from the photograph.

THE PUSH-THROUGH

Hitting the ball at a smaller (less than 45°) angle above the equator results in a

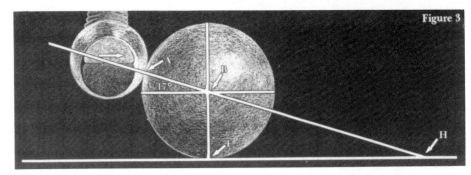

In the "push-through", the vertical component is small enough for the ball to move out fast and the mallet head to stay behind the ball.

"push-through" hit where the ball squirts out like the inside of a pinched grape.

Again, the mallet's contact at A exerts a force through the center B in the direction AH. But when the ball is hit 17° above the equator (Figure 3), as much as 76% of the mallet force is the "down-the-field" horizontal force. A 120-yard hit then would go 91 yards if the remaining 34% vertical force would not drive the ball into the ground. Driving a polo ball into grass at the angle shown in Figure 3 will transfer 50% of its energy to the grass, and that will reduce the distance to only 45 yards. Any degree of topping will not only rob some of the desired horizontal force, but that lost force will then act as a counter-force to actually slow the ball down by propelling it into the ground.

There are other adverse forces, too. The mallet slightly deforms the ball and the vertical component of AH is applied at E, creating an interesting occurence. The ball skids before it bounces, and the skid consumes more of the distance. How much energy is transferred to the ground by skidding is difficult to determine experimentally, but it seems to be around 10 to 15%. The 45-yard distance is now down to 40 yards. Better, but still poor considering that there was enough muscle there for 120 yards.

Let's examine step by step the hit in Figure 4. On most "push-through" hits the mallet usually strikes a few degrees higher than the equator, driving the ball down into the grass. The ball in Flash II is much lower than the ball in Flash I and the mallet follows behind. The "push-through" ball travels much faster than the topped ball but it's still a disappointing hit, rarely exceeding 40 yards. Note also that the wrist is between Cane Images III and IV, far ahead of the ball at the moment of impact.

When the mallet strikes just above the equator (Figure 5), the ball rebounds from the surface an instant before Flash II. The near-vertical cane indicates the wrist was *not* ahead of the ball this time.

When the ball is struck on its equator the force is all in the "down-the-field" horizontal direction. But unlike Amarillo Slim who won a bet sending a golf ball a mile by hitting it on ice, the grass surface of a polo field will create enough drag to substantially arrest the ball's velocity. So pray for clumps, lumps or horse manure to get it off the ground. Stiff grass also helps but wet or long turf will smother the ball. The skid eventually converts to roll but the ball transfers energy to the earth in the process.

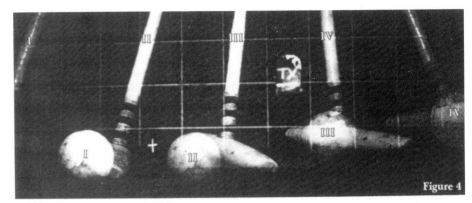

A strobe view of the "push-through" hit

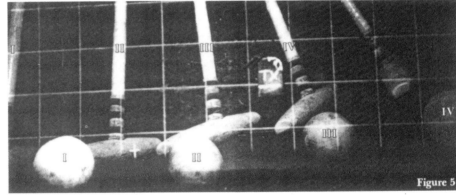

The just barely "push-through"—the head strikes just above the equator.

THE LOFT

It's with the lofted ball that the payoff begins. By striking the ball below its equator (Figure 6) we again have a vertical component in the distribution of the force, but this time it's away from the ground. Whatever is lost here to the vertical force is more than offset by the elimination of the grass drag.

A 15° loft is an excellent hit by comparison to previous examples, but is is not the optimum. You ex-ball players will remember that it's a 45° throw that gives maximum air time and maximum distance. With a round mallet head 1¾ inches in diameter, however, the maximum loft angle hitting the ball off a hard surface is only 22° (Figure 7). The mallet head will hit the ground before it can get any lower under the ball. Reducing the diameter of the mallet head won't help either because the cane will strike the ball first if the head is too small. The present head diameter (1½ to 1¾ inches) is just about optimal even if the shape is not.

We must strive, though, to loft the ball. Distance is related to the loft angle and the velocity of the ball, thus both values are important. Although the low-angled ball has more horizontal force it doesn't roll farther because grass resis-

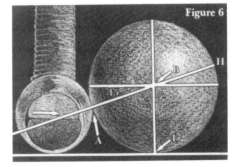

When the mallet head connects below the ball's equator, the vertical force (AH) will produce a loft.

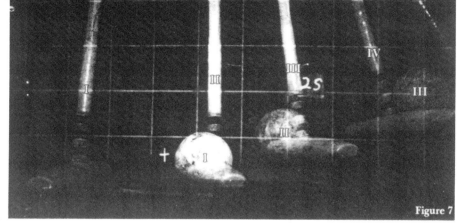

Figure 7

With a vertical cane and a modest loft, a reasonably good hit will result.

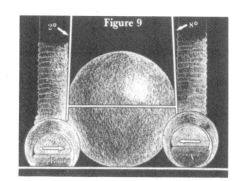

Figure 9

A hard hit dents the ball and worsens the critical cane angle.

tance is much greater than air resistance. A ball lofted less than 20° is vulnerable to opponents' mallets most of the time, but a ball lofted over 25° is generally out of reach. A player expends approximately the same amount of energy for each hit shown in the Table. A ball velocity of 98 ft/sec (67 mph) is relatively easy to obtain and with good loft provides a satisfactory hit.

Angle Of Loft And Distance Table at ball velocity of 98 ft/sec (disregarding air resistance)	
Angle of Loft	Distance in Air
45°	99 yards
35	94
25	76
20	64
15	50
10	34
5	17

THE CRITICAL CANE ANGLE

Is the loft then the final answer to our problem? Yes, but the very effort to bring the mallet head below the ball's equator has an adverse by-product. We'll call it the *critical cane angle*. It's the angle between the cane and the ball which would cause the cane to come in contact with the ball at about the *same instant* as the head.

Think of it for a moment. If you top the ball, the cane will never touch the ball. But if you connect below the ball's equator the cane may connect at the equator or above, thus nullifying in part the loft you thought you had achieved. In Figure 8 you can see the angles that separate you from that undesirable critical point. The lower the head the more likely you are to reach the critical cane angle, but there are other contributing factors, too.

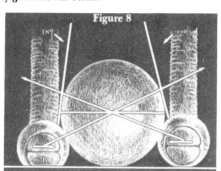

Figure 8

Loft and critical cane angles with round and flat heads. The flat head will produce a better loft, but is more vulnerable to the "wrist-ahead" syndrome.

A hard hit causing a ⅛-inch dent in the ball will bring you about 15° closer to the critical cane angle (Figure 9). A thick cane will also aggravate the situation (Figure 10). If your wrist is ahead of the ball at the point of impact, then the hit is altogether doomed: the critical cane angle

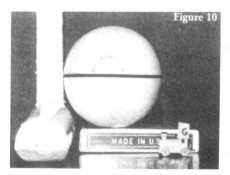

Figure 10

The ⅝-inch tee is too high for the cane diameter, or the cane is too fat for the height of the tee. Note that the cane makes initial contact.

is exceeded and the cane strikes the ball before the head does. Examine Figures 11 and 12 and you'll see the price you pay for a leading wrist: a poor loft and a disappointing hit.

For those players who are prone to lead the mallet head with the wrist (and it is safe to assume that unless compen-

"Wrist-ahead" at impact (note the cane leaning forward) exceeds critical cane angle. The result is only 7° loft.

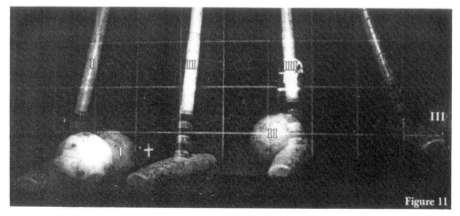

Figure 11

Another critical cane angle exceeded with predictable results. 7° loft.

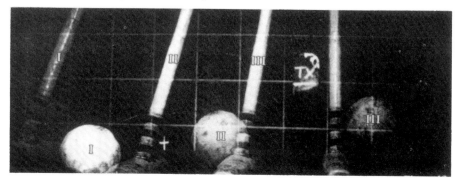

sated for by early timing a whippy cane will aggravate the tendency), there is another bit of bad news, as Figure 13 illustrates. If you tee the ball up in search of the longer hit, no matter how much muscle you put into your stroke, if your wrist is ahead of the ball at the moment of impact your chances of a better hit are reduced or even eliminated. And the higher you raise the ball the worse the outcome.

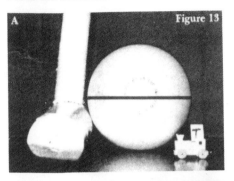

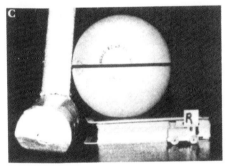

The effect of the "wrist ahead" on a teed-up ball.

Loft in Figure 13A will be about 22° if we assume no cane interference. The cane will probably ruin the hit in Figure 13B, and there is no hope for the one in Figure 13C. The wrist is five inches ahead in each of the above photos.

THE REVERSE CURVE

We see then that all efforts to create contact with the ball below its equator, from an oval mallet head to a teed-up ball, will be in vain unless the mallet head reaches the ball before the wrist passes it. Harold Edgerton of MIT, a pioneer in motion analysis through stroboscopic photography, demonstrated

to the world's golfers in the late '30s that the club head was *ahead* of the shaft in a good hit. Bobby Jones and other fine golfers were baffled. The only way to get the club head ahead of the shaft is to bring about a reverse curve in the club; in other words for the head to lead the shaft. But the only way to accomplish that is to slow down the swing after it has begun, and thus allow the head, which travels faster than the grip, to advance from the normal curve, ahead of the shaft for a reverse curve. But wouldn't the slower club speed also shorten the distance the ball will travel? they argued. Edgerton's evidence, however, was beyond doubt. It is not only the speed that matters but also how the shaft and the head impart their energy to the ball. Isn't science wonderful?

The same science applies to hitting a polo ball. For a long hit the mallet head *must* get to the ball before the wrist crosses the vertical. This turns out to be quite difficult because we only have one hand on the mallet. Golfers cheat on more than just their scorecard—they use the left arm as a brace to keep the right wrist from getting ahead of the ball. We in polo have to manage this critical position in some other manner because the left arm is usually busy fending off another player.

One cannot emphasize enough the "wrist-ahead" problem in low-goal hitters. Analysis (by strobe, video and camera) of thousands of strokes by dozens of players at the Salinas Polo School in California shows that players rated 1 goal and below have their wrist ahead of the ball at impact over 90% of the time. A few of the better players in the U.S., recognizing the similarity in appearance of "wrist ahead" to late timing, have tried to help by suggesting the ball be hit well in front of the stirrup iron. Unfortunately for the low-goal player this most often means hitting in front of his own shoulder as well. If the diagnosis of consistent late hitting were correct, then the suggested solution is also correct. If the initial problem were merely "wrist ahead," then the solution is pure disaster. Careful observation shows that most of the time the "wrist-ahead" player is not a late hitter; his shoulder is over the ball at impact and he is a strong competitor who is "By God" going to hit that ball and hit it hard. Therein lies his problem—his enthusiasm and his muscle get his wrist well ahead of the ball by the time the mallet head gets there.

We at Salinas have made considerable progress in developing techniques to

correct the "wrist-ahead" problem. A forthcoming article will deal exclusively with "wrist ahead." In the meantime, if you wish to find out whether "wrist ahead" is your problem, there are two very simple tests to check your swing.

First, locate a little bare spot near your polo field and use your mallet to make a ½-inch dirt tee for the ball. Gallop past and hit the ball. Hit it hard; if your stroke is good, you'll get 100-plus yards. If you are a typical "wrist-ahead" hitter, you will flatten the dirt tee (by driving the ball downward) about 90% of the time. A second check is to have a friend photograph you while you hit. Use Tri-X film at 1/500 second or faster, and locate the camera just far enough away to get both the shoulder and the ball in the picture. This will give you a permanent, eye-opening record.

For a final image, look at Figure 14. This is what you are trying to accomplish. The reverse cane angle is exaggerated in the illustration so there will be no mistaking the direction. The tee is 9/16 of an inch and the wrist is five inches *behind* the ball. In reality the wrist need be only one or two inches behind at impact, with the ball teed up as shown to obtain a loft angle of 35° or more.

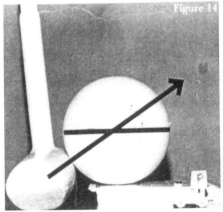

The optimal position: with the reverse cane angle, the mallet head reaches the ball before the cane could.

There are other questions raised by this research that need further study by fellow scientists and engineers. But what we need most is an awareness by all players of the elements that affect our sport. ○

Exhibiting a scientist's fascination with the game of polo, Mel Bristow is Chairman of the Geology Department at California Monterey Peninsula College as well as a player himself. For more information on ball-hitting physics, call him at (408) 646-414 or 449-6116 or write to the Salinas Polo School, Box 371, Salinas, California 93902.